Praise for *"What Does Injustice Have to Do with Me?"*

"At the present moment, both politically timely and morally important."—**Jonathan Kozol, National Book Award winner and author of** *Savage Inequalities* **and** *Death at an Early Age*

"Nurenberg reminds us that white, upper-middle-class students also have a stake in justice and equity in a society—indeed in a world—that reflects increasing economic, social, educational, and political disparity. More important, *'What Does Injustice Have to Do with Me?'* speaks directly to the role of teachers in ensuring that the fundamentals of democracy are understood by all students."—**Gloria Ladson-Billings, president of the National Academy of Education, member of the American Academy of Arts and Sciences, professor emerita in the Department of Curriculum and Instruction at the University of Wisconsin, and author of** *The Dreamkeepers: Successful Teachers of African American Children* **and** *Beyond the Big House: African American Educators on Teacher Education*

"With compassion, nuance, and a critical perspective, Nurenberg draws on research and his own experience to help fill a gap in the educational literature—how to educate white privileged students about social justice. He offers extensive, clear, and practical activities and suggestions for engaging these students. Written in an accessible and personal style, this book is a welcome and needed resource for educators working with white privileged students."—**Diane J. Goodman, diversity and social justice training and consulting and author of** *Promoting Diversity and Social Justice: Educating People from Privileged Groups*

"We need this book. Teaching starts with understanding the learner, and that requires caring about the so-called privileged as well as the disadvantaged. Nurenberg got me caring too."—**Deborah Meier, former senior scholar at New York University's Steinhardt School of Education, MacArthur Award-winning founder of the Central Park East Schools in New York and the Mission Hill School in Boston, author of** *The Power of Their Ideas: Lessons for America from a Small School in Harlem* **and** *In Schools We Trust,* **and cofounder of the Coalition of Essential Schools**

"For educators concerned about how to engage affluent white students in conversations about questions of social justice, past and present, look no further than David Nurenberg's book. Full of creative teaching examples intended to foster critical thinking, it is a valuable resource for an important audience of educators and their students."—**Beverly Daniel Tatum, president of Spelman College and author of** *Why Are All the Black Kids Sitting Together in the Cafeteria? and Other Conversations about Race*

"In the movement to penetrate the limiting lens of privilege, this resource offers a range of fresh ideas and tactics. Through storytelling, sample classroom activities, and pedagogical framing, Nurenberg demonstrates how engaging privileged white students in an exploration of power and privilege is far more than knowledge acquisition; the process itself demands the critical self-awareness that makes us better students, teachers, friends, and citizens."—**Debby Irving, author of *Waking Up White, and Finding Myself in the Story of Race***

"What Does Injustice Have to Do with Me?"

"What Does Injustice Have to Do with Me?"

Engaging Privileged White Students with Social Justice

David Nurenberg

ROWMAN & LITTLEFIELD
Lanham • Boulder • New York • London

Published by Rowman & Littlefield
An imprint of The Rowman & Littlefield Publishing Group, Inc.
4501 Forbes Boulevard, Suite 200, Lanham, Maryland 20706
www.rowman.com

6 Tinworth Street, London SE11 5AL, United Kingdom

British Library Cataloguing in Publication Information Available

Library of Congress Cataloging-in-Publication Data

Names: Nurenberg, David, author.
Title: "What does injustice have to do with me?" : engaging privileged white students with social
    justice / David Nurenberg.
Description: Lanham, Maryland : Rowman & Littlefield, 2020. | Includes bibliographical references. |
    Summary: "This book provides educators with strategies for engaging privileged, affluent white
    students in developing competencies for social justice. The education of such students is not only
    critical for our society, but also for helping those young people transcend anxiety and cynicism
    to find meaning and self-confidence as activist allies"—Provided by publisher.
Identifiers: LCCN 2019050830 (print) | LCCN 2019050831 (ebook) | ISBN 9781475853735 (cloth) |
    ISBN 9781475853742 (paperback) | ISBN 9781475853759 (epub)
Subjects: LCSH: Social justice—Study and teaching (Secondary)—United States. | Social action—
    Study and teaching (Secondary)—United States. | High school students, White—United States.
Classification: LCC HM671 .N867 2020 (print) | LCC HM671 (ebook) | DDC 361.2071/2—dc23
LC record available at https://lccn.loc.gov/2019050830
LC ebook record available at https://lccn.loc.gov/2019050831

HALLY: I don't know. I don't know anything anymore.

SAM: You sure of that, Hally? Because it would be pretty hopeless if that was true. It would mean nothing has been learnt in here this afternoon, and there was a hell of a lot of teaching going on . . . one way or the other. But anyway, I don't believe you. I reckon there's one thing you know. You don't have to sit up there by yourself. You know what that bench means now, and you can leave it any time you choose.

—Athol Fugard, *Master Harold . . . and the Boys.*

Contents

Acknowledgments

It is very nerve-wracking, especially when one is a privileged white male, to contemplate writing a book about race, social justice, and education; there are so many places it could have gone wrong without the help of the following individuals (and, if things did wind up going wrong, it was in spite of their influence and assistance). Whether it was reading and editing, consultation, anti-racism education, or just inspiration, I express my gratitude (in alphabetical order) to Linda and Steven Brion-Meisels, Marilyn Edelson, Grace Enriquez, Jane Friedman, Jack Gilette, Danielle Georges, Shelly Hull, Andrei Joseph, Lois Levinsky, Nora Murphy, Yolanda Neville, Andrew Nyamekye, Abul Pitre, Caitlin Smith, and Amanda Wager. I also still recall the very first anti-racism training I ever attended, the Empowering Multicultural Initiatives course I took through the EDCO Collaborative—how much it forwarded my personal evolution, and how well-facilitated it was by a pair of highly capable educators, one white and one African American.

Any major undertaking stands upon the shoulders of its forerunners. Throughout this book I have stood somewhat intensely on the shoulders of Katy Swalwell and Matthew Kay, and encourage my readers to dive deep into those authors' own work.

Thank you also to Katherine Schulten for giving me the confidence to pitch this book concept, to Tess Callero for being that literary agent who finally took a chance on me, and to Noah Ballard who continued that relationship—equal parts representation, professional consultation, and amateur therapy. This Noah never lost his patience with my flood of emails (his joke, not mine!).

And thank you to Karen Lynds, Paul Sonerson, Gordon Fellman, Tommy Thompson, Paul Jablon—and to the late Maura Roberts and Thomas Hart—

for being the teachers who shaped and inspired me at various critical stages of my life. None of us can ever thank our teachers enough.

Exceptional gratitude to Jade Nicholson, Kira Hall, and Sarah Jubar for their careful editing. I am particularly grateful for the efforts that Sarah, my editor at Rowman & Littlefield, took to keep me from digging any ditches big enough to fall into. Thanks to her guidance, this book is far less idiosyncratic to my own experiences, far more applicable to its wider audience, and not 400 discursive pages long.

To my wife, Liana, thank you for being a first reader who somehow exercised compassion while simultaneously never letting me off the hook for questions I forgot to ask, factors I forgot to consider, and words I probably shouldn't have written. I credit her (and through her, her colleagues and her students) for making me aware of racial and social justice issues in education that otherwise would never have hit my "privileged white guy radar." I would not have gone this far down, or remained this far on, the path if not for her, and I couldn't ask for a better partner in the work of *tikkun olam*.

To my parents and sister, thank you for setting me on this whole path to begin with, through your words and living by those words, way back when.

Last but most, I want to thank my children, Naomi and Amitai, and all of my students from both "Oak Hills" and from my university courses. They are the reason I do this work, and theirs are the hands that I hope will carry it much further than mine ever will.

Author's Note

All names of students, teachers, parents, and schools—including the institution, "Oak Hills"—are pseudonyms. Vignettes included in the book are composites of my own experiences and those of the teachers I interviewed for this project.

At some times in this book I may employ the use of the first person plural, "we," in an attempt to invite the reader into the discussion through the acknowledgment of our presumptive common identity as educators of some sort. I do not intend it as an assumption of any other shared identity (racial, gender, socioeconomic, or otherwise) or set of experiences, and hope that it is not received as such.

Introduction

THE STUDENT PAPER THAT CONVINCED ME
I NEEDED TO WRITE THIS BOOK

Evan[1] was a straight-A student, one of the brightest minds and most adept writers in my eleventh-grade Rhetoric and Advanced Language class. Using one of many tactics I had developed over the years to get myself through grading a stack of over 100 final exams, I had saved Evan's test for last, as a reward of sorts. His writing was that engaging.

Anticipating a smooth read, I turned to his essay to find the following opening gambit:

> Martin Luther King was a highly respected, charismatic and persuasive speaker during his day. However, today's audience, in this classroom, is not the same as his original one. When King's speeches are read or watched by white high school students in a well-off town in the 2000s, as opposed to poor black people fighting oppression in the 1960s, they are no longer effective. King's words do not inspire courage or great emotion, but instead are merely boring. Because "I have a dream" was not tailored to us, it is not effective for this audience, just like adults reading the Berenstain Bears books are neither entertained nor taught morals.

I blinked. I reread the passage, skimmed the rest of the essay, and then read the whole thing again. Evan's prose was solid, his case carefully constructed, all of which I found encouraging. Yet his argument felt like a punch to the gut of my course. I had designed this course as not just a study of composition and argumentation, but also a study of their use by various figures in history (and by the students now, as the inheritors of that history) to fight for justice, sway minds, and change unfair policies.

That a serious, grade-conscious student like Evan was making such an argument—was, in fact, wagering his exam on it—could only mean that he believed in it passionately. As tempted as I was to write Evan off as a spoiled, rich white kid who had somehow "missed the point" of my oh-so-brilliantly designed course, I managed to (eventually) realize the very important lesson that his essay had taught me.

That Evan, whose every previous discussion comment and written assignment seemed to indicate that he actually "got the point" of the course, was making this argument now seemed to mean that he was using writing to protest what he saw as an injustice: the teaching of writers like Dr. Martin Luther King, Jr. (hardly an obscure, niche-specific author of color) to white students like him, at an affluent, majority-white high school like ours. If my initial reaction had felt like a punch in the gut, the irony here hit me like a brick between the eyes.

Evan was not alone. By the time I read his essay, I had been teaching for several years, long enough to see that some of my students harbored a great deal of anger when it came to discussions of social justice. And long enough to see how my frustration with what (from up on my high horse) looked like their lack of "woke-ness" was driving me to respond with some very unproductive anger of my own.

It reminded me of how, during my very first year on the job, another of my star students raised his hand after a lesson on segregation. "I have a question," he began. "Segregation and Jim Crow weren't secret, right? Everyone knew about it?"

"Yes," I said.

"But then . . ." The struggle for comprehension on his face was earnest, genuine. "If black people knew about how bad it was in the South, then why did they move there?"

It was a teachable moment. A golden opportunity. And I reacted to it by shouting, "Do the words 'middle passage' mean anything to you?"

From then on all the students just shut down, and why not?

It is unfair to blame students for deficits in their own education. The mistake was mine, in assuming that because they had such high grades and test scores in the subjects that the school chose to teach and assess, my students would somehow also be conversant in a history that they had apparently not been taught . . . or had not been taught in a way that worked.

As the years passed, my empathy extended beyond the students to include their previous teachers. Their own preparation as educators was likely suffering from glaring omissions, and I could see why: almost nowhere in the substantial literature on teaching strategies, from the driest how-to manuals to the most engaging memoirs, was there advice or best-practices for how to deal with the particular challenges and deficits that teachers encounter in schools and classrooms full of highly advantaged, primarily white students.

There was not even an acknowledgment, an articulation, of what those challenges and deficits were.

* * *

What Do I Mean by "Privileged White Students?"

Chapter 1 will interrogate and explain this label at length. For now, consider "privileged white students" to be shorthand for young people of sufficient material wealth, class background, and white racial classification who are, on balance, more advantaged than the majority of their agemates nationwide.

What Do I Mean by "Social Justice Education?"

Author and educator Diane Goodman defines social justice as the attempt to create "a society with an equitable distribution of resources where all people are safe, can meet their needs, and can fulfill their potential."[2] I am choosing her definition in part because her 2011 book, *Promoting Diversity and Social Justice: Educating People from Privileged Groups*, offers a rare look at social justice work among the kind of populations I'm talking about. "Social justice education" is a set of experiences that help learners develop the competencies to recognize and understand issues of equity, and learn a skill set for creating a more equitable society. The explicit goal of social justice education is ensuring these learners will apply these skills and knowledge to help bring about that societal transformation.

* * *

WHY SHOULD WE CARE ABOUT THE EDUCATION OF PRIVILEGED WHITE STUDENTS?

"Oak Hills?" My girlfriend's boss looked me up and down through his coke-bottle glasses. "That suburban school?"

Dr. Henry Lau was the principal of the urban high school where my girlfriend taught history. It was the end-of-year party he threw for his faculty at a trendy bar downtown. I was my girlfriend's "plus one" for the occasion, and she, as one of his star teachers, was sitting literally at his right-hand side. Lau made some noise between a chuckle and a cough. "Suburban teachers. You don't teach." He then immediately turned and struck up a conversation with someone else at the bar.

Dr. Lau at least had the excuse of his daily lived experience for wearing such blinders, but too often it seems like the rest of the country shares this myopia when it comes to national conversations about public education and schooling in general. A casual search of the scholarly literature yields over 275,000 articles and studies about urban schools, versus fewer than 30,000 on schools in the suburbs. Hollywood's depiction of schools, at least public schools, seems firmly rooted in the "blackboard jungle" narrative: *Dangerous Minds, Lean on Me, Stand and Deliver, Freedom Writers, Half Nelson*, and other films, confining the few stories about the school experiences of privileged youth and their teachers to farcical comedy (*Ferris Bueller's Day Off, Clueless*) or to private schools often set firmly in some bygone era (*Dead Poets Society, The Emperor's Club, School Ties*).

What goes on in urban schools, with students from marginalized racial and socioeconomic backgrounds grappling with all manner of structural injustices, is of course of tremendous importance to the present and future of the United States. But this picture of schooling is not the exclusive experience of either American youth or of the teachers who partner with them in their education. About one-third of the approximately 100,000 public schools in the United States are classified as "suburban," serving 17 million students, making this the largest single demographic of American students.[3]

While the United States is growing more racially diverse, this trend is largely confined to cities and exurbs; only about one in ten suburban or rural counties is majority nonwhite.[4] Our country continues to segregate even as it diversifies; thanks not only to last century's history of redlining and restrictive covenants but also to early twenty-first century Supreme Court rulings like *Capacchione v. Charlotte-Mecklenburg Schools, Parents Involved in Community Schools v. Seattle School District No. 1*, and *Meredith v. Jefferson County Board of Education*, American schools were as segregated by race in 2018 as they were in the 1960s,[5] and are heading toward further segregation in the future.[6]

If you are teaching white students, the odds that you are teaching almost exclusively white students are increasing. At present, the average white student in the United States attends a school where 77 percent of the student body is white.[7] While not all suburban residents are wealthy, suburbs have a substantial lead over cities and rural counties in terms of economic prosperity.[8] Wealthy, predominantly white enclaves exist even outside of areas officially designated as suburbs, including in certain urban neighborhoods and in magnet, exam, and charter schools situated within otherwise racially and economically diverse neighborhoods.[9]

Then, of course, even within schools that boast a diverse population, there is the "bleaching" of classrooms through so-called ability grouping, documented for over 30 years since Jeannie Oakes's *Keeping Track: How Schools Structure Inequality* was published, which describes honors and Advanced Placement (AP) classrooms composed mainly or even solely of white students and/or those whose families possess comparatively greater-than-average wealth.[10]

This doesn't even take into account the affluent white majority in most private/independent schools.[11] Although the comparatively high representation of East Asian and South Asian Americans in all of these contexts does deserve mention, with the exception of California and some pockets in states like New Jersey, only 0.6 percent of American communities have an Asian American population exceeding 25 percent, and in most cases that percentage is much smaller.[12]

In short, it is still very possible, even in the twenty-first century, to be teaching at a school (or at least in a classroom) that looks like mine at Oak Hills, with its nearly 90 percent white student population and median income almost double the state average. Hundreds of thousands of students comprise this demographic, and every day, thousands of teachers struggle to find ways to work with them.

Dr. Lau was correct in thinking that the struggles of teachers like us are very different than his own. My class sizes were small. I had all the copy paper, pens, and computers I could ever want. The kids didn't come to school carrying weapons. They didn't (usually) mouth off to my face. Most of the time, they even did what I asked them to do. A 2017 article in the *Atlantic* paints a picture of students like mine:

> [S]uburban students tend to enter school with the early literacy and numeracy skills necessary to learn the prescribed curriculum . . . [and] are likely to have absorbed school-ready behaviors and attitudes from role models at home and in the community. Children in these environments, in short, don't need to be explicitly taught the value of school. They hear positive school messages all the time and quickly develop the sense that doing well in school matters. When it comes time to take tests, such students tend to score quite well, and their schools tend to get the credit.[13]

So, a breeze for teachers, right? What pictures like these leave out is that my part of the bargain as the teacher is also inescapably clear. Sometimes it seemed that my job was to keep these young people moving along a conveyor belt, one that often started with a high-priced private preschool with a waiting list, and ended with admission to a competitive private four-year college or university. As they passed by me, I was expected to buff them up a bit, add some polish and detailing, then write them a glowing letter of reference and collect my nice pile of "thank you" gift certificates at the end of the year. I was supposed to rest easy with the fact that they "understood the value of school," and to not engage them in interrogating just what that "value" was, and could be.

What I was to never, ever do, was hold them too accountable or make them too uncomfortable. I learned this very early on, from conversations like the one that follows.

* * *

Airplane Lessons

"She has to graduate. We bought her a plane."

I looked to the eight other adults sitting around the table, all speaking with the gravity one would expect at a major strategic arms-reduction negotiation. Four teachers, two parents, one guidance counselor. Their nonplussed faces were all looking to me to make a reply.

I cleared my throat. "You . . . ah . . . bought her a plane?"

Clearly, one could tell I had earned a master's degree in English from a top-notch university.

"We've been paying for flying lessons," said the man in the Armani suit. At least, that's what I decided it was. It looked expensive, and what I didn't know about suits was matched only by what I didn't know about planes. "We thought they might motivate Susannah to keep going to school. You know how hard it is with second-semester seniors."

No, I didn't. This was my first year of teaching. My only knowledge of second-semester seniors came from having been one just five years earlier. Back then I was the kind of student who, right up until graduation, panicked in Hermione Granger-esque fashion at the thought of having missed a single check box on a single homework assignment.

"How much do flying lessons cost?"

Immediately, I could tell from my colleagues' remonstrating expressions that I was heading in the wrong direction. Thanks a lot, guys. You've been at this for two decades or more. How about you take the reins of this meeting?

But no, I was the one who had convened the parent-teacher conference. Mine was the class Susannah had elected to attend only on every third or fourth day this term, and mine was the subject, English, that was required for graduation. Mine had been the phone call home.

Have fun, kid, my colleagues' faces all seemed to say.

Susannah's father quoted a figure dismissively that made my eyes go wide. "The whole point was to have a carrot on the end of the stick, you know?"

I chose not to correct his scrambled cliché. "That was, the um, plane?"

"Yes. We already went ahead and bought it. A single-engine Cessna, nothing crazy." He paused, then added, apparently with no small amount of exasperation for my making him say it out loud, "We can't return it. She has to graduate."

"Well," I said, "that's really too bad, but it's not really relevant here. Really." I swallowed. "I mean, school policies are pretty clear. Students are only allowed so many unexcused absences before they automatically fail a course, and Susannah's had 27. She wasn't sick. She even told me a few times that she'd spent the period at Starbucks."

Silence.

"I called you about it several times during the semester. I left messages—"

Susannah's mother, until now content to sit silently murdering me with her impeccably made-up eyes, finally spoke. "Look, can't we work something out here?" Her voice held no trace of embarrassment, only irritation. Clearly, there was a script here to be followed, and I was breaking from it. She probably thought I was drawing this out just to be a jerk.

"I really don't think I have any leeway," I said. "There are summer school options. . . ." I went on, but I could tell they weren't listening to a word of it. The bell rang, and the meeting broke. Everybody shook hands and excused themselves.

"Can you believe those guys?" I tagged after Ken, Susannah's social studies teacher. He did not slow his pace as we weaved in, out, and around hundreds of students flowing through the hall at passing time. I felt like that smartass driver who makes use of the wake of a speeding ambulance during rush hour.

Ken smiled at me. His wrinkle-rimmed eyes and avuncular demeanor always put me in mind of a friendly Basset hound. "Have a good class, Rookie," he said. Then he rounded the corner and entered his classroom, and I walked a few doors down to mine. After all, I had just two minutes before I needed to "go live" with 25 students, for the fourth time that day.

The next day I received a note from the vice principal's office, written in the perfect-as-typesetting hand of Mrs. O'Neil, the five-foot-tall septuagenarian secretary whose glare could cow rowdy 18-year-old football players. The note told me that Susannah's absences from my class were to be excused. I was to issue a grade based on the work she had completed.

I re-read the note. All 27 absences were now labeled as legitimate. The cause was listed as "allergies."

"Yeah," I groused to Ken later on, "allergic to work."

Ken waited very patiently, hands folded in his lap, as I vented and fumed. I got the distinct sense I was on the receiving end of the mien he employed when his students threw fits.

I finally expended my head of steam. "I mean, aren't you concerned at all?"

"Of course I'm concerned," Ken said. "I sure as hell hope she had better attendance at her flying lessons."

* * *

There are at least two lessons that teachers can draw from this incident:

Airplane Lesson #1: Those who educate privileged students must frequently do so absent the structural authority to hold those students accountable.

Airplane Lesson #2: Nevertheless, there are very serious consequences potentially waiting in the real world for these students, and not just for them personally. A pilot who does not attend flight school does not just put herself at risk when it comes time at last to fly. Even if she has surefire parachutes, there will be others, less fortunate, upon whom flaming wreckage will fall.

I could not yet, at that dinner with my girlfriend's principal and urban teaching colleagues, begin to articulate how two decades of teaching at Oak Hills would teach me those two airplane lessons over and over. These lessons are seldom propagated in schools of education, and never even alluded to in public discourse about "fixing our nation's public schools."

These were the lessons that no one ever taught a star urban teacher who gained momentary infamy when he came to work for an exclusive Boston-area private high school. This was a man who had won awards. Yet he reportedly "raised his voice threateningly" to a disruptive student, and was summarily fired before the end of the first semester.

The teacher of privileged students is often placed in the role of Aristotle, employed by Phillip the Great as tutor to his 14-year-old son, Alexander. On the one hand, what an amazing chance to influence the next ruler of the Macedonian Empire, to help make his a more informed and enlightened reign. On the other hand I'm pretty sure, had Aristotle yelled at Alexander to get the hell off Bucephalus and finish his homework, history would swiftly have been deprived of a famous philosopher, and Jacqueline Kennedy's second husband would have had some other memorable name.

The fact that Aristotle kept his head attests to his wisdom, a wisdom that I had to slowly and sometimes painfully develop over the course of my career: how to teach cause-and-effect in an environment that often banned consequences. More importantly, in the case of my subject area, English, how to help students identify with the characteristically alienated protagonists of literature when, perhaps unique from all other teenagers, they felt little of that kind of alienation themselves. I had many students who saw Holden Caulfield, *The Catcher in the Rye*'s famous rebel lost-boy protagonist, not as a stand-in for us all but as simply a whiner who needed to "grow up and move on," who derided Langston Hughes and Maya Angelou for "complaining so much" and not appreciating "all the good things about America."

Why was I worried about any of this, when the job I was hired to do was to prepare these young people for state tests, graduation, and college? The thing is, thanks to highly educated parents, and years of tutors and after-school academic clubs and world travel, most of my students arrived in ninth grade already fully prepared for everything the state could ask of them as graduating seniors. It is no exaggeration to say that some of my ninth graders were more skilled writers than the graduate students I would years later be training as English teachers.

Theoretically, I could do nothing but read aloud from *People* magazine all year long and most of them would still "succeed." Dr. Lau, in this sense, was correct.

So what was my purpose here?

At some point I decided the answer had something to do with Airplane Lesson #2.

WHERE "SUCCESSFUL" SCHOOLS FAIL

During my own undergraduate teacher preparation program I fell in love with Paolo Freire, the Brazilian activist teacher who saw the traditionally conservative institution of school as, in fact, a place ripe with opportunities to empower students, to motivate them to learn with the promise that their education could be relevant to their own personal struggles against injustice. Freire enjoined teachers to make the curriculum about the students' lives, to turn the classroom into a democratic space where students coeducated the teacher and one another in the mechanics of activism and social change. Don't fight against students' outrage, he said. Instead, help them channel it as motivation for learning and action.

But at Oak Hills, I discovered that I had to learn how to *actually motivate my students to feel outrage*—something I had previously thought was absolutely syntonic to adolescence—at the injustices I habitually assigned them to study.

I wouldn't have made it through even a semester, let alone 20 years, if not for the fact that the kids were so damned likable. They were fun, articulate, put on professional-quality plays and concerts, held fund-raisers for cancer charities. Some were internationally ranked competitive skaters, musicians who had already released successful albums, aspiring teenage scientists who had taken part in Antarctic expeditions and gene therapy research.

All kids have dreams, but the amazing thing is that kids at places like Oak Hills, through accident of birth and intense development of talent, actually have a very good chance of fulfilling them. Their greatest obstacle isn't poverty or racism, but their very affluence itself, and the subtle disadvantages that affluence confers.

Across the country, many affluent white students arrive at high school already prepared to pass state graduation tests, but not at all prepared for the world beyond their expansive green lawns. Some are not only conscious but terrified of that fact, of all the questions they don't even know how to ask. Yet many of my students could carry on intellectual and political conversations more nimbly than most adults, could make you believe—not wrongly—that they were actually able to fulfill what is too often just a quixotic platitude we foist on teenagers: go out and change the world.

I had to learn compassion for them. I had to learn how to comfort children who seemingly had every material comfort, except the ones that mattered most.

To be sure, there are many happy, well-adjusted students at affluent, high-powered schools. But there are also many, too many, who would trade their palatial homes and designer wardrobes in a second for some actual contact time with their perpetually busy parents . . . or who wither under well-intentioned but oppressive parental attention and expectations. Kids who seldom have a say in being booked passage on the breakneck train to college, and beyond it, some vague notion of "success." They remain on board, stressed out and miserable, because they can't even articulate what an alternative life would look like. These kids do suffer, yet their suffering is often rendered invisible by the hedges that gird their houses and the designer clothes that gird their bodies.

At least some of the root of this suffering, I am convinced, lies in the particularities of the environments in which these students live and learn. The same frosted-glass bubble that keeps the more racially and economically diverse outside world from intruding on their lives, except via distorted stereotypes, also keeps these young people from seeing a world of possibilities and potentials that could ease some of that hopeless, stifled feeling that so many of them seemed to express so regularly.

Teachers do have difficult and important work to do here. We have to do it carefully, subtly, saving kids from drowning without ever rocking the boat.

Remember Airplane Lesson #2: more is at stake here than just these kids' lives, even though that in itself would certainly be reason enough to persevere. Teachers at schools like Oak Hills do not merely, as the late Christa McAuliffe said of her own work as an educator, "touch the future." We touch the future's leaders.

THE AFFLUENT WHITE ELEPHANT IN THE ROOM

Nationwide, students from affluent schools are almost twice as likely to go to college as students from economically impoverished ones, especially elite colleges. Just 11 percent of high schools that sent graduates to Harvard accounted for over one-third of Harvard's class of 2017—6 percent of the class, in fact, came from just 10 schools. Harvard is no outlier: At 38 of America's most prestigious colleges—including Dartmouth, Princeton, Yale,

Penn, and Brown—more students came from the top 1 percent of the income scale than from the entire bottom 60 percent.[14] The 116th U.S. Congress, at the time of this writing the most diverse one in our nation's history, is more than 70 percent white, and more than half of the elected officials within have a net worth of $1 million or more. Ninety percent of Fortune 500 CEOs are white.

To note this trend is not to approve of it, nor is it to ignore the strides that people of color have been making for decades in changing this picture. It is also not to argue that the only people who make a difference or who have influence in society are Ivy League graduates, elected representatives, and CEOs. But to ignore this reality is to close our eyes not just to an elephant in the room, but to one that is stampeding.

That students like the ones in my classroom will disproportionately go on to hold positions of great influence is a statistical reality. The question is, whom do we want them to be when they do? Warren Buffet, or Kenneth Lay? Bill Gates, or Bernard Madoff? Eleanor Roosevelt, or Leona Helmsley? Someone needs to help ensure that this rising elite class develops the tools to think critically about their power, and perhaps use it—or even give it up—for the sake of creating a more just society.

Of course, students from less well-advantaged backgrounds can and do go on to change the world, but it is naive to imagine that they can make those major changes without the assistance (Freire even called it a "fundamental role"[15]) of at least some cooperative members of the existing power structure. You can call that elitism, but short of some sort of wholesale communist-style revolution, it's also realism. You may prefer how my girlfriend, the urban school teacher whom I eventually had the good sense to marry, once put it to me: "I'll work on fomenting social change from below. You train your kids to step aside when mine come calling."

George Mason University professor Katy Swalwell, whose pioneering exploration of the social justice education of affluent white students has informed and inspired my own work, puts the situation in less hyperbolic but no less important terms:

> If we are to interrupt the reproduction of unequal opportunities and outcomes, we must understand how poverty is not just about poor people, but the relationship between people of all social classes. . . . Studying "up" as well as "down" thus enriches one's understanding of the consequences of privileging/ marginalization and how oppression operates.[16]

As the director of multicultural services at an elite independent school once told me, diversity efforts at his school tended to focus most or even all of their energies on improving conditions for, and/or encouraging the assimilation of, students of color. He said that almost no work was being done by or with the "70 percent of students who were white," as if one could achieve an environment of racial equity and justice without doing so!

Yet this is precisely what the vast majority of existing literature on social justice work in schools seems to be attempting.

Swalwell makes an additional point that "studying privileged students' schooling helps to demystify the assumption that privileged schools are inherently good and in no need of change."[17] Schools like Oak Hills, in other words, do not represent the goal to which all American schools must aspire, despite their habitual top rankings from state departments of education and the independent assessment of prominent magazines. Schools like Oak Hills are in many ways wonderful places to teach and learn. But there are also ways in which these kinds of schools, in a very different fashion than their urban and rural counterparts, are failing their students and, in the final analysis, all of America.

THE EDUCATION CRISIS THAT SELDOM MAKES THE NEWS

This book exists to both call attention to the problem and to offer, if not solutions, at least tools to help teachers, policymakers, and concerned citizens who have until now been facing this problem isolated and in the dark.

This book also exists to help those of us engaged in Aristotle's work, constantly afraid we'll exhaust the largesse of our masters and engineer our own demise—or, worse, the demise of our students. When a student of mine wrote a poem entitled "I Hope Your SUV Explodes," it was a chilling promise that, unless something changed, someone was going to get hurt, big time.

It is an underreported fact that the vast majority of school shootings, including the infamous Columbine and Parkland massacres, take place in schools that look much more like Oak Hills than the one in *Dangerous Minds*. Teen suicide rates are higher outside big city limits,[18] where students feel less connected to community and, in the particular case of affluent suburbs, are under ever-increasing pressure to earn high grades, take on extracurricular activities, and gain admission to ever-more competitive colleges.[19] Several states, including California, Colorado, and Utah, have seen much higher-than-average suicide rates at some of their wealthiest schools.[20] Serious depression, on the rise among young people nationwide, has risen most dramatically (a 79 percent increase in the last decade) among adolescents in income groups making $75,000 or higher.[21] Privileged adolescents are disproportionately likely to engage in "self-medication" through substance abuse and self-harm.[22]

Engaging these kids in studying social justice isn't just justifiable through high-minded ideals about changing the shape of our nation's leadership. Helping students realize their power as potential change agents can also be a way to help them find meaning in what they are learning, beyond just "I need to get good grades in order to get into a good college and get a good job and then grow old and die." If such engagement can help these students see school as something more than an absurd set of rituals that they have to slog through in order to get to some vaguely defined future payout, that alone would make the endeavor worthwhile.

As I advanced in my career, earned my doctorate, and became a scholar and teacher educator, I found resources galore to help support teachers engaged in the important work of urban education, and in particular, supports for white teachers working in racially diverse classrooms. I found almost nothing that helped suburban educators navigate the challenges I've been describing, particularly that of engaging an all or mostly white classroom in meaningful study of social justice. Yet at professional development events, conferences, and consultation gigs, I have met so many other teachers at suburban and independent schools who are taking on the task of social justice education in one form or another, often doing amazing work—but also often doing it in a vacuum, constantly reinventing the wheel.

In March 2018 I was privileged to deliver a TEDx talk in Washington, DC, coincidentally on the same day that tens of thousands of idealistic young people were conducting the March for Our Lives. What an inspiration those kids were, boldly attempting to accomplish what seemed impossible. Watching and listening to them speak recharged my batteries . . . as, I was surprised to learn, my TEDx speech apparently did for some teachers of privileged students. All of this convinced me that there was demand for a resource like this book.

A colleague once summed it up as we were leaving a district professional development event featuring a popular anti-racism speaker: "For 29 years," he said, "I've been hearing this exact same speech. I think by now I understand the 'big picture' problems very well. What I'm still waiting for is someone to give me specific things to do about it."

On the rare occasions when such speakers did offer specific tools, those tools seemed built to fit schools and communities that were nothing like Oak Hills. So I decided to create the tools that just might work for students like ours, and attempting to do so has been far from easy. Despite how the Mr. Laus of the world might characterize our work, teachers like me are also very much in the trenches; the fact that our trenches are often lined with white picket fences and shiny SUVs obscures our particular challenges, as well as those of our privileged students.

NECESSARY DISCLAIMERS

The strategies in this book, and the reasoning behind using them, are informed by a combination of research and personal experience. I do not present them as guaranteed effective tools for every classroom, and I did not conduct rigorous experimental studies to systematically assess their impact. These strategies have worked well for my classroom, and are meant to serve as examples and starting points for teachers looking for practical ideas on how to engage their own affluent, privileged white students in learning about social and racial justice.

Issues of race, social justice, privilege, and pedagogy are multifaceted, nuanced, and controversial. By nature, any recommended action that touches on these issues is a worthy subject for interrogation and critique.

Lilia Bartolomé warns of "methods fetish" in education, a myopic focus on pedagogical interventions that leave structural systems of oppression in schools and in the larger society unchallenged.[23] I will strive in this book (particularly in chapter 6), just as I attempt in my own teaching practice, to not forget that larger mission. But the world of a teacher—as opposed to that of an academic—is one that demands constant, immediate, concrete actions, thousands of them every day.[24]

I do realize what an incredible act of hubris writing this book may seem, so I want to start by positioning myself as a voice of some knowledge and experience, but not necessarily one of authority, despite the third-person narration that most of the chapters beyond this introduction employ. Anyone reading this book has had knowledge and experiences with schools, either as educators or, at the very least, as students. A teacher looking to implement any of the suggestions I've offered knows far more about her students, her colleagues, her school, and her community than I do.

So first, I will say to my readers what I say to every teacher candidate who takes my graduate courses: YKYS-YMMV, which I pronounce "Yikes-Yumvy." This awkwardly cutesy acronym stands for "You Know Your Students—Your Mileage May Vary." Teaching and learning are complex, dynamic, and highly contextually dependent processes. I can offer research and experience as guides, but ultimately there is no such thing as a "one-size-fits-all" approach, only proposed tools for your toolbox that you can adopt, modify, or discard per the needs of your students.

Second, when it comes to understanding inequities and working to remove them, I am myself very much a work in progress—a white heterosexual cisgender man struggling to understand how I fit into our world's patterns of privilege, oppression, and activism, continually developing my sense of when to listen and when to speak, and how to do more good than harm. No matter how much I engage in this sort of study and reflection, there will inevitably be limits to my understanding, imposed by my own privileged experience.

Rochelle Gutiérrez, like Bartolomé, is wary of the danger of "teachers who feel compelled (either intrinsically or merely to be 'politically correct') to address issues of equity but who are unwilling to think about their role in perpetuating" those inequities.[25] The mandate to critically examine and address and own one's responsibility, culpability, positionality, and blinders is an ongoing prerequisite for doing social justice work anywhere, especially in such hierarchically fraught environments as schools.

Before and while engaging in a mission to do social justice work, I would caution teachers to make sure that they take some classes in equity and active anti-racism training, to read literature in the field (particularly in critical race theory and also in whiteness studies), and importantly, if this is not a part of your existing experience, spend some time observing, learning, and interacting in diverse environments. But at some point, human beings concerned with these issues still need to act—even withholding action, pending further study and self-reflection, is an action that in some ways argues for maintenance of the status quo. While well-intentioned but deeply flawed acts of "doing something" may not always lead to a better state of affairs than "doing nothing," one must also acknowledge the fact that some kinds of "doing nothing" are worse than even imperfect and incremental attempts at change.

What I will attempt to do in this book, and to model for others, is two things:

1. Lean heavily on the work of those scholars, teachers, and activists with better credentials and deeper understandings of these topics than I have.
2. Make my best effort to be vigilant, to continually contextualize the advice I present in this book within the experiences I have had, the person I am, the journey I am on, and the students whose journeys have intersected with mine for a brief time.

There have been many times in my life when I have failed, when I have—despite the best of intentions—merely reinforced and replicated patterns of oppression, labored under harmful assumptions and misperceptions, offended without even having the presence of mind to understand that I did so. Despite my best efforts, and those of my friends and colleagues who served as first readers, there may well be times in this book where I fail in that mission. At those times, my hope is that some kernel of value can still be found in my admittedly imperfect attempts.

I do not assume that those reading this book are white, male, heterosexual, or cisgender. I do assume that the reader serves in a teaching or mentoring role, formal or informal, with affluent, primarily white students in a subur-ban, or elite urban or private school setting, or is at least interested in the topic of the education of that population. While some of these strategies may be applicable to elementary school–aged children, the majority are most appropriate for use with high school or middle school students. I hope that, although the material here is influenced by the particular identity contexts in which I operate, that it is to some degree also "portable" and adaptable for others—YKYS-YMMV of course in mind.

That said, I do want to make the case that there are particular opportu-nities for privileged white teachers who are working with privileged white students, and that some of the strategies in this book might have a special kind of effectiveness when employed by someone like me.

True, there is some merit to the argument that it is simply impossible for a person with as much privilege as I have to make any meaningful or useful contributions to social justice, whether in a classroom or in writing a book—that only a person with direct experience of marginalization, which by most definitions I lack, can advance our understandings and offer strategies that do more good than harm. The best thing I can do, some might say, is keep quiet and get out of the way.

On the other hand, I think there is some danger when white, privileged educators—including myself at times—yield *sole* responsibility for anti-ra-cist work to people of color. There are many valid arguments for why white educators should look to people of color for both leadership and guidance roles. But however unjust it may be, it remains that

> experiences of racism articulated by a person of color is more often than not discounted [by some white people] . . . [they are] received as an attack on an individual's personal character and bias is assumed. However, coming from another white person, there is no perceived conflict of interest, and the idea of racism outside of slavery and Jim Crow seem more plausible. [26]

Or, as a student recently put it in her blog, "If you are a white person, it is even more important that you take the time to have this conversation with other white people. Sometimes it means more coming from another white person because it feels like less of an attack and more like advice." [27]

"BUT I'M A [PICK YOUR SUBJECT MATTER] TEACHER! THIS ISN'T MY JOB!"

Today's teachers are not only called on to help students acquire and master academic content, but also to teach pro-social behaviors and executive func-tioning skills, or even hygiene; to serve as emotional counselors; to be advo-cates in legal or family troubles; to help students navigate the job world, the criminal justice system, or their friendship circles. Adding social justice issues to the mix, particularly with the inevitable volatility that discussions of race and privilege bring, may seem like the straw that breaks the camel's back.

But this is necessary work, especially in an era where divisions and inability to take the perspectives of "the other" are threatening the very fabric of our nation. We have a mandate to teach students skills in analysis and critical thinking, to help them be able to synthesize multiple points of view and problem solve with vastly complex challenges such as climate change and international terrorism. As Kathryn Short, a Los Angeles school administrator puts it,

> from an academic standpoint . . . talking about race is an important lesson in critical thinking. When students learn about the history of housing, job, and education policies in the United States, they can begin to understand why their home community looks the way it does—is everyone mostly the same, or is the community more diverse?—and to question whether today's policies are similarly discriminatory or more inclusive.[28]

That description may seem to make discussions of inequity the sole province of social studies classes, or perhaps classes that examine the human experience through literature. Certainly my own background and default perspective is that of a humanities and social sciences teacher, and many of the activities here revolve around or otherwise involve student responses to fiction and nonfiction texts and films, through reflection- and discussion-heavy modalities. They are easily portable to youth groups, book groups, and discussion groups of all kinds—but this is not to say that such tools are not also of potential use to teachers in other subjects.

The Common Core State Standards have placed increasing emphasis on reading, writing, and discussion across the curriculum,[29] and in many places this book will highlight specific plug-ins for science and math educators who are wondering how the heck any of this stuff interfaces with algebra or chemistry. Mathematics and mathematical thinking provide tools for understanding the economics of inequity plus methods to employ, understand, and critically examine statistics and economics as these both inform us about, and influence, social policy. As math educator Jonathan Osler reminds us, many of the world's biggest social problems have significant mathematical components:

> The systemic and structural oppression of low income and people of color in the United States is worsening. The number of people in prison continues to grow, as do unemployment rates. Billions of dollars that were once available for social programs and education have been diverted to pay for war. Rents are skyrocketing, while affordable housing is becoming even scarcer. Over 35

million people lack health insurance. . . . [I]n math classes around the country, perhaps the best places to study many of these issues, we continue to use curricula and models that lack any real-world, let alone socially relevant, contexts. A great opportunity to educate our young people about understanding and addressing these myriad issues continues to be squandered.[30]

In other words, practical applications are crucial to help students learn math concepts anyway, so why not seize the opportunity to make those contexts ones that actually help students understand, and perhaps even begin to combat, real-world problems of inequity?

The sciences have a vital role to play in helping humanity address the largest problems of all: climate change, health and epidemiology, food production and security, innovative means of obtaining and using energy, coping with disruptive technologies like artificial intelligence, genetic engineering, and more. No progress in the social, political, and economic dimensions of these problems can be made without a population that comprehends the science that undergirds them.

As in math, practical application is key to understanding and mastery in the sciences, yet too often science concepts are taught out of a textbook rather than through living the scientific practices of experimentation and scientific method. Without engaging in these practices to learn for yourself the theories and understandings that the professional scientific community has discovered, then "debates" about issues like climate change, the evolution of species, and the value of vaccinations become dead-end prospects of "my book (religious text, conspiracy website, etc.) says this, and your book (science textbook) says something else, so it's all a matter of where you put your faith."

Similarly, studying the evolution of science, and how it differs from pseudoscience, is vital for understanding the role that eugenics and other apparently scientific practices played in creating and perpetuating the constructs of race, and assumptions of racial hierarchy, that inform the world today.

All students need and deserve this kind of education, in all of their subjects. Teachers at "high-powered, high-performing" schools have a special opportunity, as many of their students possess such thorough on-or-above-grade-level understandings of so many basic concepts that they are in many ways well-prepared *scholastically* to apply those concepts to real-world issues. The challenge, as described throughout this book, may be more about working through their cultural baggage (and perhaps your own!) than in overcoming academic challenges.

THIS BOOK'S GOVERNING FRAMEWORKS

Social justice educator Matthew Kay argues not only for the necessity of social justice conversations, but also notes that successful conversations about justice, particularly those involving race, "depend on a very specific ecosystem . . . without healthy classroom relationships and sound conversational structures, race conversations cannot thrive,"[31] students and teachers alike cannot safely take risks, and teachers' well-intentioned efforts can easily do more harm than good.

Kay is one of many educators who emphasize the importance of avoiding "pop-up race conversations," and instead invest significant time in setting norms and in having students practice elements of respectful disagreement, empathy, mutual support, conflict resolution, and clear discussion protocols before attempting to launch into emotionally challenging material. I'll expand upon these ideas in chapter 2.

A key part of creating and maintaining this environment is for teachers to model their own status as a work-in-progress, as someone who, in the words of Melody Hobson in her 2014 TED talk, "Color Blind or Color Brave," is attempting to become "comfortable with being uncomfortable."[32] Doing so, says Kay, "removes a lot of pressure from students. . . . It positions [the teacher] not as an intimidating authority about to publicly expose their ignorance, but as a fellow traveler, someone else who has also been exposed"[33] to all of the subtle indoctrination, the institutionalized racism and oppression, the harmful myths that all of us—but especially many of us white people—struggle to even recognize, let alone combat.

Teachers, or any authority figures in the room, cannot position themselves "above" questions of race, class, gender, and the other elements of their identity, along with all of the baggage that carries and all the ways in which it shapes their thoughts, words, and actions. This is one of critical race theory's biggest contributions to social justice work, and should serve as a reminder that "meaningful race conversations depend upon teachers understanding the implications of their own racial and cultural perspectives."[34]

This book will attempt to model norms for teachers to establish for both their students and themselves when discussing issues of justice, specifically:

Norm 1: Speak for one's self and one's own experiences.

Norm 2: Validate the experiences of others. Recognize that they are speaking what is, for them, a truth—this includes how they might feel about something said in class, even if the speaker had different intentions.

Norm 3: On the other hand, assume good intentions. We all have "permission to fumble."

Norm 4: Respond to something that upsets you by asking honest questions (e.g., "What do you mean by that, precisely?" "Where did you
learn that information?" "What personal experiences led you to think/
say that?")

Norm 5: Practice reflexivity and reflection. Regularly ask yourself what
led you to the beliefs and positions you hold, and what informs the
actions you take.

These norms have been assembled and synthesized from a wide variety of
authors, classes, and workshops. Kay's book is a particularly useful and
accessible resource for those interested in an in-depth exploration of norms,
structures, and mind-sets for navigating the fraught but necessary territory of
race in the classroom.

This book will also use Diane Goodman's "Cultural Competence for
Social Justice" to help frame the work being described. Goodman defines
"cultural competence" as "the ability to live and work effectively in culturally diverse environments and enact a commitment to social justice."[35] This is
the clearest articulation of the goals that inform and guide the work we just
do with privileged students and the practices detailed in this book.

Goodman divides the "range of awareness, knowledge and skills" necessary for doing this as follows:[36]

Competency 1: Self-awareness: awareness of one's own social identities,
cultures, biases, and perspectives.

Competency 2: Understanding and valuing others: knowledge of and appreciation for others' social identities,[37] cultures,[38] and perspectives.

Competency 3: Knowledge of societal inequities: understanding of how
social identities and forms of oppression affect people's experiences
and access to power, resources, and opportunities.

Competency 4: Skills to interact effectively with diverse people in different contexts: ability to adapt to and work collaboratively with different
cultural groups.

Competency 5: Skills to foster equity and inclusion: ability to identify and
address inequities and create environments, policies, and practices to
ensure diversity and fairness.

While these competencies are interrelated, each later competency builds on,
and requires a solid footing in, the ones that precede it. The work we do with
our students can proceed according to this progression, and so too do the
chapters in this book.

CHAPTER OVERVIEWS

Before going too deep into those competencies, chapter 1, "Who Are 'Privileged' Students, and How Should They Be Taught?" will provide some grounding context in the theory and philosophy for this book. The practical strategies begin in chapter 2, "Warming Up the Room," which will discuss the particular, and vital, preparations that teachers undergo with their classes in order to create the kind of environment where students can engage in difficult conversations about race and privilege in meaningful, nontoxic ways.

Chapter 3, "Self and 'Other,'" will then explore Goodman's first two competencies, offering tools a teacher can use to engage white, privileged students in identity work so that they can see themselves as participants in, as opposed to detached (and perhaps uninterested) observers of, the operations of race in American society. White, privileged students need to see purpose and meaning in learning about "the Other," recognizing common human connections while acknowledging and valuing difference.

Chapter 4, "What Does Injustice Have to Do with Me?" takes up the work of helping privileged white students to not only recognize social inequities, per Goodman's third competency, but also to recognize how these inequities include, affect, and even harm people like themselves.

Chapter 5, "Privileged Victims," explores this last point in detail, suggesting lessons and resources that illustrate how privilege can actually damage as well as advantage its possessors, arguing for actual self-interest in working for a more equitable society.

Chapter 6, "Struggling to 'Be the Change'—Allyship, Activism, and the Dangers of the 'Savior' Trap," provides advice for teachers about how to navigate the difficult roads of Goodman's final two competencies, helping their white students see roles for themselves in addressing social and racial injustices without merely replicating those same patterns of oppression with their well-intentioned attempts to make change.

Chapter 7, "Choosing Between What Is Easy and What Is Right," reminds teachers that their classroom operations need to reflect the social justice competencies they have been teaching their students about, and presents structures for democratic classrooms and other socially inclusive teaching strategies. It then zooms the camera lens out beyond the classroom, to the school and community in which that classroom is situated. Would-be activist teachers will need to negotiate with their colleagues, administrators, and the community of parents and guardians whose support is both pragmatically and ethically necessary to secure. The chapter then closes the book with some final thoughts about the value and necessity of doing the extremely challenging work of teaching all these social justice competencies to privileged white students.

FOUR KEY PROPOSITIONS

Having laid out all of these borrowed and adapted frameworks, I now want to outline the four key ideas of my own articulation that guide this book, namely that the successful teacher of privileged white students must engage them with these propositions:

1. Racism and other forms of oppression are not "someone else's" problem (just people of color, just economically disadvantaged people, etc.)—well-off white people play a part in this story as well.
2. While the part they play is often as beneficiaries of an unjust system, that part can be transformed into the role of ally, someone who can question and help disassemble and transform that system. As marginalized peoples fight for their rights, their allies can support them, follow their lead, and remove some of the barriers they face.
3. It is worth investing time and energy into making the previous two propositions into learning goals for students. This material is not mere supplement to "real" content and skill learning. Not only can it be woven into "mainstream" curriculum and instruction, but actually enhance them, make them more authentic and engaging.
4. It is worth rocking the boat, challenging and changing some of the tried-and-true structures that ironically make many "high-powered" schools actually lag behind the cutting edge at a time when education is transforming around the country and around the world. More diverse schools, by necessity, have had to develop more culturally responsive, pedagogically nimble ways of reaching all students. Research-based practices involving more student-centered teaching and democratic classroom management methods are rarer in schools like the kind I teach in, yet the students in such schools can benefit immensely from them.

The bell is about to ring, so let's begin.

NOTES

1. All names, including that of "Oak Hills," are pseudonyms.
2. Goodman, 2011, 29.
3. According to the U.S. Department of Education, the other demographic categories are: 14 million in cities, 12 million in rural areas, and 6 million in towns. See https://nces.ed.gov/programs/coe/indicator_tla.asp.
4. Parker et al., 2018.
5. Harris and Curtis, 2018.
6. Chang, 2018.
7. Spatig-Amerikaner, 2012.
8. Parker et al., 2018.

9. Bui and Dougherty, 2017; Logan and Burdick-Will, 2017.

10. Lewis and Diamond, 2015; see also Oakes, 1985.

11. "Private School Enrollment," National Center for Education Statistics, 2018. However, 87 percent of families with children in grades K–12 with annual incomes of $75,000 or more (the highest income bracket measured) have children only in public schools, with another 3 percent having children in both public and independent schooling situations (Council for America Private Education, n.d.).

12. Chowkwanyun and Segall, 2012.

13. Schneider, 2017.

14. Aisch, Buchanan, Cox, and Quealy, 2017.

15. Freire, 2000, 60.

16. Swalwell, 2013, 12.

17. Ibid.

18. Maynard, 2015.

19. "Challenge Success," 2019.

20. Rosin, 2015; Hyde, 2016; Brown, 2018.

21. Twenge, Cooper, Joiner, Duffy, and Binau, 2019.

22. Luthar, Small, and Ciciolla, 2018; Yates, Tracy, and Luthar, 2008.

23. Bartolomé, 1994.

24. As long as we are discussing positionality, I will cite my experience as both an academic and a high school teacher: *nothing* in my experience as a scholar and professor comes *anywhere close* to the nonstop pragmatic demands and on-the-spot judgment calls of the hight school classroom. The nature of that job does not afford the kind of omphaloskepsis that is the privilege, perhaps even the duty and purpose, of those in the ivory tower. Ideally, the practitioners in each of these worlds should respect and access the expertise of the other to their mutual benefit.

25. Gutiérrez, 2000, 214.

26. Williams, 2016.

27. Dahl, 2017.

28. Quoted in Shafer, 2017.

29. Rebora, Ogle, and Lang, 2012.

30. Osler, 2018, 2.

31. Kay, 2018, 13.

32. Hobson, 2014.

33. Kay, 2018, 45.

34. Ibid., 42.

35. Goodman, 2013.

36. Ibid.

37. Social identities include race, ethnicity, sex, gender, sexual orientation, religion, socioeconomic class, ability/disability, age, and national origin.

38. Culture includes traditions, values, beliefs, and patterns of behavior.

Chapter One

Who Are "Privileged" Students, and How Should They Be Taught?

Although popularized by Peggy McIntosh's famous 1988 essay, "White Privilege: Unpacking the Invisible Knapsack," the concept of privilege as used in social justice circles has its roots in 1935, when W. E. B. Du Bois wrote in *Black Reconstruction in America* that white workers, even those who earned low wages,

> were compensated in part by a sort of public and psychological wage. They were given public deference and titles of courtesy because they were white. They were admitted freely with all classes of white people to public functions, public parks, and the best schools. The police were drawn from their ranks, and the courts . . . while this had small effect upon the economic situation, it had great effect upon their personal treatment and the deference shown them. White schoolhouses were the best in the community. . . . The newspapers specialized on news that flattered the poor whites and almost utterly ignored the Negro except in crime and ridicule. [1]

McIntosh wasn't even the first white author to take up the idea of white institutional advantage. That was probably Theodore Allen, who in the 1960s coined the term "white skin privilege." [2] Both Allen and, later, Weather Underground leader Bernardine Dohrn, who also used that phrase, [3] were considered part of the far-left fringe.

What McIntosh did was bring this term more or less into the mainstream, offering a redefinition of systems of oppression, moving from "this group of people is disadvantaged" to "this other group of people has too much advantage." She described her journey from a focus on how her status as a woman disadvantaged her to a growing awareness of the advantages she enjoyed as a white person, "an invisible weightless knapsack of assurances, tools, maps, guides, codebooks, passports, visas, clothes, compass, emergency gear, and blank checks" such as

- I can arrange to be in the company of people of my race most of the time.
- I can avoid spending time with people whom I was trained to mistrust and who have learned to mistrust my kind or me.
- I can turn on the television or open to the front page of the paper and see people of my race widely represented.
- When I am told about our national heritage or about "civilization," I am shown that people of my color made it what it is.
- I can be pretty sure of having my voice heard in a group in which I am the only member of my race.
- I can expect figurative language and imagery in all of the arts to testify to experiences of my race.
- I will feel welcomed and "normal" in the usual walks of public life, institutional and social.[4]

McIntosh originally listed 46 of these advantages, yet marvels at how her schooling "gave [her] no training in seeing myself as an oppressor, as an unfairly advantaged person, or as a participant in a damaged culture. I was taught to see myself as an individual whose moral state depended on her individual moral will."[5]

Warren Blumenfeld expands on McIntosh's focus on race and gender as privileging factors, citing how a system of advantages

> confers dominance on some social identity groups, for example in a U.S. context, males, white people, heterosexuals, cisgender people, Christians . . . while subordinating and denying these privileges to other groups, for example, females, racially minoritized (*sic*) peoples, lesbians, gays, bisexuals, trans people. . . . These systemic inequities are pervasive throughout the society. They are encoded into the individual's subconscious and woven into the very fabric of our social institutions, resulting in a stratified social order privileging dominant groups while restricting and disempowering subordinated group members.[6]

Katy Swalwell, concerned that those who ascribe to the theory of privilege may develop an understanding of privilege as some mysterious "force of nature," forwards a modified definition of the term that emphasizes the forces that create and maintain it: "Elite or privileged students," she writes, are "those positioned by power relations within systems of supremacy that are continually shaped by historical, social, political and economic factors [which] are made stronger when rendered invisible, consciously or not, to those who benefit from them most."[7]

This is in many ways the position of critical race theory, which "recognizes that racism is engrained in the fabric and system of the American society. The individual racist need not exist to note that institutional racism is pervasive in the dominant culture," as evidenced in the legal frameworks and institutions of our nation as well as in subtler systems of social norms. [8] This process, as Swalwell says, "does not require nefarious intentions to work; in ways both subtle and explicit, these systems condition people to think of themselves as normal." [9]

Another key element of critical race theory is the way in which it recognizes and emphasizes the *intersectionality* of privilege, the idea that "people can be privileged in some ways and definitely not privileged in others. There are many different types of privilege, not just skin-color privilege, that impact the way people can move through the world or are discriminated against." [10] As Diane Goodman writes, "Our social identities are not a balance sheet in which one can just compare the number of identities on the dominant side and know how much power, privilege or freedom one has." [11]

Privilege is both intersectional and, in some senses, contextual. I am a white man raised by college-educated parents, even if their chosen profession as social workers meant, in my father's words, that "we would be middle class except for the lack of money." Indeed, we lived paycheck to paycheck, and during some lengthy periods where my father was out of work, our ability to make the mortgage payments was often in doubt.

Nevertheless, I always considered myself to be comfortably middle class. My parents worked in offices as opposed to on a farm, or in the last dying gasps of western Massachusetts' factory economy, as was the case with many of my peers. By the fifth grade, if not earlier, many of my classmates would spend after-school hours picking cucumbers and asparagus in the fields, returning to class the next day showing off the scratches, bruises, and under-the-table cash they'd acquired. I never had to do that. As I grew into my teenage years, my whiteness gave me "free passes" in the eyes of everyone from law enforcement to hiring managers, advantages that my counterparts in the sizable Puerto Rican population in our region did not have.

When I became a scholarship student at an elite preparatory school, however, I became keenly aware how inferior my economic situation was to that of most of my peers there. It was everywhere: in the clothes they wore, the places they had traveled, the sports and instruments they had been trained to play since toddlerhood, the way none of them ever seemed to sneeze or trip or stutter.

More saliently, my Jewishness became far more marked at this school than it had ever been, even though there were barely any other Jews around me in my childhood. Here, students slipped swastikas into my mailbox on several occasions. Anti-Semitic prank phone calls, particularly during the time of Germany's reunification, were commonplace. A teacher once gave me a detention for challenging her assertion that all Jews were responsible for the death of Jesus Christ. Less overt were the myriad subtle, unintentional reminders that I was "othered," distinct, invalidated.

So attendance at that school was both a marker of privilege, in the education and credentials it let me acquire, and also a reminder of some ways that, relative to those around me, I was marginalized. Even then, my maleness, whiteness, and heterosexuality still conferred certain advantages over classmates who didn't share those characteristics. However, if I were living in Eastern Europe during the 1930s and 1940s, none of that would have saved me from state-sponsored murder in the gas chambers. Context and intersectionality can literally be life-and-death distinctions.

It is this contextual and intersectional nature of privilege that leads to criticism of the concept's validity, from progressives and conservatives alike. Since this book lacks the space to engage in a full exploration and interrogation of various definitions of, and challenges to, the concept of privilege, I will place my own flag in the ground bearing a particular definition for my purposes: In this book, I define "privileged students" in the way Swalwell did, as

> net beneficiaries . . . whose experiences in the aggregate tend to afford them greater access to resources and opportunities . . . [versus] net maleficiaries . . . whom we call marginalized. [12]

At times this book will use the term "privileged" as shorthand for "white and affluent." To be sure, not all privileged students are white, and not all white students have the same degree of privilege vis-à-vis other white students, or even in particular situations, vis-à-vis students of color.

However, we should not kid ourselves: "[I]n American society . . . there are few ways in which the process of privileging operates more powerfully than the racialization of people and the stratification by social class,"[13] and because of this, I will follow in Swalwell's footsteps and make race and affluence the prime focal points of my book. To be sure, whiteness still confers some privilege on white people of meager economic resources, but adding wealth to the picture magnifies that privilege immensely.

While always keeping in mind that intersectionality and context can and do create hierarchies even within a white, well-off population, and that affluence is of course a relative condition, there is nevertheless a net benefit that justifies my categorizing the populations I focus on in this book as "privileged," vis-à-vis anyone else who lacks these attributes. I would certainly count myself among this "net beneficiary" group, at least in the time, place, and context in which I live now.

The most insidious quality of privilege may well be its invisibility to those who possess it. Without a conscious understanding of one's advantages, efforts to address injustices to "net maleficiaries" may appear more like preferential treatment than restoring a balance. This perception might explain sentiments like those expressed by a white Bostonian protesting, during the 1974 busing crisis, "I'm white, and I want *my* rights!"[14] It might lie behind one white man's explanation of why he voted for Donald Trump, namely that "everything [about the Democratic platform] is about illegals, and the poor, and everything else. They don't care about us anymore. They just don't. It's just like we're irrelevant, you know?"[15] It might explain the "All Lives Matter" white backlash against the Black Lives Matter movement. Unless whites like me become conscious of our advantages, then we will likely always feel either attacked or "abandoned" by social justice efforts.

PROBLEMS WITH THE "PRIVILEGED" LABEL

Swalwell cautions that "privilege . . . does not look the same everywhere and we are wise to understand its differences, particularly in terms of how its residents position themselves"[16]—for example, the meritocratic mind-set of a "new money" white suburban student versus the "aristocratic elites" attending private schools. Social justice pedagogy needs to assume different forms to cater to each group, she argues.

There are probably dozens of shades of nuance and difference even within privileged white groups, and rather than attempt the Herculean task of creating some sophisticated typology to track all the subtypes of privileged white student and match them with recommended approaches, this book's advice will be general, placing trust in individual practitioners who know their own students and their communities well enough to adapt accordingly.

One additional, dangerous effect of labeling a group as "privileged" is that this demands an opposite pole of those "net maleficiaries." Those labels—marginalized people, underprivileged people, subaltern people—inevitably dehumanize and degrade, defining these people mainly by their lack of what the privileged group has. The harm of this dichotomy in some senses cuts both ways. In his essay, "On Being White and Other Lies," James Baldwin (echoed recently by Ta-Nehisi Coates when he speaks of "people who think they are white"), challenges the validity of the construct of whiteness:

> Because they think they are white, [whites] do not dare confront the ravage and the lie of their history. Because they think they are white, they cannot allow themselves to be tormented by the suspicion that all men are brothers. Because they think they are white, they are looking for . . . stable populations, cheerful natives and cheap labor. . . . White being, absolutely, a moral choice (for there are no white people).[17]

By this same mode of thinking, the category "privileged" can be seen as simply a denial of the common humanity of others, an identity dependent on the subordination of one's fellow human beings. In fact, this system, in its own way, is also dehumanizing to the privileged. As white anti-racist educator Tim Wise once put it:

> To define yourself, ultimately, by what you're not, is a pathetic and heart-breaking thing. It is to stand denuded before a culture (whiteness) that has stolen your birthright, or rather, convinced you to give it up. And the costs are formidable, beginning with the emptiness [the privileged] so often feel when confronted by multiculturalism and the connectedness of people of color to their various heritages. That emptiness then gets filled up by privileges and ultimately forces us to become dependent on them. We are not ourselves anymore, but the overpaid, overfed, overstuffed slaves to a self-imposed, self-chosen system of cultural genocide. . . . I can't help but think that at the end of the day, we, too, got played. [18]

Know that I indulge in these labels, like "privileged" and "marginalized," conscious of their dehumanizing nature. It is because of that very nature that this book is so important; social justice work has the potential to engage privileged students in the act of breaking apart the inequities which, for all of the benefits they confer, also rob those privileged students of their own humanity.

Finally, I am conscious of the additional dangers of equating the privileged/marginalized dichotomy with white/African American, as this book is frequently guilty of. Because the inequity gap between those two groups is the largest in American society (in wealth, in health, in educational outcomes, in relationship with law enforcement), and because of the particular inheritance of slavery that has done so much to shape both white and African American heritage, these are the two groups I discuss the most with my students, and this book will place the majority of its focus on them as well.

I sincerely ask my readers' forgiveness for contributing to the erasure of the particular experiences of non-African American blacks, the Latinx population, indigenous peoples, and Asian Americans and Pacific Islanders, but since those experiences and these Americans' relationships with privileged white culture(s), as well as with one another, are so varied and nuanced, all deserve more exploration than this one book has the space to afford. I would rather do justice to those explorations in future books, than shortchange them here just to give token "checks" in all possible "boxes" for discussing marginalized peoples. One has to start somewhere.

TO SHOCK, OR TO TEACH?

This book does not suggest the direct, head-on, "shock therapy" approach to confronting privileged white students with the "real facts" of oppression, privilege, and justice. I take this position even though it might at first appear that those very tactics "worked" on me, in the earlier stages of my ongoing personal evolution. My instructors in college and graduate school spent hours preaching about patterns of privilege and oppression, interrupted by "discussions" where any student voicing an opposing perspective got immediately pounced on. "After several thousand years," a graduate teaching assistant once said to shut me down, "we've already heard everything that you men have had to say."

Oh, how I hated those classes.

Yet my "road to Damascus" moment came when I bemoaned to a friend how far I felt from the center of power in that classroom, so un-listened-to. So seen and judged for what I was, not who I was as an individual.

"You know," said my friend, an economics major, "that's what I feel like, as a woman, in all of my classes, all the time."

And just like that, some of what my professors had said started making just a little more sense. Why? Because, even in a very limited way, I had been *living* it, having an experience that my privilege had until that moment kept me from having, and therefore, kept me from learning. (Years later, I would also come to learn the phrase, "when you're accustomed to privilege, any move toward equality can feel like oppression.")

What we learn deeply is what we learn through experience. If you know how to drive a car, think about how you learned. Was it from reading that little booklet the Department of Motor Vehicles handed out in driver's ed classes? Or from actually getting behind the wheel and driving, expanding your knowledge and competency as you acquired new experiences?

The current education buzz phrases for this kind of learning include "coming to knowledge," "active learning," "student-centered learning," "inquiry-based learning," and "constructivist learning." While there are shades of difference between these terms, what they share is a refutation of what Freire calls the "banking" model of instruction. This model—still, unfortunately, the dominant one in American public school classrooms and even more so in most of the rest of the world—envisions knowledge as something that exists in the mind of the teacher, or in a resource like a textbook or article, and sees education as the art of "transferring" that knowledge into the minds of the students. Hallmarks of this model include teacher-directed, lecture-based instruction, along with activities that the entire class pursues in a standardized, one-size-fits-all fashion, according to a standardized timetable and assessed through standardized testing.

This is the model we have inherited from the industrial age when schooling was restructured in the image of factory work, complete with ringing bells to signal "shift changes." Decades of research have shown this approach can be effective for learning that involves rote memorization, but far less effective for helping students acquire mastery of complex, higher-order types of thinking.

But at least since the late 1990s, there has existed "a general—if somewhat loose and shifting—consensus" that schools must teach "21st century skills [that are] essential to prepare all students for the challenges of work, life, and citizenship in the 21st century and beyond, as well as ensure ongoing innovation in our economy and the health of our democracy."[19] Skills such as analysis/critical thinking, problem solving, synthesizing and evaluating information, and working successfully in groups are seen as "skills [students] need to thrive in a world where change is constant and learning never stops."[20]

Methods that have been shown to be effective for this kind of learning do not follow the "banking" model, but rather engage students in discussions and simulations, present them with problems to solve, have them create and test theories, and drive them to collaborative endeavors with their classmates in order to codevelop knowledge.[21] Such methods position students in the role as cofacilitators of their own education. Rather than being expected to just absorb knowledge from readings and lectures, students instead assemble their own understandings, supported by and developed through interactions with materials, problems to solve, classmates, and teachers.[22]

In this model, the teacher is a facilitator and colearner—as the clichéd phrase goes, "not the sage on the stage but the guide on the side." The teacher sets up the conditions for learning, letting students develop as best an understanding of the new material as they can on their own—or in groups—before the teacher steps in to nudge them further. Under this model, "vocabulary comes at the end of the week. . . . Only after students uncover the concepts and have some ownership of them does [the teacher] drop some academic names during discussions."[23]

As teacher educator Paul Jablon says, "The hardest part for a teacher," in a classroom like this, "is to stop talking. . . . Every time you answer a student's question you stop them from learning."[24] When this model works, in the words of teacher Eeva Reeder, students "really deeply learn concepts . . . [not just] so that they could spit back formulas and so on, on a paper and pencil test . . . [instead] they own it."[25]

For all of these reasons, indoctrinary "shock tactics" (although I have read many writers who demand their necessity in issues of injustice) still read to me like poor teaching strategy. My college professors and graduate TAs spoke, and our job was to write down what they said and agree—period—or face the consequences. My learning-through-experience in their classes came somewhat by accident, by pondering the meta-level implications of the classroom structure as opposed to through classroom assignments they designed.

If we want to really help our students develop critical thinking and evidence-based analysis, then we should never ask them to accept a theory as uncontested fact, as the only valid lens through which to view systems of power in our country and in the world at large. What we should require is that students demonstrate understanding of a given argument, and genuine engagement with the questions and implications that the argument raises. A student who passionately disagrees with, say, the theory of white privilege, and studies it hard in order to counter every point of it, should earn a higher grade in a class than a student who parrots back everything critical race theorist Derrick Bell says without evidence of detailed exploration.

Besides, on both legal and ethical grounds, middle and high school teaching is not college teaching. Indoctrination, or anything that smacks of it, flies better in a postsecondary setting where students have freely selected your course and are paying for the privilege of "tough love." It is less professionally and ethically defensible when your students are minors who are forced by law to sit in your classroom for 50 minutes every day.

Also, ever since the No Child Left Behind Act in 2001 ushered in the era of "outcomes-based education," the responsibility for learning and achievement in public schools was shifted—and remains shifted—from the student to the teacher. Rightly or wrongly, the assumption ever since is that if the student has not learned a required skill or concept, the teacher has failed. They must try and try again, in as many ways as it takes, until that student has mastered it.[26]

In the name of students' right to an education, teachers in any kind of public school classroom (and increasingly, in independent schools as well) have become positioned as salespeople, desperate to convince students of the value of what they are learning, and evaluated on the basis of their students' achievement. In some ways this is a good thing; as we will explore in detail later on, students really do deserve an answer to the time-honored question of, "Why do we have to learn this?"

This paradigm gives even more strength to a power that students have always possessed, the power of what Herbert Kohl calls intentional "not-learning":

> Not-learning tends to take place when someone has to deal with unavoidable challenges to her or his personal and family loyalties, integrity and identity. In such situations there are forced choices and no apparent middle ground. To agree to learn from a stranger who does not respect your integrity causes a major loss of self. The only alternative is to not-learn and reject the stranger's world.[27]

Kohl is writing primarily about children of color from underprivileged back-grounds, finding in "not-learning" a rare—if sadly self-destructive—avenue to seizing some power and agency in a school system that devalues and dehumanizes them.

But privileged white students retain that same option. They too can exert that same defense mechanism when they encounter challenges to the beliefs and assumptions they hold . . . and unlike most of the parents of the students Kohl studies, their parents wield considerable political, economic, and social clout. A teacher can make their students only so uncomfortable before they push back, demand and almost inevitably obtain sanctions against that teach-er, up to and including removal—as was the case with the "threatening" star teacher mentioned in the introduction. Remember, we are Aristotle to Alex-ander.

Teachers of privileged students might find themselves on somewhat more solid ground if they are using "tough love," confrontational-type methods to help students learn, for example, effective essay writing, or factoring using the quadratic formula. Students need to learn these concepts in order to pass state tests, the SATs, and the AP exams. But there is no state test for social justice competencies, no curriculum framework with any teeth that requires students to learn them; quite the contrary, in fact, as the majority of texts in humanities courses reinforce the perspectives of the dominant race and class.

In short, teaching social justice in affluent schools, even more than in traditional academic subjects, can only proceed with the consent of the stu-dents and their families, and of administrators and colleagues who have their own vested interest in keeping those two parties happy.

Even in a community and power structure that supports teachers doing such work, even where overt student resistance is minimal, there is still the danger that the shock approach might not accomplish anything. As Matthew Kay writes, such shock

> often causes student expressions that can *look* like breakthroughs . . . but may not be . . . we can think so much of our classroom communities that every show of raw vulnerability is regarded as evidence of progress. *They're crying, so I'm good.* This inch-deep Hollywood metric has more potential to feed our egos than help our students. [28]

Along with this sort of disabling emotion, such "shocks" can also produce counterreactions, as Boston University Education professor Scott Seider en-countered with a study group of privileged suburban students, including "suspicion, resentment and desire to trivialize" the issues. Seider concludes that "teaching privileged teens about societal inequity and the interplay be-tween dominant and marginalized groups is a tremendously complex endeav-or." [29]

It's a dance, what we would-be social justice educators do with privileged students—how to "comfort the afflicted and afflict the comfortable"[30] just enough to open minds, but not enough to open cans of worms we cannot close. While this argument is unlikely to evoke much sympathy in the minds of those for whom oppression is a daily lived reality, this book argues nevertheless that white fragility, male fragility, upper-class fragility, and their ilk are conditions that, like it or not, a teacher has to work with and around, just as effective teachers in less affluent schools need to know how to work with students who didn't have enough to eat that morning. Those teachers—often at their own expense—may know that they have to show up with bagels and orange juice if they want their kids to be able to learn geometry that day.

The advice in this book constitutes "breakfasts" that are designed to be digestible for privileged white students, so I would advise those seeking spicier fare to look elsewhere.

GETTING "TOO POLITICAL"

On the other hand, there may be those who will find this book too extreme. These readers may argue that its lessons are "too political," and that the classroom is no place for such content. What this argument, however well-intentioned, fails to recognize is that students inevitably receive a political education in school, whether or not it is made explicit. Students in highly privileged school environments inevitably learn political lessons along the lines of what Shamus Khan describes in his ethnographic study of an elite boarding school:

> [L]essons of privilege that students learn [are that] hierarchies are natural and can be used to one's advantage; experiences matter more than innate or inherited qualities; the way to signal your elite status to others is through ease and openness in all social contexts. Inequality is ever-present, but elites now view it as fair. Hierarchies are enabling, not constraining. It is the inherent character of the individual that matters, not breeding, or skin color.[31]

The default political education that privileged students receive is that our nation is an essentially just meritocracy, where the elite have earned their high status and that only individual decisions, and not institutionalized barriers along racial, class, and/or gender lines, are responsible for inequities. I am not claiming that no truth lies anywhere in this political position, but it is a political position nonetheless, and to not engage students in exploring alternate narratives is to promote that one political position to the exclusion of all else.

For Paolo Freire, there is no such thing as a classroom free of political content. He writes that "to be in the world without making history, without being made by it, without creating culture . . . without being political, is a total impossibility."[32] He maintains that "it is impossible to humanly exist without assuming the right and the duty to opt, to decide, to struggle, to be political,"[33] and therefore the teacher has some responsibility and duty to help students become aware of and empowered by their own ability to make these choices.

We have choices as teachers, too. This book is for those who have chosen to, or are considering choosing to, engage students in a conscious exploration and deconstruction of social injustice. It is for those who are willing to brave the inevitable criticism from all angles, to take risks that are not required to take, to help work with a population of students whose needs are unrecognized and invalidated by just about everyone—but who, I am convinced, represent a piece of the social justice puzzle without which the full picture will never be assembled. To those who take up this mantle, I salute you, and I'll do what I can here to help.

NOTES

1. Du Bois, 1935/1995, 700–701.
2. Allen, "A Call to Join with Sponsors of This Call in a John Brown Memorial Pilgrimage to Harper's Ferry, West Virginia on Saturday, December 4, 1965" (New York: John Brown Commemoration Committee), cited in Perry, 2010.
3. As described in Randhawa, 2015.
4. McIntosh, 1988.
5. Ibid.
6. Blumenfeld, 2013.
7. Swalwell, 2013, 6.
8. "What Is Critical Race Theory?" UCLA School of Public Affairs, 2009.
9. Swalwell, 2013, 7.
10. Crosley-Corcoran, 2014.
11. Goodman, 2011, 29.
12. Swalwell, 2013, 7.
13. Ibid.
14. Hampton, 1990.
15. Glass, 2019.
16. Swalwell, 2013, 52.
17. Baldwin, "On Being 'White' . . . and Other Lies," 1998.
18. Wise, 2011, 171.
19. Great Schools Partnership, 2016.
20. Partnership for 21st Century Learning, 2016.
21. A starter here: Baloche, 1997; Burden, 2016; Chall, 2000; Delialioğlu , 2012; Gilboy, Heinerichs, and Pazzaglia, 2015; Jablon, 2014; Johnson and Johnson, 1997; Larmer, Mergendoller, and Boss, 2015; Lieber, 2009; Markham, 2003.
22. Vygotsky, cited in Van der Veer and Valsiner, 1991.
23. Jablon, 2014, 29.
24. Ibid., 21.
25. Reeder quoted in Edutopia, 2010.
26. McNeir, 1993.
27. Kohl, 1995, 6. See also Toshalis, 2015.
28. Kay, 2018, 90.

29. Seider, 2019, 7–8.
30. Attributed to Progressive Era muckraker Finley Peter Dunne's character of "Mr. Dooley," although the internet is full of misattributions to, among others, Karl Marx, Abby Hoffman, and Bob Dylan.
31. Khan, 2012, 194.
32. Friere, 1974/1998, 58.
33. Ibid., 53.

Chapter Two

Warming Up the Room

It's hard to say which response teachers fear most when trying to engage students in a conversation or learning activity about social justice: that the students will not be able to grasp the concepts, that they will unleash destructive and toxic emotions on one another, or that they will just clam up and produce 50 minutes of awkward silence. Grasping the concepts is the concern of any teacher with any kind of lesson, and the remaining chapters of this book will deal mainly with that goal. However, the other two worries (yes, the silent classroom is a worry, as heavenly as it might seem if you've got a particularly rowdy class) need to be dealt with first, or else our ability to help our students achieve that goal of understanding concepts will be severely curtailed, if not impossible.

Before you can ask students to engage in challenging and demanding work, you must help them become part of a safe and supportive community. Conversations about race, class, and justice can be charged and uncomfortable for students and teachers alike. It is both important and difficult for a teacher to walk that line between not scaring students away from the conversation by leaping in with admonishments or "corrections," and also responding appropriately to inappropriate comments and steering the conversation away from becoming toxic.

Recall Matthew Kay's advice about the "very specific ecosystem" that conversations about race and justice require, especially with white fragility to take into account. The fact that most white people have little to no experience in navigating conversations about race is a problem compounded by the fact that most students—and too often, their teachers—have insufficient tools for creating and maintaining climates where meaningful and generative race discussions can happen.

Some of the groundwork for this ecosystem needs to be laid out early in the school year, before any discussion of race or justice even enters the picture, and it takes time—merely declaring your classroom a "safe space," says Kay, doesn't make it so. Any conversation in which students' personal views and experiences come into play, says Kay, asks those students to

> be honest about fears, hopes and anger [and] mine their own lives instead of assigned texts for source material. Teachers here break a tacit agreement to keep our class conversations detached. This paradigm can be changed, but only through effort and practice of building genuine *house talk* relationships.[1]

Small groups of four or five can provide students a more intimate, safer, and more productive space to have these discussions. Teachers will need to weigh that advantage with the disadvantage that the teacher will not be present at all times with all groups to intervene in or moderate potentially fraught situations.

Robin DiAngelo is very critical of "the need for so many white progressives to 'build trust' before they can explore racism," which she fears can too often result in "accommodations made to coddle white fragility." She cautions that "the very conditions that most white people insist on to remain comfortable are those that support the racial status quo (white centrality, dominance and professed innocence)." With respect to Dr. DiAngelo's concerns, a wealth of psychological and educational theory attests to how adolescents require a sense of safety for learning. However difficult, it is still very possible to, as she says, "combine kindness with clarity and the courage to name and challenge racism."[2]

Either in small groups or as a full class, the kinds of activities that help students develop and maintain the "house talk" environment will vary, based not only on the students in the room, but also on *when* during the year these activities occur. Bruce Tuckman's work on small groups[3] and Mary Ann Jensen's Stage Theory of Group Development[4] posit that groups, small or large, go through various stages of evolution—forming, storming, norming, performing, and adjourning. At each stage, the group will have certain distinct needs that must be met in order for the group to function safely and effectively. The teacher can provide activities tailored to the needs of each stage, with the goal of helping the group achieve and maintain what Srogi and Baloche call "positive interdependence."[5]

* * *

Group Work That Doesn't Stink

All through middle school, high school, and even college, I hated group work. It took me years to realize that I hated group work because no one ever taught me how to do it.

Working effectively in a group requires as specific a skill set as learning a sport. No teacher in his right mind would hand a basketball to a student who had never learned the discrete skills of dribbling, passing, and throwing, tell her to "go play basketball," and expect any degree of success. Yet we are doing something quite analogous every time we just put students in groups and say, "go work together," and then we wonder why it so often turns into a train wreck.

Just as every sport has specific drills for practicing the skills necessary for success, so too does cooperative learning. The activities described in this chapter can be thought of as "batting practice" or "speed trials" that help students develop the skills necessary to work together, be it on a major project or in a difficult conversation, but conducted in low-stakes settings long before "the big game," as it were. Just as such practice is necessary for athletic success, so too is it a prerequisite for, in the spot-on words of one of my students, "group work that doesn't stink."

We owe it to students to teach them these skills, both because nearly any professional setting will require them to work interdependently in some sort of team, and because citizenship by definition requires productive cooperative interactions with others. These very competencies are often explicitly described among those twenty-first-century skills students need to acquire, and if more adults possessed these skills, our workplace and political cultures might be far healthier than they currently are.

* * *

As always, YKYS-YMMV ("You Know Your Students—Your Mileage May Vary"—see the introduction for a refresher) applies and, depending on your students, you may need more or less scaffolding, or may need to set more or fewer specific parameters or ground rules for behavior, in order to ensure that the activities don't devolve into chaos or are not otherwise abused or distorted.

These activities, in increasing order, require students to work cooperatively, to pay close attention to one another and to fine details, to adapt to the actions of others and modify their own actions accordingly, and even to engage in problem solving. These skills will serve students in any number of academic arenas, which can serve as consolation and justification for teachers who are understandably concerned about spending so much time in the early weeks of the year doing activities that may seem unrelated to the official subject-area content they are required to teach.

The activities are to some extent "brain hacks" that don't smell like schoolwork (and are therefore more appealing for many students), but covertly build and strengthen their neurology when it comes to cooperative work and higher-order thinking.[6] In short, spending this time is an investment that will not only yield dividends when it comes to sharing uncomfortable conversations about race and justice, but also when it comes to any number of learning goals and activities. Some of these activities can be infused with subject-area content as well, serving those two aims simultaneously.

FORMING ACTIVITIES

During this first stage, students need to develop a sense of safety and shared identity. Activities that help them do so often resemble popular icebreakers from summer camp or corporate teambuilding, and a quick Google search can reveal dozens of them. The following are just a few examples.

Toothbrush: Students go around in a circle sharing the color of their toothbrush, and "what that says about them." This gives them the opportunity to reveal a personal but low-stakes[7] detail about their lives, the specifics of which they are largely in control of.

Mirror: The classic theater exercise where students face each other in pairs and, in silence, one leads with slow, easy-to-follow hand motions that their partner must mirror. The goal for the leader is to not lose their mirror-partner through any rapid or unpredictable actions. They later swap roles, and eventually are challenged to keep on exchanging leadership until it is no longer clear who is leading and who is following, but the two are moving as one.

What's my story? Active listening: One student shares a brief story from their lives about a low-risk, innocuous topic (e.g., what is their favorite food or TV show, and why). One or more other students listen, then restate what the speaker just said in their own words, using as much detail as possible. The speaker then decides if the listener has indeed heard and understood them, and the activity repeats until all parties are satisfied.

Similarities and differences: Students in a given group must come up with three "things you can't tell by looking at them" that everyone in that group has in common. In addition, each student must also provide one quality unique to just that student, shared by none of their groupmates. This activity helps students learn that they might actually have more in common than they suspect, and get a peek at some of the "iceberg beneath the surface of the water" that could revise stereotypes they have of their peers. At the same time, the unique qualities are a reminder that every single person brings something special to the table that no one else can provide.

STORMING ACTIVITIES

The storming stage comes when students attempt group activities with a shared goal and, predictably, conflict occurs. Some students might vie for power or control, some might become dictators, some might withhold participation out of either anxiety or laziness. Typically in middle and high school this is the stage that most group work reaches and never evolves past (see "Group Work That Doesn't Stink"). The mission of the storming stage is to help groups go through this necessary period of conflict in a low-stakes setting, with mandated opportunities to reflect and improve on the mechanisms by which they work together.

Don't drop the ball: In this game, students must create a collective sentence, each one adding a new word as they go around the circle (sometimes they pass an actual ball—hence the name of the game—to indicate whose turn it is to speak). The pace should be quick, and each new speaker needs to add a word that advances the story of the sentence in a way that makes sense. If their word does not make sense, or if they freeze, or add two words, or laugh, the ball is dropped and the next student in line must immediately take over and restart the sentence. The goal is to keep the sentence going for as long as possible. Active listening and quick adaptation are the skills that this activity builds. The sentences also tend to get hysterically funny, so even though laughing drops the ball, it also builds cohesion among the group.

Tower of power (aka *Bridge over troubled waters,* etc.): Each student group is responsible for building some sort of simple structure (e.g., a tower, a bridge) using certain specific materials (e.g., index cards, popsicle sticks, pipe cleaners, LEGO blocks) with certain constraints (e.g., must be free-standing, must support the weight of an eraser) within a tight time limit (usually five minutes or less).

This is usually a high-energy activity, and some groups will be more successful than others, but the real goal here is to have a postgame analysis in which students discuss and determine who showed leadership, how roles were assigned and divided, how the group dealt with new proposed ideas or with conflicting desires.

The teacher then runs the activity *again*, with the same groups, either later that class period or the next day. The groups attempt to change what didn't work for them the last time while repeating strategies that were successful. By the time students are ready for high-stakes cooperative assignments, they will have learned a series of strategies for working with one another that they know will be effective for their particular group.

Practicing conflict: Conflict, at heart, is simply a disagreement, a clash of perspectives. Carol Miller Lieber calls it "a natural and essential part of living," and yet in the classroom, "we usually perceive conflict as a negative phenomenon instead of an opportunity for change and growth."[8] Since most adolescents (and to be fair, most adults) lack tools to successfully and nonviolently navigate conflicts, it is usual practice in classroom management for teachers to attempt to suppress conflict as much as possible, through both prevention and intervention.

But if we want students to engage in collaborative practices, from discussions to group projects, we can't protect them from conflict, nor should we want to—if there is no conflict, no clash of ideas, then why have the students share their ideas at all? Echo chambers do not produce quality learning. Editors argue in a newsroom, generals disagree about battle plans, doctors clash over diagnoses and treatment regimens. Ultimately from this struggle may emerge a solution that no single person could have found on her own, a "eureka" moment sparked by something someone else said.

Yet, as Lieber writes, "young people rarely have an opportunity to learn a systematic way of thinking about conflict or a practical process for handling [it],"[9] so chances are that when students arrive in your classroom, they will need to be taught these skills. Lieber's book, *Conflict Resolution in the High School* (1998), William Kreidler's *Conflict Resolution in the Middle School* (1994), and David and Peter Johnson's *Teaching Students to Be Peacemakers* (1995) are three great resources that offer a full curriculum with suites of activities for helping students handle conflict in a generative rather than toxic way, including:

- Practicing taking multiple points of view in a conflict situation
- Communicating using "I statements"
- Discerning the difference between interests (actual needs and desires) and positions (someone's stated wants)
- Recognizing anger triggers and practicing anger-defusing strategies

These skills are often best developed through role-playing exercises, where students can have some fun pretending to be characters in fictional conflict scenarios. Role plays provide low-stakes, safe places to practice conflict resolution skills, and can serve as valuable anchors to hold on to when real conflicts arise ("Remember the scenario where Brenda was convinced Sasha had stolen her phone?").

Even if you have never discussed issues of race and justice in your classroom, these would be valuable skills to inculcate in the next generation. Given how our elected officials, media stars, and other public figures too often model nothing but disdain for those who hold different views, the classroom may be the one place where students can learn more constructive approaches to conflict. If you are discussing issues of race and justice, then the tools to encourage constructive conflict are absolutely prerequisite.

Despite the name of the stage, not all storming activities are about conflict and abrasive situations. "Storm damage prevention and recovery" (i.e., building resilience) also needs to be a part of this process. Below are three regular activities I use with my students throughout the year, but which are particularly important during their "storming" time:

Check-ins: Every day, class begins with every student, one by one, weighing in with a one-to-five word "check-in" about how they're feeling that day. The teacher establishes and enforces norms from the outset about what sort of language and content is acceptable. The check-in has several benefits, which the teacher can explicitly discuss with the students, including:

- Reinforcing the norm that the teacher considers the students (and students should consider each other) to be human beings, not just an aggregation of attendance marks and test scores. The message is that their feelings and state of mind matter to both the teacher and the rest of the community. Check-ins can provide a forum for the entire class to both cheer their successes and be concerned about their challenges; they can remind students that they are not alone.
- Reinforcing the norm that students' feelings and state of mind matter from a learning perspective as well. Students who check in, honestly, as hungry or tired or in some way distressed will have trouble focusing, acquiring new material, and participating in class activities. Teachers who have a "heads up" about these concerns from the outset can plan for ways to support these students, and take their condition into account during the class period. Too many teachers wind up treating student disengagement or noncompliance of any sort solely as behavior problems, when sometimes such issues stem from unmet biological and emotional needs that interfere with a student's ability to participate appropriately. The conversation becomes about detentions and other consequences, and the teacher misses the chance to employ more effective strategies to get the student in a state to learn again.
- If certain students repeatedly check in as distressed in some form, the teacher can follow up with the student, a parent/guardian, a guidance counselor, and/or other supports to attempt an appropriate intervention, defusing some potential conflicts before they happen. It is natural and developmentally appropriate for adolescents, especially younger adolescents, to have a highly self-centered worldview.[10] If a student comes into the room glowering, it is very possible that one or more of her classmates could take offense, assuming that glowering look was meant for them, and begin to react defensively. If, on the other hand, the glowering student checks in at the start of class with something like "Having a tough day," it

can provide an important, empathetic reminder that what appears to be hostility may actually be pain.

To be certain, check-ins are not and should not be times for students to bare embarrassing, overdetailed, or inappropriate accounts of their situations. They are for providing clearer direction for the rest of their community as to how to interact with them that day.

Compliment a Classmate: On regular occasions, especially before or after large or difficult projects, the teacher can convene a "compliment" session. The goal is for students to share earnest, specific positive feedback with their peers, both to help boost their self-esteem and also to encourage the recipient to continue practicing the benign behaviors and qualities that were complimented.[11] There are any number of mechanisms for doing so, including:

- Written notes, signed by the students who write them but read aloud by the teacher without revealing authorship. This combination of anonymity and accountability also allows the teacher to serve as a "gatekeeper" to prevent or modify inappropriate contributions. Alternatively, the teacher can curate a bulletin board where such compliments are posted.
- One-on-one sessions where students are paired, purposefully or randomly, and deliver compliments to one another face to face. This method permits and reinforces more direct connections between students, which is both a positive (potentially stronger bonds) and a negative (potentially more discomfiting).

Setting norms and parameters ahead of time could include, in addition to the usual cautions about taking the assignment seriously, a mandate to compliment *actions* and *personal qualities*, versus *possessions* or *appearance.* Kay presents a typology of compliments[12] where the "highest grade" statements are very specific, detailed, and serve the goal of communicating a sense of respect, admiration, or strong relationship. Teachers may need to train students in the difference between general praise ("Sarah is a great student") versus the more valuable and effective forms of specific praise, centered around specific behaviors ("I like how Laney always lends me her pencil when I forget one" or "yesterday Joel made a really great comment about individual rights"). Praise from a teacher can sometimes be a source of embarrassment to a student, but (sincere) praise from a classmate indicates an entirely different variety of earned respect from a constituency that, for good or ill, tends to be much more important for students' self-esteem than their teachers.

* * *

On Compliments

I've been having my students engage in "Compliment Friday" for over a decade, ever since I first read about the idea in Charlie Abourjilie's Developing Character for Classroom Success *(2000). Many of my students really respond well to it, look forward to it, and are genuinely upset on occasions when they miss the chance to take part. Like any classroom tool, it has its shortfalls as well as its benefits, including:*

Time: *Writing and reading the compliments aloud, in total, takes about 5 to 8 minutes of class time once a week. I consider it time well invested, but add it up throughout the year and it's not insignificant.*

Distribution of compliments: *Inevitably, some students will receive more compliments than others. Sometimes that is because these are clearly individuals who consistently go above and beyond to be helpful and supportive of their classmates, in which case I don't have a problem with that; they should be a model to others. But sometimes the "popular" kids accrue compliments simply by virtue of their privileged social status, while other students receive few to no compliments. Therefore, I sometimes institute a condition to "compliment someone different than you did last week," or "compliment someone you've never complimented before." Sometimes I assign small groups the responsibility for making sure that everyone in their group receives a compliment. I have seen some teachers go around the room naming each student, and not moving on from that student until someone gives them a "shout out" compliment. On rare occasions, I will secretly manufacture a compliment and say it is from another student.*

Sarcastic or otherwise inappropriate compliments: *I would be lying if I said all my students always take the activity 100 percent earnestly. Some treat it as an obviously artificial chore, and a few try and use the opportunity to take subtle (or not-so-subtle) potshots. When this happens, I will both speak to the offending student one on one, and address the issue in general with the class: I'm giving you the forum to celebrate and value one another, I will tell them. Would you really prefer if we didn't have this? Would our class be better for it? Never has a class of mine ever risen to make that argument, and sometimes other students will even speak up and urge their classmates to behave better.*

* * *

Gratitudes: As a variation on the same sorts of mechanisms for delivering compliments, ask students to deliver statements of gratitude to one another. The thanks can be for things that happened in class ("Thanks for helping me with my research project, thanks for checking my work"), in a different teacher's class, or even for something not at all related to school ("Thanks for giving me a ride when it was raining out, thanks for babysitting my little brother last week"). Although Kay's advice about the power of specificity holds here as well, there is also something to be said for the power of a simple expression like, "Thanks for being my friend."

These sorts of activities, when made routine parts of the classroom, can serve as a kind of inoculation against deliberate antagonism when the time comes for difficult, emotional classroom conversations . . . and a means of reassurance and reintegration after those difficult conversations shake things up.

NORMING

The norming stage comes when students settle into routines and patterns that guide their interactions. Now that they know and to some extent trust one another, students are more likely to uphold these norms on the grounds that doing so maintains the positive functioning of the group. These norms can be set out by the teacher, but are often more effective when codeveloped with student input.

Developing Listening Norms: Students practice a given set of listening *behaviors*, physical indications that send a message to a partner that they are respectfully engaged with what the partner is saying. The teacher can lay out these behaviors from the outset, but it is often better for the teacher to help students develop that list together—what are the signs, the teacher can ask, that indicate to *you*, the students, what listening looks like? How do *you* know when someone is listening to you? Usually, some sort of list emerges that looks like:

- Eye contact or facing the speaker
- Nodding, mm-hmm-ing or giving some other nonverbal sign of response
- Refraining from talking or texting (I encourage students to frame "don'ts" in positive terms, which is why this doesn't read as "don't talk or text." "Keep my phone put away" is a good one)
- Asking follow-up questions

Depending on students' cultural backgrounds, some of these may differ— eye contact in some cultures, for example, may be taken as a sign of disrespect or brazenness, while others might engage in "talkback" that is affirmational and not perceived as an interruption. Hammering out norms that the class can agree on may take some doing, but it is worth the investment.

These norms can be negotiated verbally, or with sticky notes that students can (signed or anonymously) place on chart paper, perhaps with circle diagrams labeled "behaviors that communicate respect" and "behaviors that communicate disrespect."

* * *

How Many Norms?

My graduate students often raise this question: If every teacher followed advice like this and coconstructed norms with their students, how could the students keep track of shuffling all those different norms in their different classes? It's a valid concern. Schools already give students a kind of intellectual and emotional whiplash with their endless series of "jump-cuts"—now we're studying evolution, whoops, a bell rings, now we're writing about Romeo and Juliet, *whoops, bell, now we're factoring equations, whoops, bell, now we're playing dodge ball.*

At most middle schools and even some high schools, teachers work in teams, and could commit to sharing a common set of basic norms. Ideally, a whole school, led by a purposeful administration, could agree on and reinforce a common set of norms—and some of the most effective schools do just that. School leaders take note: Community norms can be made far more ambitious than "no hats anywhere in the building," and far more specific than "treat everyone with respect." Consider norms like "We stand up for our classmates when they are being treated badly" and "We take intellectual risks, knowing that our mistakes help us learn."

* * *

Developing Conversational Norms: How will discussions be moderated? Will students raise hands? Will the previous speaker pick the next one? What if someone is speaking too much, or doesn't want to speak at all? How will the group respond to speech that a student finds offensive? What if some find it offensive, but others do not?

Creating these norms ahead of time provides a roadmap, a set of guidelines to prevent and mitigate some of the dangers that lie in what Kay calls "pop-up" conversations. While the teacher of course has final say in these matters, and can and should veto or amend norms that appear to be recipes for disaster, the more the students have a hand in codesigning and voting on their norms, the more invested they are likely to be in upholding them.

Since no battle plan survives its first encounter in the field, you, and the students, should expect to revisit and revise norms if and when some of them don't seem to be working. But to not have a plan at all invites disaster. As a general set of guidelines, here again is the set of norms outlined in the introduction that have served me and my students well:

Norm #1: Speak for one's self and one's own experiences.

Norm #2: Validate the experiences of others. Recognize that they are speaking what is, for them, a truth—this includes how they might feel about something said in class, even if the speaker had different intentions.

Norm #3: On the other hand, assume good intentions. We all have "permission to fumble."

Norm #4: Respond to something that upsets you by asking honest questions (e.g., "What do you mean by that, precisely?" "Where did you learn that information?" "What personal experiences led you to think/say that?")

Norm #5: Practice reflexivity and reflection. Regularly ask yourself what led you to the beliefs and positions you hold, and what informs the actions you take.

Norms for Safety in the Mixed-Race Classroom

It is likely that even classrooms populated by majority white, privileged students will have at least some students of color, or even, as is too often the case, just one. As college student Lamar Bethea describes,

> Whenever I'm the only black student in class . . . I sometimes find it difficult to contribute to class discussions. It's not that I feel that what I have to say isn't worth saying, but that my opinions won't have the same weight as those of my classmates. [13]

Reaffirming and encouraging discussion procedures like exchanging compliments and shout-outs are especially important for reassuring students who have these concerns, and the teacher should model showing respect and serious consideration for the contributions of their students of color. Teachers also need to be aware of the "representation pressures" that minority students in a largely white classroom often find themselves under. Bethea continues:

> My opinion is the only black opinion involved in the discussion. That means that each of my ideas has to be articulate and well thought out. I often feel that if I make any missteps, it not only reflects poorly on me, but on my race as a whole. . . . These feelings only intensify whenever the subject moves to sensitive racial topics. In these situations, I wonder if it's expected of me to contribute to the conversation, especially when the subject matter is relevant to contemporary events or my own personal experiences. [14]

Such pressures are hard to dispel when the racial demographics of your classroom are like this. Here is where explicitly inculcating and reinforcing the norm of "speak only for yourself" (and perhaps an extension, "do not expect others to speak for anyone other than themselves") is especially important in your classroom.

One option for engaging privileged white students' empathy for the importance of this norm is to ask them to think of a time when they felt unfairly judged for the actions of others in their group—this could be their sports team, their family, their school—and to reflect on that discomfort, with an eye toward not causing that discomfort for anyone else in the classroom community.

* * *

The Coin Scenario

When going over this particular norm with my students, I will often use the example of what happens when I find a coin lying in a hallway or on school grounds. Before I pick it up, I will usually look around to see if anyone is watching. Although I know it's silly, I still worry, since my "Jewishness" is a very public part of my persona at school, about reinforcing the anti-Semitic stereotype in some gentiles' minds of Jews as being money-obsessed. This is a pressure I am under that Christians never need to worry about.

I emphasize how minor this inconvenience is when compared to the more serious and pervasive pressures on other groups, but I bring it up to illustrate a point. I want my students of color to be aware that I am aware of this issue, and for my white students to keep it somewhere in their minds.

I will also bring up how much I would dread, as a middle or high schooler, any time the subject of the Holocaust came up, because sooner or later the teacher or another student would single out me to contribute a "Jewish perspective." Not only could I not speak for all Jews, I didn't even have any Holocaust victims or survivors in my family! Again, an annoyance at best, but it's also a signal flare I want to send up, early and often, that this is not a mistake that I will be making with my students . . . and I will quickly intervene should I see anyone else making this mistake.

* * *

Public declarations of these norms, and enforcement of them throughout the year, cannot possibly counteract the weight of pressure that singular students of color might feel in a mostly white classroom, but some studies suggest that what social psychologist Claude Steele calls "stereotype threat"—the worry that one is "at risk of confirming, as a self-characteristic, a negative stereotype about one's social group"—can be reduced if teachers make public assurances that students' race, gender, and other identity characteristics will not be used against them in assessments. [15]

Depending on the situation, when you are constructing small discussion groups, putting more than one student of color together in the same group—so long as the group is not *solely* composed of students of color, and therefore readily recognizable to all as a segregated "minority group"—might be helpful for identity support, as student Amanda Cross describes:

> Having another person with skin like you is helpful, especially when people start spouting racist stereotypes and tropes. [At minimum] you can stare at them and they can stare back at you, and you know, your feelings weren't just in your head.[16]

Remembering, of course, that students are individuals regardless of their race, you obviously want to consider all of the usual factors (readiness level, interest, other students with whom they do or do not get along) when assigning students of color to groups.

The norm that may go the farthest toward bolstering the emotional safety of students of color in a majority-white classroom and school, though, may well be the teacher consistently including positive and humanizing images and examples of people of color—without the appearance of tokenism or exceptionality—throughout the curriculum and the classroom,[17] something explored in more detail in chapter 3. In addition, consider the following practices:[18]

- Know who your students are. Undertake as much effort as necessary to learn how to properly pronounce their names and use that proper pronunciation in class. Find out what their personal heritage is, and seed culturally relevant information from that heritage into the curriculum you create for class. For example, for math problems that use names and cultural referents such as, "How many apples will John have if he gives three to Mary?," perhaps every so often the fruits could be guavas, and the names could be Juan and Maria.
- Be careful of assuming "we" are all the same "we." In other words, monitor your statements carefully to make sure you are not assuming everyone in the room has the same cultural referents, or racial or ethnic identity. Just as most teachers are trained to use the phrase "parent or guardian" instead of assuming all students live with parents, think carefully about phrases like "when your ancestors chose to come to this country"—were some of your students' ancestors brought here in chains, against their will? Assuming that all of your students listen to the same music, have a shared knowledge of TV characters, or have the same standard of living always runs the risk of marginalizing some individuals. Be particularly careful of unconsciously conflating your Asian, Latinx, and biracial students with your white students. Light-skinned and/or economically prosperous mem-

bers of those groups often end up being swept up into the "default" assumptions of the white experience, which further marginalizes them.[19]

- Don't tell students of color not to worry. Discussions involving race and inequity, especially in a majority-white classroom, can raise anxiety and activate trauma for students of color in a way that white educators may not be able to understand. "Let them be the experts of their own experience," Karen Kelsky writes. "Your first, and most important, job is to listen and acknowledge their fear, distress, and anxiety."[20]
- Don't expect or push your students of color to always be in a place where they can immediately open up to you (especially if you are a white teacher) about how they are feeling in class. Asking them if there is someone they want to talk to and facilitating their ability to reach this person may be more helpful. Don't expect your students of color to be responsible for making suggestions as to how to create a safer environment—that's your job, not theirs—but if they do make suggestions, consider them seriously.
- Utilize conscious classroom management techniques to ensure that white students don't dominate discussions. This does *not* mean putting on the spot a student of color who has been silent and inviting them to comment. However, if a student of color is raising a hand, then making a space for that student, even if it jumps the set order or procedure for turn-taking, can be a sign of support. You could alert students early on that you reserve the right as facilitator to "tweak" speaking order for a number of reasons, such as privileging the contributions of students who have not yet spoken, or ensuring a back-and-forth exchange of ideas as opposed to just repeating the same positions. This way, using race as one factor in turn-taking is not quite as obvious.
- Respond immediately to comments that could be perceived of as hurtful. This doesn't mean jumping down the throat of a white student who in all likelihood did not mean offense (recall Norm #3: Assume good intentions). However, respectfully yet firmly interrogating certain statements, especially referring back to your classroom norms as you do so, can send a message to students of color that you are aware of the potentially hurtful nature of these comments and are responding by challenging them. Examples include responding to comments like "black people do X" or "Asian people are like X" with a calm but firm reminder of Norm #1: Speak only for one's own experience; or responding to comments like "Black Lives Matter is a terrorist group" by using Norm #4: Ask honest questions ("What do you mean by that, precisely?" and "What sources are you drawing on that make that argument?").

On the other hand, if one student makes an outright attack on another, slings racial slurs, or in some other way violates the norms of respectful discourse, you have a responsibility to stop the conversation, call out the offense immediately, and institute a consequence. That said, determining in "borderline" cases whether a particular remark rises to this level is not an exact science. Students often make comments without any intention to harm, or consciousness of potential trauma to, their fellows. The section on microaggressions in chapter 6 offers some guidance on engaging students in a discussion of that difficult reality.

- Don't be defensive. If students express critique or skepticism of a particular belief you hold, really listen to them, and respond without strong emotion. This is good advice for dealing with all of your students, but especially for your students of color, who already face barriers with reactions of authority (especially white authority) to their concerns. This can be difficult, of course, but you cannot teach critical thinking while holding your own positions exempt from it.
- Along those lines, when you screw up—and you will, because we all do— take responsibility, apologize, and resolve to do better. As counterintuitive as it might seem, especially for a young teacher trying to establish their own legitimacy, admission of your own humanity and continuing evolution makes you look confident and strong. It is the fragile teacher who never dares to admit mistakes. It also shows students that you care enough about them to change your ways if you realize you're doing something that poorly serves them, and that their needs matter more than your vanity.

Some authors recommend that teachers "wear visible symbols of support" (e.g., a Black Lives Matter T-shirt). Exercise caution here. As detailed in chapter 7, any appearance of political endorsement or indoctrination can at minimum shut down students who hold differing views, and at worst can bring down administrative or community consequences on you. In some schools, hanging a GLSEN "Safe Space" or "Hate Has No Home Here" sign in your classroom may be considered a statement of support, while in other schools it could be considered favoring a certain political party or position. It's up to you to negotiate the lines as applied to your own community. For example, in my school, I often wear a sweatshirt bearing the logo of the program that uses voluntary busing to bring students of color from the city into the suburbs. Although not all students of color at Oak Hills come via this program—some do live in the community—many students and faculty associate the logo with support for our students of color in general.

These kinds of actions, used as regular routines, can set a powerful norm that you as the teacher care about the particular needs of students of color in your classroom.

PERFORMING

At this stage, the students are ready to be enacting the discussions and activities detailed in the rest of this book. Knowing when the students are ready for this stage can be tricky, but having lots of low-stakes simulations can at least give you a sense. Since no student ever advances in lockstep with anyone else, you may well need to provide extra supports and scaffolds for certain individuals even when the majority of the class seems ready and able to handle potentially uncomfortable conversations. Postgame analysis with the students, either together as a class or through anonymous feedback mechanisms, can help you make adjustments that keep the class in this "good performance zone." Don't forget the power of those aforementioned compliments, either, to restore positivity and equilibrium after difficult conversations.

ADJOURNING

If students have spent a semester or year doing the hard work of coming together as a community, and the even harder work of sustaining that community in such a way that it can successfully grapple with conversations about social justice, then you don't want to just end on the last day of class with, "Bye, have a great summer!" Some sort of concluding ritual is required, and one that is more ambitious than just a pizza party (although pizza can certainly be included!). As *Habits of Mind* authors Arthur Costa and Bena Kallick put it,

> Most of us go through life viewing our experiences as isolated, unrelated events. We also view these happenings simply as the experiences they are, not as opportunities for learning. . . . [This] is not a habit we want to pass along to children. Instead, we want students to get into the habit of linking and constructing meaning from their experiences. Such work requires reflection. [21]

Effective adjournment activities give opportunities for both teacher and students to formally recognize the positive achievements of individuals and of the class as a whole, to recognize difficult events and congratulate the class on having endured and overcome them, to express statements of gratitude (perhaps in a more extended and elaborate fashion than was done throughout the year), and to reflect on learning, a metacognitive process that represents some of the highest orders of thinking. [22] According to Costa and Kallick,

> Reflecting on work enhances its meaning. Reflecting on experiences encourages insight and complex learning. We foster our own growth when we control

our learning, so some reflection is best done alone. Reflection is also enhanced, however, when we ponder our learning with others.[23]

Finally, adjournment activities can and should provide an opportunity for students to plan "next steps": follow-on learning and activism. Their goal is to both continue to develop their understanding of the ideas and concepts they have been learning, as well as to put them into practice in the immediate reality of their lives.

But that's the ending, the scenario toward which you are working. The students, and their teacher, have a long, long way to go before getting there, and that road begins with the next chapter.

NOTES

1. Kay, 2018, 29–30.
2. DiAngelo, 2018, 126–28.
3. Tuckman, 1965
4. Abudi, 2018.
5. Srogi and Baloche, 1997. Also see Baloche, 1997; Putnam, 1993.
6. See Jablon, 2014, 145–82.
7. Once again, YKYS-YMMV. Perhaps there are students in your class who do not regularly engage in oral hygiene and might be embarrassed by this activity, in which case you could choose another, even more innocuous question.
8. Lieber, 1998, 9.
9. Ibid.
10. There is no end to resources for further reading about this. As a starting point, I recommend Bleiberg's (1994) "Normal and Pathological Narcissism in Adolescence," followed by a tour of more contemporary research in neurology as outlined in Louise Carpenter's (2015) "Revealed: The Science Behind Teenage Laziness."
11. Smith, 2010.
12. Kay, 2018, 32–37.
13. Bethea, 2016.
14. Ibid.
15. Stroessner and Good, 2011; "Best Practices to Reduce Stereotype Threat in the Classroom," 2014; Ngoma, n.d.
16. Cross, 2017.
17. Ngoma, n.d.
18. Kelsky, 2017.
19. Ong, 2003.
20. Kelsky, 2017.
21. Costa and Kallick, 2008.
22. For some concrete, research-backed strategies for scaffolding student reflection, see chapter 12 in Costa and Kallick (available online at http://www.ascd.org/publications/books/108008/chapters/Learning-Through-Reflection.aspx).
23. Ibid.

Chapter Three

Self and "Other"

This chapter will address the first two competencies in Diane Goodman's "Cultural Competencies for Social Justice":
Competency 1: Self-awareness—awareness of one's own social identities, cultures, biases, and perspectives.
Competency 2: Understanding and valuing others—knowledge of and appreciation for others' social identities, cultures, and perspectives.

Davis, a tenth grader, wrote in his reaction to *Walkout*, a 2006 HBO historical drama about the 1968 Chicano student protests in East Los Angeles:

> It [does not seem] reasonable . . . for Mexican students to come to America and then demand a better education. You can't control the color of your skin, but you can control your demands [of] another country.

Davis's teacher had a lesson ready about California's former status as a part of Mexico, and how many of the ancestors of those students might have "come" when the United States annexed their land after the Mexican War, adding another layer of explanation for why so many of those Chicano students demand the right to speak Spanish in school. The teacher was able to focus any shock or outrage she may have personally felt into productive, educational channels.

However, what should that teacher do about Davis's outrage? That is precisely the word used to describe the reaction of many privileged white students who read the narratives of those who, in one way or another, have been poorly served by the U.S. power structure. Comments that their teachers regularly hear or read, in one way or another, include:

- Stop whining!
- I hate when [people of color] knock America. People have it so much worse in other countries.
- The whole racism/sexism thing got settled in the 1960s.
- The only problem with racism now is that people won't stop making race into an issue.

* * *

Not Another One!

Once, as I was handing out copies of Richard Wright's Uncle Tom's Children, *one of my white students was unable to stop himself from muttering, "Not* another *book about poor black people in the South!"*

Most students, mine or yours, do not articulate their discomfort so bluntly. But that doesn't mean their discomfort isn't there; I saw it whenever I anonymously polled my students at semester's end and found that they consistently rated the books by authors of color as the least engaging, least appealing, least relatable. These are the books that a significant number of my students listed as "texts we should replace." There is often an anger and dissatisfaction here, even when it is not expressed directly.

* * *

Paolo Freire wrote about how teachers could engage students by validating and responding to their anger. "The kind of education that does not recognize the right to express appropriate anger against injustice," he wrote, "fails to see the educational role implicit in the expression of these feelings."[1] Freire worked with the children of impoverished sugarcane workers, helping them see education as a tool for critiquing, and changing, the injustices in the very structures of their schooling.

The anger that privileged white students routinely exhibit seems different, though—more like an angry determination to discount the narratives of marginalized Americans. It may stem, at least in part, from these students' perception of their education as being inundated with such stories. One teacher once encountered a white parent who complained that the curriculum had "hit saturation point" with multicultural authors, even though a review of the reading lists still revealed a majority focus on the histories and narratives of wealthy white males, particularly in honors-level classes.

From some privileged white students' point of view, it might seem that they are learning "someone else's" history and stories that have no relevance to their own lives.

Even the teachers of privileged white students can fall into the trap of thinking "that multicultural education is primarily for students of color," like the teachers in Dr. Ashley de Waal-Lucas's study who "acknowledged that they would probably include more multicultural content into their curriculum if they had a more diverse student population."[2] No less than their students, teachers can "believe Martin Luther King Jr. Day is a holiday specifically for African Americans and that it makes as little sense to celebrate it in a school where there are hardly any African American students as celebrating Ramadan would be at an all-Christian school."[3]

How can we reconcile the need to diversify our curriculum to include the full spectrum of human experience, with the simultaneous imperative to make learning "authentic," to make it correspond to students' real lived experience, when that experience is one from which multicultural voices are largely absent?

Teachers of adolescents from all walks of life can tell you that "student engagement is at the core of teaching and learning, at the core of classroom and school culture, and at the core of reaching all students in a school,"[4] and the best way to engage students is to connect the material to what they care about. The cornerstone of student engagement is helping students to "make concrete connections between what they have read and what is happening in the world, country, or the local community."[5] So what do adolescents (and, let's admit it, many of us adults) care about most? Themselves. You have to make it all about *them*.[6]

* * *

Amandla!

I shouldn't have been baffled at what happened once when I showed my students Amandla!, *a 2003 documentary that interviewed dozens of South African activists who fought to destroy apartheid—but I was. In our Socratic circle discussion[7] the next day, my white students focused nearly exclusively on a five-minute segment where the filmmaker interviewed retired white Afrikaner riot policemen whose job it had been to suppress (beat, arrest, shoot) such activists. I couldn't understand what my students found so compelling about this throwaway scene where the police barbequed meat while mocking the songs the activists had sung, clearly only included in the film to demonstrate the racism that the ANC and its allies were fighting against. I was incredulous at the thought that my students might somehow have been identifying with those ugly sentiments.*

Looking back, I think that I may have missed a much more fundamental reason for their fixation: These were the only people in the movie who looked like my white students. They spoke English as opposed to subtitled Zulu or

*Xhosa; they were eating the same hamburgers and sausages that my white
students also ate. I have come to understand that the first task in engaging
privileged white students in meaningful exploration of multicultural voices is
to lower that identification barrier.*

* * *

A teacher whom Katie Swalwell had studied struggled with his privileged
white students when it came to

> exoticizing Others, romanticizing their plight, or reifying deficit stereotypes. It
> was quite easy for [privileged] students stepping out of the bubble for the first
> time to veer into non-critical terrain such as color blindness (See? The kids in
> the ghetto are just like you and me!) or patronizing charity (Those poor kids in
> the ghetto—I am so lucky! I should help them!) as they reject fear of or apathy
> about Others.[8]

Swalwell concludes from this teacher's experience that any attempt to burst
or expand the "bubble" of isolation that privileged white students occupy
must involve "a scaffolded, critical analysis of the bubble as a human-made,
historical construction with deep connections to the real suffering and thriv-
ing outside of it."[9] In other words, there is a danger in presenting a diverse
series of voices without also doing some work with students in critiquing the
way in which concepts like "diverse" (as opposed to . . . white?) are formed
and understood.

What follows, then, are a series of scaffolds and lessons to attempt these
challenging tasks. They are presented here as bases from which educators of
privileged white students might grow and adapt lessons that will be effective
in the particular classrooms and environments in which they work.

WORKING WITH WHITE IDENTITY

Recall from the introduction Diane Goodman's "Cultural Competencies for
Social Justice": While a clear goal for privileged white students may be
Competency 2: Understanding and valuing others, Goodman cautions that
they may first need to work on Competency 1: Self-awareness. In turn, both
of these are necessary phases before (as the next chapter deals with) the
students can move into Competency 3: Knowledge of social inequities. In
other words, the first step toward someone seeing value in the perspectives of
people of other racial identities is to explore what "racial identity" means to
begin with.

However, a formidable obstacle to overcome is the idea that many white
people—and I count myself as no exception, for much of my life—consider

race to be a construct that only applies to people of color. Robin DiAngelo, author of *White Fragility*, explains how, when white people try to address questions about race,

> [W]e tend to organize our answer around people of color—a story about my first cross-racial friendship, something someone said about people of color, what my parents thought about them, etc. What this reveals is how deeply we associate race with people of color. If they are not present or we are not referring to them, we believe that there is no race at play. [10]

So for discussions of race, racism, and justice, to "have something to do with them," white students need to see themselves as also possessing a racial identity.

The following activities, as with all activities detailed in this book, have been used in the author's own practice. They carry the perpetual YKYS-YMMV[11] caveat for teachers to let their own knowledge of themselves, their students, and their environment guide how much of these activities they wish to use and how best to adapt them.

Lesson: Identity Circles

Goal: Students will gain insight regarding the ways in which they construct their own identities, both in terms of what they include and what they exclude.

Time: 15–30 minutes.

Materials: Writing implement and paper, either blank or with preprinted "four interlocking rings" graphic organizer. There are many other popular graphic organizers available for use with this kind of activity; you may also wish to consider using manipulables, like forming shapes with pipe cleaners or blocks, or even with digital art tools. [12]

Step 1

If you are not using a preprinted graphic organizer, ask students to draw four interconnecting rings in an Olympic logo style, and provide a model for reference.

Step 2

Ask students to individually brainstorm as many aspects of their identity as they can—"things" that they think they "are." They should come up with as many ideas as they can within a specified, short amount of time, and write these anywhere on the paper *outside* the rings. The teacher can model responses like (in my own case): "Male. Father. Teacher. American. Jewish. Baseball fan," and so on. However, the teacher should not yet include or mention race. Defer all student questions of "are you looking for X" or "is it okay if I say X" to the individual student's own personal judgment.

Step 3

Ask the students to pick four, and only four, of the identity aspects that they came up with in step 1, the four that they feel are *most important and central* to who they are, and to write one inside each of the four rings. Acknowledge that this task might be challenging, but express confidence and reassurance that the students can do it.

Step 4

When the students have finished or when time is up, ask for volunteers to share what they came up with. Don't put students on the spot or force them to reveal things they might not be comfortable sharing with the class.

Step 5

Using slips of paper, survey apps, or other methods of anonymous polling, ask the class how many of them chose to include something about their family. About their interests or hobbies. About their favorite music or sports teams. About their religion. About their gender. Eventually, ask them how many included race.

Step 6

It is very likely, in a room of all or mostly white students, that few to none will have included race. Ask the students why they think this might be. Ask the students if they think the results might have been different in a more racially diverse classroom.

Step 7

Students complete reflection writing and/or exit ticket.

While the issue of identity is most often explored through literature and poetry, or perhaps through social studies in the sense of cultural or national identity, the concept manifests all across the curriculum. In mathematics we consider identity as a relationship of equality: $A = B$, such that A and B produce the same value regardless of what we substitute for the variables. In another sense, identity is an equality between functions that are differently defined.

In the sciences, the idea of taxonomizing organisms, or of defining the identities of elements, molecules, and substances based upon their unique and/or shared properties, is in some ways an issue of identity. A conversation about conceptualizations of identity in STEM (science, technology, engineering, and mathematics) fields could lead into one about personal identity, or vice versa, as a way for students to make those all-important "bridges" between seemingly abstract concepts in math and science, and the daily reality of their favorite subject of all: themselves. [13]

Science, of course, is both responsible for outdated notions of "racial identity" and, in more contemporary times, for debunking the notion of race as something purely biological. Later in this chapter I list some opportunities for science educators to directly engage their students in exploring the differences between meaningful biological distinctions and social constructions.

Of course, social constructions still wield power, and the construct of whiteness ironically wields the most power when it is rendered invisible to whites themselves. DiAngelo notes that "white people often say that since they lived in an all-white neighborhood or rural setting, they know nothing about race. We have to understand that white space is teeming with race . . . every moment I spend in all-white space I am being reinforced in a white worldview." [14]

At some point the teacher should steer the post–Identity Circles conversation toward the idea that white people in our society *do* possess a racial identity. White teachers can explain how this identity has impacted them personally, taking the opportunity to model for and remind the students of Norm #1: Speak for one's self and one's own experiences.

The teacher can ask the students, as a part of or subsequent to this activity, what they think a "white racial identity" is or entails, first as an individual writing assignment, shared only with the teacher. Then the students can build off their thoughts in this assignment, perhaps after (nonjudgmental!) teacher feedback, in a paired or small-group conversation, and finally as a whole-class discussion. To build from their existing knowledge, they can then read, together or as homework, texts relating to the field of whiteness studies, particularly in terms of historically changing definitions of whiteness, including excerpts from:

- Theodore Allen's *The Invention of the White Race* (1994)
- Rich Benjamin's *Searching for Whitopia: An Improbable Journey into the Heart of White America* (2009)
- Noel Ignatiev's *How the Irish Became White* (2012)
- Jon Meacham's "The New Face of Race," and Ellis Cose's "What's White, Anyway?" (both from *Newsweek*, September 17, 2000)

The previous chapter's advice on setting up and maintaining an appropriate "ecosystem" for potentially fraught discussions like this one is key. It may also be useful to have students first watch Mellody Hobson's TED Talk, "Color Blind or Color Brave?" [15]

Lesson: Color Blind versus Color Brave

Goal: Students will identify and critique the notion of "color-blindness," and be able to both articulate and critique Mellody Hobson's argument that color-blindness is not a useful strategy for dealing with issues of race.

Time: One or two class periods

Materials: Writing implement and paper, Mellody Hobson's TED Talk, "Color Blind or Color Brave?" Mellody Hobson is the former chairperson of DreamWorks animation (whose movies many students are familiar with), and president of Ariel Investments. She is the first African American woman to chair the Economic Club of Chicago, not to mention being the spouse of *Star Wars* creator George Lucas. [16]

Step 1

In keeping with the constructivist ethos of always starting learning with the students' own present knowledge and experience (as explained in chapter 1), the teacher can begin the lesson by asking the students if any of them have heard the term "color-blind" used in association with race, what they understood the term to mean, and whether and how any of them identify with the idea of being color-blind in the sense that "race isn't a part of how I see people." The teacher is encouraged to share personal anecdotes where relevant.

Step 2

The teacher can then ask students (first in writing, then in paired discussions, and finally as a class) to think of any times or ways in which being color-blind in this sense might be beneficial, and where it might have drawbacks and deficits.

Step 3

From student comments, the teacher can then segue into Hobson's TED Talk, in which she explains how

> researchers have coined this term "color blindness" to describe a learned behavior where we pretend that we don't notice race. If you happen to be surrounded by a bunch of people who look like you, that's purely accidental. Now, color blindness, in my view, doesn't mean that there's no racial discrimination, and there's fairness. It doesn't mean that at all. It doesn't ensure it. In my view, color blindness is very dangerous because it means we're ignoring the problem. [17]

Hobson cites statistics about white overrepresentation on corporate boards and in government as evidence of such a problem. The teacher may wish to supplement with data more immediately relevant to students: high school graduation rates, school suspension rates, college completion rates, and of course the "achievement gap," or the disparity between African American, Latinx, and white students in terms of grades and standardized test scores, even when income and other factors are held constant. For example, according to the Stanford Center for Policy Analysis, "Even in states where the racial socioeconomic disparities are near zero . . . achievement gaps are still present. This suggests that socioeconomic disparities are not the sole cause of racial achievement gaps."[18]

Teachers should exercise caution when pursuing this line of discussion, though, as doing so might unintentionally reinforce white students' conscious or subconscious conceptions of African American or Latinx people as somehow mentally "inferior" to whites. The complex work of analyzing the reasons behind these gaps is best handled later, because at this point we're still mainly working with Goodman's first competency of self-awareness. Jumping into an exploration of the larger picture too early risks eliciting all manner of ill-informed responses based on stereotypes and half-remembered history classes.

Instead, the teacher can focus on Hobson's argument that race is something that Americans, particularly white Americans, need to talk about openly, despite the fact that "this subject matter can be hard, awkward, uncomfortable. But that's kind of the point. I think it's time for us to be comfortable with the uncomfortable conversation about race."[19]

Step 4

Hobson cites, as an example of the benefits of confronting one's own discomfort, her swim coach who had told her to hold her breath at all times, as a way of building stamina and tolerance for discomfort. The teacher can ask the students again to reach into their own experience: where have they encountered the benefits of this kind of conditioning? In sports? In practicing a musical instrument? In dealing with homesickness at sleep-away camp?

There has been much attention given recently to the idea of "resilience" in children. The privileges enjoyed by the wealthy too often allow well-meaning parents to "save" their children from uncomfortable situations, or from facing the consequences of the choices those children make. Chapter 7 will detail some of the many ways in which affluent schools continue this enabling process, one which can ultimately stunt those children's ability to develop true resilience and tenacity. Given how important such resilience is to so many arenas of life, according to social scientists and psychologists such as Paul Tough, Judy Willis, and Carol Dweck, this is one more way in which tackling issues of multiculturalism and social justice in the privileged white classroom serves these students' learning and development needs. Hobson's enjoinment to be "comfortable with being uncomfortable," therefore, is a mantra that the teacher can come back to year-round—perhaps even posting this on a classroom wall—but it is especially useful in discussions of race.

* * *

Embracing the Discomfort

Acknowledging that discomfort is not always something to run away from is especially vital for a population that so often has the privilege of avoidance. As a white person, I really don't have to think about race unless I choose to . . . in a way that, as a Jew, I don't have the privilege of being able to not think about being in a minority religion, particularly if I am inhabiting any public space, or consuming any broadcast media, during the six weeks between Thanksgiving and Christmas. I can't demand an audience with the general manager of every shopping mall, the CEO of every television and radio station, the owners of every house with robotic reindeer statues on their lawns, complain that I've "hit saturation point" on Christmas stuff, and expect any kind of relief. I cannot help but feel personally attacked when pundits and politicians demand an end to "Happy Holidays" in favor of the exclusive "Merry Christmas." I can, however, withdraw from a class that focuses on the subject of race, and be pretty well assured that I need never be "bothered" by it again.

* * *

Step 5

Choosing to abandon the construct of color-blindness permits discussion of race and racial identity, including white racial identity. Returning to the Identity Circles activity, ask students to update their chart with "markers"—outward signs, behaviors, activities, and objects that someone observing them might associate specifically with that aspect of their identity. For a hobby or pursuit (say, baseball or painting), students could list tools (bats, gloves, paintbrushes, easels), clothing (favorite team jersey, Van Gogh "Starry Night" print T-shirt), language and terms (home run, no-hitter, shading, Impressionism), music ("Take me out to the ballgame," Don MacLean's "Vincent"), even foods (ballpark franks, Georgia O'Keefe's fruit portraits). Some of these can get a little silly, and that's okay.

Step 6

Move on to cultural markers that students identify with their ethnicity or religion—symbols like a cross, Star of David, or Star and Crescent. Languages spoken for prayer, or by people in your family, or by your ancestors prior to arriving in America. Everyone except 100 percent Indigenous Americans has ancestors who came (willingly or not) to the United States from somewhere else, and white students, especially affluent white students, are far more likely than African American students (whose ancestral origins are often obscured by the history of slavery) to have access to knowledge about their ancestry that dates back many generations. This is never a guarantee, however—some white students may be adopted, or for some other reason may not have access to this information. Your activity has to find a way to make cognizant and respectful allowances for such possibilities. Conversely, you may have African American students whose family identity is in fact informed by voluntary immigration, or by voluntary moves within the United States. Remember, YKYS-YMMV!

Step 7

Eventually, get to race. *Are there certain qualities, beyond skin color, that you associate with white racial identity?* The students can brainstorm, perhaps aided by some pages from Christian Lander's satirical book, *Stuff White People Like: A Definitive Guide to the Unique Taste of Millions.* Lander's examples ("coffee," "film festivals," "organic foods") are skewed toward a certain "hipster" stereotype subset of white identity, and Rochelle Gutiérrez warns that failing to address various ethnic identities among white students "maintains the potential to reduce ethnic groups of color to deviant status or categories of 'other,'"[20] so encouraging students to make distinctions within different subsets of "white" identity can be a good idea as well.

Indeed, white students may argue that "white" is too large a category to be somehow essentialized into certain typical behaviors and qualities, and they would be in some sense correct. A conversation about the absurdity of essentializing the cultural identities and behaviors of white people can open the door to white students asking that same question about essentializing other cultural and racial identities. On the other hand, the very concept that some behaviors and cultural facets might get labeled as "white" is a novel one for many white students. Many things that Lander or others might label as "white" are marked for them simply as "normal." As Joshua Nguyen puts it:

> Whiteness in America goes by unnoticed because we often don't think about it appearing or happening. . . . Many of us never question why we usually default

to a white perspective since it is the norm for many of us, and has been the norm all our lives. [21]

The teacher can ask students the same question Nguyen poses to his readers: as it is predicted that by midcentury, white Americans will be a numerical minority, will public discourse still categorize nonwhite people as "minorities"? "This," says Nguyen, "is symbolic of how America constructs racial categories as 'whites versus everyone else.'" [22]

As Plato figured out a few thousand years ago, our perceptions are always shaped by the "caves" in which we are raised. Plato's "Allegory of the Cave,"[23] which your students can study earlier in the year, outlines the challenges of seeing beyond blinders that we're not even aware exist (for a long time, the movie *The Matrix* was, and may still be, a more student-accessible vehicle for discussing this concept). What is "normal" to you, especially if you see it constantly reinforced by the media you consume and (importantly) the highly segregated circles you move in, is very hard to see as just one possible set of qualities out of many.

EXPANDING BEYOND THE "SINGLE STORY"

The following lesson involves students reading Horace Miner's classic mock essay, "Body Ritual among the Nacirema" (1956), designed to engage students in challenging the idea of any particular cultural practices as "default" or "normal."

Lesson: "Meet the Nacirema"

Goal: Students will recognize the concept of ethnocentrism, and understand that the concept of "normal" or "default" can be relative, and is defined by the dominant culture.

Time: One or two class periods.

Materials: "Body Ritual among the Nacirema" article.[24] Given the length and some of the high-register language used, the teacher will likely wish to shorten or otherwise modify it into a more accessible, one- or two-page document (some such modifications are freely available online).

The article describes outlandish rituals practiced by "an obscure and primitive culture," which include kneeling before a holy font of water in a household shrine each morning, sticking magical materials in their teeth in a vain attempt to halt decay, and "witch doctors" who banish demons in "exorcism sessions."

The punchline, of course, is that this essay describes middle-class "American" culture (for which "Nacirema" is a backward anagram). Practices as familiar to many American students as washing their face in their bathroom sink, getting a dental filling, and having a session with a therapist are described in great detail—Miner's narrator is nothing if not a careful observer—but through an outsider's ethnocentric lens that clearly defines his subjects as "alien" compared to the "norm" that the narrator assumes his readers identify with.

Step 1

Announce to the students that they will be learning about a unique and very peculiar culture called the Nacirema. You may wish to ask if any student has studied this culture before (a subtle test to see if any of them might already know the "secret," in which case you may wish to ask them to hold back and let their classmates have the pleasure of discovering this "mysterious culture" for the very first time). Pass out copies of the article, and/or project an image of it onto the board.

Step 2

The teacher can read the article aloud, have the students take turns reading it aloud in parts, or some combination. Don't let the students in on the joke until and unless they figure it out on their own, and interrupt the reading at times to ask the students for feedback as to what they think of the "bizarre customs and practices" of this "strange and primitive tribe."

Step 3

Alternatively or in addition, engage the students in a close read: ask the students to circle words or phrases that stand out to them. If they don't see it on their own, call their attention to ways in which the author attempts to prejudice the reader's opinions of the Nacirema people, such as using words like "shocking" or "horrifying" to describe cultural practices, describing the people as "superstitious" and possessed of "magical beliefs," and putting scare quotes around words like "houses" to imply that Nacirema dwellings would not meet the author's definition of a proper home.

Step 4

If some students speak up in defense of the Nacirema or are critical of the narrator's voice, the teacher may even wish to play devil's advocate, picking one or more Nacirema practices and asking whether or not this ritual is objectively horrifying and bizarre?

Step 5

If no student figures out the secret on their own, return the students to the early paragraph that describes the location of the Nacirema's territory. Although obscured through convoluted language, if students look at a map to find these places, they will discover the "Nacirema" live all throughout the United States! Asking a student what "Nacirema" spells backwards can seal the deal.

Step 6

Now, the fun lies in going back through the article and figuring out what "ordinary" American practices it refers to—for example, "lacerating the skin of the face or legs" is shaving.

Step 7

In pairs, groups, and/or as a class, engage the students in a discussion. What is the flaw in the narrator's approach? Is he not looking carefully enough? What is he missing, and why? Whose voices are not included in the narrative? How might the article read differently if some "Nacirema" were allowed to include their perspectives on their own culture?

Step 8

The discussion can then be expanded to the larger question of why the author, Horace Miner, might have wanted to create a work of satire like this.

Miner's article is a critique of the way Western anthropologists had traditionally examined other cultures through the lens of how they were different from, and inferior to/less legitimate than, Western cultures.[25] Despite being over 50 years old, the piece still resonates. Perhaps this is because much popular media still centers white cultural referents and "Others" differing practices. The very idea that someone from "elsewhere" could describe things that privileged white students understand to be normal and sensible as "strange and superstitious" is novel for many white people.

Lesson: Your Own Personal "Nacirema" Writing Assignment

Goal: To get out from under ethnocentric biases—to ask not, "Why are *they* different," but ask, "Why are *we* different?"

Time: One to three classroom periods (depending on students' writing skills).

Materials: Something to write with/on, and the following assignment.

Part 1

Option A: In at least 50 words, describe, in some detail, all of the things you did after you came home from school last night. We'll call this your "evening activities."

Option B: Draw a scene of your "evening activities." Show effort and detail—no pencil-drawn stick figures!

Part 2

In at least 150 words, describe how your evening activities would look to an observer from a radically different culture (let's say an alien from Mars). Write it in a form like the Nacirema article, a report from someone studying you from afar, who sees what you do but who makes very different assumptions and conclusions because they know very little (and haven't bothered to ask you!) about *why* you do what you do.

Encouraging white Westerners to question assumptions of normalcy that they may not even realize they have is not just a matter of being "politically correct"; it's a prerequisite for making any real meaning out of the experiences of people whose culture might look and feel different from theirs.

When reading, for example, Chinua Achebe's *Things Fall Apart*, if white students cannot get past the fact that the characters, who are nineteenth-century Ibo tribesmen in West Africa, live in huts and worship spirits, they will not take much from the novel beyond a sense of, "Wow, what a weird bunch of people."

But if they do the mental and emotional work of positioning what is familiar to them as just one possible way of life out of many equally legitimate and internally consistent ways to live, then it opens up more chances for students to see "what this stuff has to do with me." In the case of *Things Fall Apart* in particular, "this stuff" includes conflicts related to the gap between parental expectations for their children and the children's own dreams, the challenge of trying to make a name and a reputation for oneself, social pressures to put on a public show of behaviors one might not actually want to do, and plenty of other situations that a white American high school student—or really, nearly any human being—experiences.

And if a privileged white American high school kid can gain insight into the issues that affect her own life by reading about life in a nineteenth-century Ibo village, it's probably even more likely she will find connections to authors and characters from contemporary America who are not of her race.

* * *

DeVante, Seven, and Starr

We come back to the "Nacirema" a lot in my classes, even when reading contemporary American fiction, like when we discuss a scene in Angie Thomas's The Hate U Give *in which Chris, the well-meaning but slightly clueless white boyfriend of African American protagonist Starr, asks, "Why do some black people give their kids odd names? I mean, look at you guys' names. They're not normal."*

The boys he's talking to, DeVante and Seven, reply, "What makes . . . our names any less normal than yours?"[26]

This conversation got my attention, I always tell my students, because I have been Chris so many times, looking at the names on the rosters of my wife's urban classrooms and wondering how on Earth those names could have arisen. As Seven tells Chris, "Most of the names white people think are unusual actually have meaning," whether from cultural roots, or combinations of names of people whom parents wished to honor, or something else. I realized I had fallen into the "Nacirema" trap, assuming a practice to be nonsensical just because it didn't look familiar.

* * *

Lesson: "The Danger of a Single Story"

Goal: For students to resist the temptation to generalize or essentialize from a certain set of experiences.

Time: Steps 1–5 will take one to three class periods. Subsequent steps are meant to expand into a multiweek unit, or become a recurring thread to pick up in future units.

Materials: YouTube video of Chimamanda Ngozi Adichie's TED Talk, "The Danger of a Single Story."

Step 1

Ask the students to brainstorm/free write about a time when they either felt someone misunderstood them and/or drew inaccurate conclusions about them.

Step 2

Ask the students to do a second brainstorm/free write about a time when they misunderstood or drew inaccurate conclusions about someone else. This activity should not be presented, at this stage, through a lens of race, culture, or privilege. Anecdotes about teachers, parents, siblings, and friends are rife with such moments, whether or not race or cultural misunderstandings are involved, although perhaps stories of this nature will surface anyway.

Step 3

Taking the students' comfort level and classroom norms into account, the teacher could have some students volunteer to share their stories with the class, with partners or groupmates, in the form of the teacher reading them aloud anonymously.

Step 4

Show Chimamanda Adichie's TED Talk, in which she defines the "Danger of a Single Story" as depicting a group or individual "as one thing, as only one thing, over and over again, and that is what they become."[27] Prime the students to be on the lookout (perhaps with graphic organizers as scaffolds) for accounts in which Adichie feels the victim of a single story, such as:

- A white college roommate who asked the Nigerian-born Adichie about her "tribal music" and was shocked when Adichie played Mariah Carey
- A professor who told her that her writing "wasn't African enough" because the characters were too prosperous
- Where Adichie, too, discovered she had "single stories" about others, including being surprised that the boy from a poor family who worked as a domestic servant for Adichie's family was capable of creating beautiful art
- Viewing Mexicans solely through the lens of illegal immigration.

While the full video is 20 minutes long, time-pressed teachers could show just the first 9½ minutes, which contain the core of Adichie's message as well as all of the above anecdotes.

Step 5

After checking for comprehension, ask the students to apply this idea back to the personal anecdotes they wrote. Who was the victim of a "single story" in their anecdote, and how?

Step 6

Ask the students to also examine who had more *power* in the interactions they described in their stories, and to explain their reasoning.

Step 7

Return to Adichie's statement from her TED Talk:

How they are told, who tells them, when they're told, how many stories are told, are really dependent on power. Power is the ability not just to tell the story of another person, but to make it the definitive story of that person. . . . Start the story with the arrows of the Native Americans, and not with the arrival of the British, and you have an entirely different story. Start the story with the failure of the African state, and not with the colonial creation of the African state, and you have an entirely different story. [28]

Step 8

Introduce (or return to, if the class has studied it before) the distinction between subject and object of a story. The experience of an individual or group can look very different depending on whether the narration is shaped by their point of view and voice, or by an outsiders' voice seeking to describe them. Ways to pursue this goal could include some of the following resources:

- There are many modern retellings of classic Western children's tales, such as *The True Story of the Three Little Pigs* by Jon Scieszka (1989), which re-present these well-known stories from the point of view of the character traditionally labeled as the antagonist (e.g., how the wolf describes the fable). Students can examine, through the use of easy-to-access texts dealing with presumably familiar characters and plots, how a story differs depending on who tells it.
- A more sophisticated children's book that could serve such a lesson is Anthony Browne's *Voices in the Park* (1998). Browne's book is divided into four separate narratives, each from the point of view of a different character, retelling the same story from their own point of view, *Rashomon*-style, complete with judgments about the other characters they meet. [29] Groups of students could be given photocopies of the pages of just one of the four narratives, and each group asked to draw conclusions about the narrator and the characters. Then, as all of the groups share their portions, the students can, "jigsaw" style, keep updating and reinterpreting the original narrative as they hear more perspectives. For example, a wealthy narrator views a down-on-his-luck man as an "unsavory type" to be avoided, while the man's own narrative reveals him to be a loving father.
- A key goal in social studies classes is to help students develop an understanding of primary versus secondary sources. Textbooks are the quintessential "secondary source" that present and mediate most students' understanding of history, and their use generally constitutes 75–90 percent of classroom instruction. [30] Engaging students in comparing two or more different textbooks' depictions of the same events, and examining what

events each book chooses to include or leave out and how these events are framed, can be excellent fodder for exploring "single stories."

- Particularly dramatic contrasts can come from comparing traditional textbooks' narratives with those told in books such as James Loewen's *Lies My Teacher Told Me* (1995) or Howard Zinn's *A People's History of the United States* (reissued 2015), both of which tell stories of American history through the lenses and perspectives of marginalized peoples as opposed to the usual focus on those in history who wielded formal power.
- In English class, pairing multiple texts that deal with the same or similar groups from different perspectives and authorships can provide similar material. Using the aforementioned *Things Fall Apart* as an example, students could examine the ways in which white British writers in the heyday of colonialism such as Joseph Conrad or Rudyard Kipling depicted African characters as dangerous, unknowable, and not-entirely human "savages," and then compare it with the complex and identifiable Ibo characters of Achebe's Umuofia. In turn, they could then compare Achebe's portrayal of female Ibo characters in the village with that of Chimamanda Adichie's "The Headstrong Historian" (2008), a story set in the same fictional universe but with a women-centered focal point, or Yaa Gyasi's Asante women characters in the early chapters of her novel, *Homegoing* (2016).
- Even keeping within white Western traditions, authors such as Margaret Atwood, Marion Zimmer Bradley, and Madeline Miller are just three of many who have retold classical Greek myths through a feminist lens.

First recognizing that one's understandings are informed by particular stories, and that those stories always leave out information and skew our understanding depending on perspective, is an important aid toward understanding and appreciating the "Other." It removes the white self from the center of the universe, and opens the door to legitimacy and respect for those whose traits and norms may differ.

Literature's advantage is that it can allow students to explore new perspectives from the comfort of their own chairs, but in reality, all academic subjects offer opportunities for this process to take place. The remaining sections of this chapter will explore English language arts (ELA) applications a bit further before detailing opportunities for teachers of other subjects to help their students identify and expand beyond the "single story."

We always need to keep in mind the all-important question for the teacher of privileged white students: what is the value of all of this to a student? And if there is value, how can we help those privileged white students get over the hurdle of engaging with the stories and achievements of people who do not necessarily look and speak the same way they do?

ELA/LITERATURE—WHOSE VOICES WILL WE HEAR?

In 1992 Ellen Swartz decried what she called the "master script" in American education, the "classroom practices, pedagogy, and instructional materials, as well as to the theoretical paradigms . . . that are grounded in Euro-centric and white supremacist ideologies." This script, she continues,

> silences multiple voices and perspectives, primarily by legitimizing dominant, white, upper-class, male voicings as the "standard" knowledge students need to know. All other accounts and perspectives are omitted from the master script unless they can be disempowered through misrepresentation.[31]

The history of American education, according to Swartz, is one of "the struggle for inclusion and representation of historically omitted race, class, and gender groups in school knowledge."[32]

This struggle may look slightly different in English classes versus social studies/history classes, but at heart it remains a question of which "voices in the park" will we ask students to engage with, which histories are taught as "single stories," and which students get to see from multiple perspectives. The relevance of these questions for the classroom teacher is not simply ideological—the answers have direct impact on student engagement and willingness/ability to learn. When Rudine Sims Bishop challenged school curricula to develop reading lists with books drawn from, and depicting, racially and ethnically diverse people, her main argument was that children from outside the privileged race and culture needed figures with whom to identify:

> When children cannot find themselves reflected in the books they read, or when the images are distorted, negative, or laughable, they learn a powerful lesson about how they are devalued in the society of which they are a part. Our classrooms need to be places where all children from all cultures that make up the salad bowl of American society can find their mirrors.[33]

Although implementation varied widely, the push to expand reading lists beyond the traditional canon did bring significant changes in the curricular content of the humanities. For example, by the 1990s, representation of minority "ethnic American or non-American" authors in some popular middle school literature anthologies rose to somewhere between 21 percent and 59 percent.[34] Yet in the late 1980s, a survey of nearly 500 public and independent schools conducted by the Center for the Learning and Teaching of Literature revealed that nine of the top ten most-taught texts in American high school curricula[35] were authored by white men from either the United States or the United Kingdom (the tenth being by a white American woman):

- *Romeo and Juliet* by William Shakespeare
- *Macbeth* by William Shakespeare
- *Huckleberry Finn* by Mark Twain
- *Julius Caesar* by William Shakespeare
- *To Kill a Mockingbird* by Harper Lee
- *The Scarlet Letter* by Nathaniel Hawthorne
- *Of Mice and Men* by John Steinbeck
- *Hamlet* by William Shakespeare
- *The Great Gatsby* by F. Scott Fitzgerald
- *Lord of the Flies* by William Golding

In 2019, a massive study by Renaissance Learning[36] of almost 30,000 schools revealed that, in 2017–2018, the top ten lists still remained 80–90 percent white, with Steinbeck, Shakespeare, Hawthorne, Fitzgerald, and Lee still holding on to their slots. White women authors such as Suzanne Collins and Mary Shelley have penetrated the list, but the only authors of color to make the top ten were R. J. Palacio (ninth grade only) and Nicola Yoon (ninth though eleventh grade only). Not a single nonwhite author is listed in the twelfth-grade top ten, and there are no male writers of color in the top ten in any high school grade. Small wonder, then, when privileged white students have a hard time parsing the experiences of authors who do not look like them—they likely have had very little practice.

Critical race theory (CRT) celebrates the power of storytelling to empower the marginalized; Gloria Ladson-Billings wrote that "stories provide the necessary context for understanding, feeling, and interpreting."[37] In CRT, stories give marginalized individuals and groups the tools to "name their own reality," in Richard Delgado's words, forming counternarratives to the dominant ones promoted by the powerful. In a way, this proverbial rising tide can indeed lift all boats; if, Delgado says, "the exchange of stories from teller to listener can help overcome ethnocentrism and the . . . need to view the world in [only] one way,"[38] then the privileged might find this shattering to be liberating as well.

* * *

This Stuff Gives You an Advantage in College!

When the Oak Hills English Department first introduced a World Literature elective, the course engaged many students simply because the texts it offered seemed so different from those they had read for their entire school careers. What began as simple fascination with the "exotic" grew into a complex series of explorations of the tension between universals—elements in books by foreign authors with which white students could nevertheless, to their

surprise, identify—and what seemed particular to certain times, places, iden-
tities, and circumstances.

To some extent, this is the dialectic that undergirds all engagement with
literature, but the seeming "alienness" of the texts and their settings threw
that process into stark relief for the white students. It became a mantra to
ask, how much of what character X does is because of who she is as an
individual, how much is because of her cultural and historical influences,
and how much is because she is a human being? And what makes us think we
can determine this? The process was more complex, demanding and engag-
ing than the usual study of how X author uses Y metaphors to make Z
statement, although to be fair, we included plenty of that as well.

Alumni of the course often reported that they were the only kids in their
college classes to have had experience with the non-Western authors and
ideas—postcolonialism, appropriation, globalization—that their classmates
were just encountering for the first time. This became another selling point
for students during course-selection time, especially those concerned that
their high school education had not adequately prepared them with this thing
called "a global perspective" that they had heard is prerequisite for success
in college.

* * *

For many privileged white students, however, this process must be scaffolded. The growing adoption of young adult (YA) literature into ELA curriculum is a recognition of the fact that it is easier for teenagers to relate to
characters who are their own age, operating in a world that resembles their
own (or, oddly, future dystopias), versus the long-ago settings of Shakespeare, Austen, or pretty much any book that takes place prior to the advent
of the internet and social media.

The books by authors of color that are most frequently taught in schools
definitely fall into the "Days of Yore" category: the writings of W. E. B. Du
Bois, James Baldwin, Ralph Ellison, Richard Wright, and Zora Neale Hurs-
ton all depict times and places that can seem alien to modern adolescents,
even without the additional hurdle of an unfamiliar racialized experience.
That it is Nicola Yoon who broke into 2018's "top ten books" for high
schoolers is almost certainly tied to her youth, and to the contemporary
settings of her writing.

Popular YA literature by multicultural authors, such as the novels *The*
Hate U Give, American Born Chinese, The Poet X, Dear Martin, The Aston-
ishing Color of After, All American Boys, and the *Brooklyn Brujas* series, to
name a few, all feature teenaged protagonists wrestling with familiar issues
of identity, acceptance, school, family, and romantic relationships in an easy-
to-access context. This familiarity can then provide an anchor to steady

white, privileged students on their voyage through the elements of the stories that are highly particular to race and culture. One scaffold a teacher may wish to use is some sort of chart with two columns. See table 3.1 for an example.

Table 3.1. Scaffolding connections between self and "Others"

Places where I can identify with this character or specific connections I can make between my life and the character's life	Experiences or aspects of this character that are very different from my own

One could also take a page from Edward de Bono's lateral thinking methods, and add a third column to the right—"things that I just find interesting."[39] By using this technique, a person can perhaps avoid what he called the "intelligence trap," the kind of binary thinking that leads a student to solely focus on supporting or countering certain positions—something school asks students to do all the time in essays and debates—as opposed to allowing a person's mind its freest reign.

In addition to race, culture, and time period, social class is another potential barrier to take into conscious consideration when attempting to engage privileged white students with multicultural literature. Because of the economic history of white domination and the systematic suppression of the legal and economic agency of other groups in America, it is very common, especially in older or "classic" books by authors of color, to have protagonists of color who live in some form of poverty. It is unfortunately too easy for privileged white students to dehumanize and disassociate themselves from characters who are poor sharecroppers or families who live in slum tenements.

A growing body of sociological and psychological research reveals how images of poverty can actually engender resentment in the minds of the affluent. A recent Yale University study suggested that in "more unequal situations, wealth visibility leads to greater inequality than when wealth is invisible"[40] or, as interpreted by political columnist Hannah Brooks Olsen,

> the Haves . . . are less charitable, less generous, and less emotionally drawn to help when they can see just how little the Have Nots have. This, I believe, is linked to the perception of scarcity, and the idea that our economy is zero-sum game. That is, if a poor person were to suddenly become not-poor, they may come for what you have and you might have less.[41]

Psychologist Claudia Hammond, author of *Mind Over Money: The Psychology of Money and How We Use It*, described a series of studies that support Olsen's theory, including a Princeton University experiment studying the neurological reactions of middle- and upper-class volunteers being shown images:

> [W]hen the volunteers were looking at pictures of rich people, the medial prefrontal cortex was activated . . . to put it crudely, the grey matter flashes up a message saying "same species here" and that tells us that we should relate to this other thing in front of us as a fellow human being, rather than a lawn mower or a pigeon or whatever. But when the people in the scanner were shown the pictures of homeless people the medial prefrontal cortex failed to do its thing. . . . [T]he brains of the volunteers didn't register that the shambling guy with the matted hair, the shapeless coat and the broken-down boots was another human being. Instead the areas of the brain associated with disgust were activated.[42]

If it is true that psychology, neurology, and culture conspire to create barriers to privileged students' ability to empathize, this may be part of the root of the sentiment, "Oh no, not another book about poor black people in the South."

This is not an attempt to use science to justify or excuse classism as well as racism; rather, it is a recognition and admission that there are real barriers that a teacher must explicitly work to address when trying to get privileged white students to connect with characters in certain books—hence, the importance of "gateway" books featuring more affluent and privileged characters of color.

For example, the Dead family of Toni Morrison's classic *Song of Solomon* (1977) are affluent African Americans, landlords who are influential figures in their town. A central conflict for Milkman, the protagonist, is that he has grown up in a wealthy household and wonders whether he will ever be able to be his own man, or whether he will always depend on his family's money. This is an immediately relatable concern to many privileged white students, especially boys.

Milkman eventually goes on a journey that slowly takes him out of his comfort zone, into the more dangerous world of the South and his family's past, and also into conflict with his best friend Guitar, who has been continually facing the realities of racism from which Milkman has been shielded for so long. The reader goes along this journey with Milkman, an "easing into the pool" versus the usual "cold-water shock" that drives some privileged white students away from engaging with a text like *Black Boy* or *I Know Why the Caged Bird Sings*.

The Dead family's affluence does not shield them entirely from white racism, any more than the Younger family's money does in Lorraine Hansberry's *A Raisin in the Sun* (1959), or the LeVay family's wealth in *Stick Fly* (by Lydia Diamond, 2008). The experiences of all of these characters ultimately have roots that go back to Jim Crow and slavery before it, just as Jin Wang, the protagonist of *American Born Chinese* (by Gene Luen Yang, 2006), is haunted by the specter of his cousin "Chin-Kee," a living embodiment of white racist stereotypes about Asians. In turn, Jin Wang draws strength from the Monkey King myths of his cultural inheritance, just as

Milkman Dead gains actual superpowers rooted in the legends of African mysticism. The influence of race, both retarding and empowering, is inextricable from the characters' experiences in all of these books . . . yet is wrapped in a package that may not immediately turn off privileged white students from even attempting to identify.

Once again, this is not to say that teachers should never ask white, privileged students to engage with texts that depict the real lived experience—complete with, at times, suffering and deprivation, along with the dignity and endurance—of oppressed people. This is also not to say that the only valuable characters of color to study are those whose traits are closest to those considered "white." This is about order of introduction, not either/or; for example, first experiencing Lilliam Rivera's *The Education of Margot Sanchez* (2017), whose protagonist attends an elite private school (yet still must grapple with racism and dual consciousness), before exploring the impoverished rural childhood of Esmeralda Santiago in *When I Was Puerto Rican* (1993).

Reading texts with comparatively affluent and empowered characters of color has another benefit for privileged white students: it contradicts the narrative, unintentionally reinforced by every book focused on slavery and poverty, that the sum total of the experience of people of color, especially African Americans, is one of destitution and deprivation. As Beverly Tatum asks, "How do white children see *others* reflected? Are they learning about people of color as equals or does the curriculum continue to reinforce old notions of assumed white superiority . . . ?"[43]

Students of color have always struggled, and continue to struggle, to find ways past temporal, cultural, economic, and racial barriers to access the traditional white-centric literary canon. A plethora of resources now exist to assist teachers in helping their students of color engage with it, from hip-hop retellings of Shakespeare to books like Stephanie Powell Watts's *No One Is Coming to Save Us* (2017), a retelling of *The Great Gatsby* through African American characters.

The kinds of bridges created to give students of color easier access to white canonical texts can be crossed in the other direction as well. With paired texts, white students and students of color alike can see how some of the themes in the canonical works by white authors that they are used to reading are both similar to, but also manifest differently in, contexts specifically dealing with the experiences of people of color.

Ultimately, this all boils down to the argument that a healthy curriculum includes a variety of authors, who present a variety of characters reflecting the full breadth of human experience. This is what will best serve students of all races in our classrooms. As Stotsky writes, our reading lists should

[i]nclude literary works that feature, across works, both negative and positive
characters who are members of particular ethnic, religious, or racial groups,
not just one kind of character. . . . Historical truthfulness is served by showing
that all groups have people who can be admired or criticized, and that different
authors in a country's mainstream literary tradition have held different points
of view about members of particular religious or ethnic minority groups. [44]

* * *

What If I Can't Choose My Own Books?

*Whether it is a matter of tight budgets or just lack of influence over how
those budgets are spent, it is often difficult for teachers to just order new
class sets of books. This is another reason why those reading lists haven't
changed for so many decades—those books still sitting in bookrooms don't
cost any extra money to use! With limited resources to buy new books,
English departments can easily get lost in waste-of-time debates about the
merits of X text versus Y text; English teachers simply love to argue about
books, and they can do so very passionately and persuasively. But it's the
wrong argument to be having.*

*The deeper problem beneath the exigencies of "what do we already have
in our bookroom" is that the classic ELA unit is built around a single book
that the entire class reads at the same time. But teaching* Great Expectations
*isn't a learning goal (unless your goal is simply not to get fired!). Learning
goals include mastery of certain standards involving textual comprehension
and analysis, written and spoken expression, and these goals can be served
equally well by literally thousands of books.*

The same money that could buy 100 copies of The Catcher in the Rye
*could buy 20 copies each of 5 different titles representing "adolescent com-
ing of age" books from a variety of authors' perspectives . . . or even 5
copies of 20 different titles. If neither departmental budget nor supplemental
grant monies are available, or if you simply cannot get permission from the
necessary gatekeepers for other reasons, at the very least you are likely to
have some discretionary ability to use short stories of your own choosing.*

*The mechanic of "literature circles," where small groups of students all
read separate texts and come back together in class discussions that link
them through thematic or structural commonalities, frees up an English
teacher to include many more voices than time or funding might otherwise
seem to allow.*

* * *

Let's circle back to Rudine Sims Bishop:

Children from dominant social groups have always found their mirrors in books, but they, too, have suffered from the lack of availability of books about others. They need the books as windows onto reality, not just on imaginary worlds . . . books may be one of the few places where children who are socially isolated and insulated from the larger world may meet people unlike themselves. If they only see reflections of themselves, they will grow up with an exaggerated sense of their own importance and value in the world—a dangerous ethnocentrism.[45]

Of course there are limits to the transformative power of literature. Richard Delgado and Jean Stefancic warn of the "empathic fallacy," which

consists of believing that we can enlarge our sympathies through linguistic means alone. By exposing ourselves to ennobling narratives, we broaden our experience, deepen our empathy, and achieve new levels of sensitivity and fellow-feeling. We can, in short, think, talk, read, and write our way out of bigotry and narrow-mindedness, out of our limitations of experience and perspective . . . however, we can do this only to a very limited extent.[46]

White, privileged students reading and discussing books about people who don't look like them isn't going to magically cure ignorance, structural racism, and inequality. It does, however, give otherwise racially isolated kids some opportunity to transcend the barriers of what is familiar and gain a more expansive understanding not only of the human experience, but of themselves . . . and also to metacognitively recognize and understand that process, and apply those learnings to their real-world attempts to get beyond their bubble.

HISTORY AND SOCIAL STUDIES: DEFINING "ACTUAL" HISTORY

The teaching of history is usually considered far more politically fraught than the teaching of literature. After all, in many people's minds, fiction and poetry aren't about "real" things, and even narrative nonfiction and memoir lie safely rooted in individual experience. On the other hand, the racial politics of how history—and *whose* history—gets taught in public schools tends to make front page news.

While most schools in the Boston area suffer from racial segregation, Cambridge Rindge and Latin School (CRLS), the public high school of Cambridge, Massachusetts, is something of an exception, with a near 50/50 split of white students and students of color (about 30 percent African American students and 10–15 percent each of Asian American and Latinx students). The students' economic diversity is also atypical for the region, with a third of the students categorized as economically disadvantaged, enrolled alongside students from some of the wealthiest (usually white) families in one of the wealthiest states in the country. [47]

In 2017 the Black Student Union at CRLS, with the aid of the organization's faculty advisor, constructed and propagated a video series called "Minority Reports" with the goal of having students of color highlight "real, brief and commonplace daily verbal, behavioral, or environmental indignities, experienced by students inside their high school." [48] Some of the most arresting stories came, perhaps unsurprisingly, from their experience in history classes, like these examples:

> I was in a class and . . . we were talking about how slaves were being raped. A white student stood up in the back of the class and said, "Slaves can't be raped because they were property."

And,

> One day people came to my class to present about Black History Month and there was a debate about whether there should be a White History Month . . . and when we started talking about it, one of the [white] students said, "Well, Black History would be more important if it was actual history." [49]

So what earns the distinction, in the minds of privileged white students, and the white power structure in which they are educated, of being "actual" history?

Recall that history textbooks traditionally constitute 75–90 percent of classroom instruction in schools. [50] The history they present is laden with certain racial and cultural biases. Donald Yacovone from at Harvard University's Hutchins Center examined nearly 3,000 U.S. history textbooks from the 1800s to the 1980s, finding that

> across time and with precious few exceptions African Americans appeared only as a problem, only as "ignorant negroes," as "slaves," and as anonymous abstractions that only posed "problems" for the real subjects of this written history: white people of European descent. The assumptions of white priority, white domination, and white importance underlie every chapter and every theme of the thousands of textbooks that blanketed the schools of our country. . . . And while the worst features of our textbook legacy may have ended, the themes, facts, and attitudes of supremacist ideologies are deeply embedded in what we teach and how we teach it. [51]

Even contemporary textbooks can suffer from these defects. Take for example a McGraw-Hill world geography text from 2015, with over 140,000 copies in use, that framed the Atlantic slave trade in such seemingly innocuous terms as bringing "millions of workers from Africa to the southern United States to work on agricultural plantations" as part of a larger chapter on immigration.[52]

Several attempts by teachers to present alternate framings of U.S. history, particularly focusing on the experiences and struggles of Americans of color, have faced organized resistance from the power structure. In 2010, Arizona passed a law banning the teaching of "ethnic studies" on the grounds that it "advocate[d] ethnic solidarity instead of being individuals" and was "designed for a certain ethnicity"—as if a white, European-centered focus was not also designed for a certain ethnicity! A federal judge struck down the ban seven years later.

In 2015, Texas, South Carolina, and Oklahoma were among the states in which legislators battled over the content and framing of school history standards; in Oklahoma, this escalated to a state representative introducing a bill to ban the teaching of the Advanced Placement U.S. history curriculum because it put too much emphasis on "what is bad about America" and did not include enough about "American exceptionalism."[53]

Media narratives tended to frame all of this as a battle, where on one side stood those who desired to present a unifying narrative among the many diverse strands of American history. Arizona Superintendent Tom Horne captures this view succinctly in his public defense of the ethnic studies ban:

> [T]he function of the public schools is to bring in kids from different backgrounds and teach them to treat each other as individuals. And the Tucson district [ethnic studies program] is doing the opposite. They're teaching them to emphasize ethnic solidarity . . . and I think that's exactly the wrong thing to do in the public schools.[54]

On the other side was the argument that the promulgation of a singular narrative, typically one with "overwhelming dominance of Euro-American perspectives," leads many students, according to a National Education Association (NEA) analysis of 30 years of research, "to disengage from academic learning. Ethnic studies curricula exist in part because students of color have demanded an education that is relevant, meaningful, and affirming of their identities."[55]

But since the current predominantly Euro-American narrative does indeed appear relevant, meaningful, and affirming of the identities of white privileged students, what is the argument—and the strategy—for broadening a social studies approach to engage them with the histories of other peoples? In other words, is there a value to, and a method for, widening these students' definitions of "actual history?" One argument, presented by Dr. Christine Sleeter, author of the aforementioned NEA report, is that

> Mainstream Euro-American studies deny all students—both White and of color—an education that takes seriously the realities of institutionalized racism

that people of color live every day, and knowledge that arises from within communities of color. Ethnic studies, by allowing for multiple voices to enter dialog constructing the narrative of this country, is critical to the development of a democracy that actually includes everyone.[56]

This is similar to the arguments presented about the world literature course described in the previous section: that the idea of not being "in the know," of not having a fuller picture, could draw on white students' natural curiosity, their learned anxiety about being properly prepared for college, or both.

However, weighing the merits and flaws of possessing a command of "traditional" versus "alternate" narratives of history is not necessarily a useful way of framing the question of how to engage white privileged students with the stories of marginalized peoples. Constructing a "traditional/white-Eurocentric" versus "alternate/ethnic" binary misses much of the value that social studies and history classes can provide to all students. As culture journalist Jacoba Urist put it, "the media and lawmakers often reduce [discussions of teaching history] to two poles: a liberal left that pursues an overly 'negative' reinterpretation of U.S. history versus a conservative right that just wants students to memorize a list of names and facts—and 'smudge out the ugly parts.'" Urist continues:

> Currently, most students learn history as a set narrative—a process that reinforces the mistaken idea that the past can be synthesized into a single, standardized chronicle. . . . [But history] is a collection of historians exchanging different, often conflicting analyses. And rather than vainly seeking to transcend the inevitable clash of memories, American students would be better served by descending into the bog of conflict and learning the many "histories" that compose the American national story.

She concludes that students should be taught history not as a single narrative, but as a *discipline* that is "about explaining and interpreting past events analytically."[57]

Urist's fellow *Atlantic* contributor, Michael Conway, argues that instead of teaching history, schools should teach *historiography*—the process by which historians assemble narratives, what they leave in, what they leave out, how they frame events, and what the effects of those framings are. "If students are really to learn and master these analytical tools," Conway writes, "then it is absolutely essential that they read a diverse set of historians and learn how brilliant men and women who are scrutinizing the same topic can reach different conclusions."[58]

"Historiography," writes James Loewen in his introduction to *The Confederate and Neo-Confederate Reader* (2010), "asks us to scrutinize how a given piece of history came to be written. Who wrote it? When? With whom were they in debate? What were they trying to prove? Who didn't write it?

What points of view were omitted?"[59] This way, the teacher need not engage in some sort of struggle to convince privileged white students that they need to be engaged in learning "someone else's history," but instead engage them in a process that gives them more tools to understand how history is constructed and interpreted. Learning and using these tools to explore and assess a wide variety of historical perspectives gives students the responsibility for *defining, critiquing, and defending* framings of "actual history" as opposed to just accepting and memorizing the definitions established by those in power, be they liberal or conservative. This can be an easy "sell" to students as adolescents in particular, and human beings in general, tend to engage positively with the idea of being given the tools of self-empowerment.

* * *

First Date Perspective

This activity I've used with my ELA students has easy portability to the social studies classroom: I tell a narrative about my first serious "date" in high school, putting a list of events that occurred on the board, including:

- *Arrived 15 minutes early*
- *Dropped a glass in her kitchen that shattered on the floor*
- *Asked for broom, helped clean up the glass*
- *Ordered pizza on the phone*
- *Forgot her address when the pizza delivery person asked for it*
- *Played Nintendo games together*

Then I ask students to select just those events that paint me in a positive light, and tell the story that way. They tend to include things like, "prompt arrival," "took responsibility for the dropped glass and cleaned it," "ensured that they would have food."

Next, I ask them to include just those events that paint me negatively. "Wrecked her property within minutes of arrival. Couldn't remember the address of the place he'd just arrived at."

Finally, I ask them to write a rendition of events as told from her point of view—how might that differ, and what information might it focus on? This opens the door to developing an understanding that even nonfiction is still the conscious product of choices as to what and how to include information, and how to frame and present it.

* * *

Students can be asked to examine primary- or even secondary-source documents in the service of actually constructing competing "textbooks," or at
least "course readers," full of resources and framings that shape the historical
narrative a certain way, and then exchange with their classmates. Everyone
would then analyze and evaluate the effects of the choices the other groups
made, and how the narratives they created differed.

Examining contemporary journalism is another way students can practice
the skills of historiography. The assignment could be to pick a news story in
print, on TV or radio, or online. They should follow the story through two
different news media outlets that are covering it (for example, MSNBC and
FOX). Students should take notes about:

- Which facts, ideas, sources, and angles seem to be present in both outlets'
  coverage
- Which facts, ideas, sources, and angles seem present in only one outlet,
  but not the other
- Other significant differences or similarities

By the end of the entire unit, students should learn and be able to both
recognize and create examples of narrative shaping via factors listed in Table
3.2.

Since students learn most fully through *doing,* as a summative assessment, groups of students could act as a real news team (or future historians
looking back on our present era), covering a real event happening in the
school community (e.g., a school dance, a new school rule, a profile of a
sports team, an investigative report about the cafeteria food). They should
compose an article or video that reports the event, and then a second article
or video which reports it with a different spin. In neither news report nor
historical narrative are they allowed to lie or make up any facts. However,
through selection, omission, and framing, they have free reign to shape each
story.

This learning-through-doing can happen before, or concurrent with, the
study of several well-established yet divergent historians whom the teacher
selects. Ultimately, says Conway, "this approach exposes textbooks as noth-

Table 3.2. Basic types of bias in news reporting

Omission	Word choice/labeling	Limiting/framing
Choice of sources	Regionalism	Placement
Headline/captioning	Institutional affiliation	Image choice

Adapted from Bass, et al. (2003). "News bias explored: The art of reading the news."
University of Michigan. http://umich.edu/~newsbias/manifestations.html

ing more than a compilation of histories that the authors deemed to be most relevant and useful." As Conway puts it,

> In historiography, the barrier between historian and student is dropped, exposing a conflict-ridden landscape. . . . Historians studying the same topic will draw different interpretations. . . . Will every perspective be afforded its due? Probably not. But the students will be better equipped to recognize weaknesses in an argument and resist the allure of a simplified national narrative. [60]

To answer, then, the white privileged student's concern about learning "actual" history: historiography is the *actual process of constructing history*, and by definition one cannot learn historiography without reading multiple narratives focusing on, and from the perspective of, multiple people and groups along the racial, cultural, and economic spectrum.

* * *

How Am I Going to Find the Time to Do All This When I Have So Much Content to Cover?

This is the biggest obstacle to effective teaching of history: that curriculum standards are inevitably framed in terms of breadth, instead of depth, of coverage. State frameworks and especially the AP exam present an impossibly long series of names, places, and events that teachers are responsible for "covering" with students.

"Cover," by necessity, ends up being defined as "there was a day when this was the topic of the lesson," then there is a quiz, and then students move on. This breakneck pace reduces students' experience of learning history to a process of memorization and recitation, versus acquiring deep understandings of social and economic forces and historiographic methods. Social studies teachers may feel they cannot afford to take a moment to "step off the conveyor belt" to spend a week or more diving into examining multiple narratives of the same event or even the same era.

It's not an all-or-nothing proposition. Even creating one unit around historiographic work, which could double as a chance to introduce content, could be valuable for your students. If all else fails, you could relegate these sorts of lessons to the realm of an elective course. Even a limited engagement is better than nothing!

* * *

MATH AND SCIENCE: WHAT DO THEY HAVE TO DO WITH SOCIAL JUSTICE?

It is tempting to consider the STEM fields, particularly math, to be "culturally neutral." After all, numbers are not socially constructed racialized phenomena, and neither gravitational forces nor Newton's laws seem to be experienced differentially based on culture or skin color. If we were ourselves just integers or subatomic particles, then the discussion would end there. But since we are human beings, then our positionality influences everything we teach and learn, including math and science.

According to Professor Omiunota Ukpokodu, ethnomathematicians like Brazil's Ubiratan D'Ambrosio remind us that "mathematics and mathematical knowledge is not culturally neutral, absolutist, or universal. Rather, it is situated within a sociocultural frame of a given cultural group."[61] This means that "students who come from different cultural backgrounds enter the teaching and learning process with their cultural thinking and processing styles when doing mathematics, and teachers must understand this."

Ukpokodu describes several examples of how culture, and cultural mismatch, can influence students' ability to learn mathematics. Sometimes this is about engagement; word problems that only use referents traditionally coded as white/Eurocentric (such as slicing a pumpkin pie as opposed to slicing a guava to teach fractions), but it can also involve fundamental differences in teacher versus student understanding of the parameters and solutions to the same mathematical problem.

Take this example from University of Wisconsin–Madison Professor William Tate's study of urban middle school students who had been presented with the following problem to solve: "It costs $1.50 each way to ride the bus between home and work. A weekly pass is $16.00. Which is the better deal, paying the daily fare or buying the weekly pass?"[62] As Ukpokodu describes:

> The predominantly African American urban students responded "strangely" to the problem by choosing the weekly pass as the better deal. Unfortunately, the students failed this item because they had contextualized their thinking within the context of their lived experiences as they thought and applied the multiple uses for the pass—working seven days a week (not just five days), going to two or more jobs, for rides to visit relatives, social events, church, and allowing relatives or friends to use it when they are not. According to the dominant, Euro-centric, and middle-class paradigm of problem solving and mathematical thinking, *the students supposedly failed this test item even though their thinking was logical and accurate, because the item was constructed based on a middle-class [white] perspective.*[63]

According to Gutstein, because the assumptions of (predominantly white) math instructors and assessors "are not consistent with the daily lives and realities of many African American students" and others, students from those groups may require explicit instruction that "the mode of response should reflect the idealized experiences of a traditional white middle-class family," instruction that few math teachers think to provide. Second, "the students had to understand the mathematics involved in solving the test item [while] using the white middle class as a frame to guide their problem-solving. This dual consciousness was required if the students were to 'succeed' according to the Eurocentric assumptions of the test designers."[64]

While white, privileged students likely experience no such mismatch or need for "dual consciousness" because, presumably, their assumptions and those of their instructors, textbooks, and test designers are aligned, this also means that they *miss out* on potential opportunities to think divergently about mathematical processes. If teachers want to prepare their students for the kind of analytic thinking that will help them use mathematics to solve real-world problems, then it is vital they help their students develop the ability to question the parameters and assumptions of a problem, or else they will be at risk for using "correct" math "incorrectly" when the time comes for actual application of their skills.

Test preparation companies figured this out long ago, as articulated here by the Melbourne, Australia–based BestTuition, which advertises training in lateral thinking, defined as:

> the skill to deduce problems via indirect and creative means. Good math students will have a sense of knowing what creative strategies they can employ for unforeseen questions just like a good writer has a knack of expressing themselves more elegantly than others. Lateral thinking also provides benefits in the exam preparation process, as an emphasis on the manipulation of concepts rather than the process of doing questions will make studying a lot more.[65]

Students are often taught math through the use of "real-world" examples that can be very effective for acquiring basic concepts, but make some implicit assumptions about context. Until and unless those assumptions are rendered conscious and obvious, then the lesson not only threatens to exclude students from certain backgrounds, but inadequately prepares students from the privileged culture for actual application to real-world problems. As mentioned earlier in this chapter, Edward de Bono made his career around developing ways to help people think laterally, and a simple internet search on "lateral thinking puzzles" can yield hundreds of resources for teachers seeking to inculcate these skills in their students. The lesson below uses a classic example.

Lesson: Digging a Hole

Goal: To encourage students to think laterally/divergently and consider context when applying math to solve a real-world problem.

Time: 10–15 minutes.

Step 1

The teacher asks the class/puts the problem up on the board: "Suppose it took two hours for two men to dig a hole five feet deep. How deep would it have been if ten men had dug the hole for two hours?"

Step 2

Students, individually or in groups, answer the question. There is a high likelihood that they will answer "25 feet deep."

Step 3

The teacher asks students to explain how they solved the problem, what equation they created, what mathematical concepts they applied, and why.

Step 4

Then the teacher will ask students (preferably in pairs or small groups): "Is there any way in which, in the real world, the answer might *not* be 25 feet deep? What sorts of conditions or questions might make the answer different?" The teacher should make it clear that they are not asking for a numeric answer here—the question is not "how deep would the pit be"—but rather, what factors might the students *not* be considering that could make the answer something *different* than 25 feet?

Step 5

Below is a list of common potential responses to this problem. If students appear stuck, the teacher can offer a few hints in the form of questions that might lead to one or more of these answers, but it is also quite possible that the students will come up with some that are not on this list:

- The deeper the hole, the more effort is required to dig it, since waste soil needs to be lifted higher to the ground level, so that might affect the rate of removal.
- The men could work in shifts to dig faster for longer than they could if they were all digging at once.
- Deeper soil layers may be harder to dig out, or the men may hit bedrock or the water table, which would slow things down.

- The more people you have working on a project, the more each person might assume they can "slack off," and/or more people to talk to could result in more distraction and less efficient and speedy work.
- The two men may be an engineering crew with digging machinery, and the ten men might just have shovels . . . or vice versa.
- There are more men, but are there actually more shovels?
- The two hours dug by ten men may have taken place under different weather conditions than the two hours dug by two men, which could affect rate of removal.
- What if one man in each group is a manager who will not actually dig?[66]

Step 6

Facilitate a discussion among the students about the assumptions laden in math problems, and the advantages and limitations of not outright stating these assumptions. Somewhere the idea should arise that two people might approach the same problem with different assumptions, and reach different answers, *even if they are both using math correctly.* This could be a moment to bring in the example of the "bus pass" problem described earlier, or the 1999 crash of NASA's Mars Climate Orbiter because scientists from the Jet Propulsion Lab were using the metric system for their calculations, while their collaborators at Lockheed Martin were using the imperial system, and each had just erroneously assumed the other was using the same units.

Step 7

Ultimately the students should be tasked with creating their own examples of this phenomenon in action, and/or taking various word problems from their textbook and coming up with lists of "assumptions" and "challenges/alternatives to those assumptions." Some of these can then be developed, with specific units and conditions, to form new problems for them to solve.

Teachers interested in using this concept to broach issues of social justice have some easy points of entry, as the key to a great many lateral thinking puzzles lies in questioning one's own prejudices and assumptions, such as in this classic riddle:

> A young boy is injured in a car accident and is rushed to a hospital. Just as he is about to undergo surgery, the surgeon stops and says, "Wait—I can't operate—that boy is my son!" Yet the surgeon is not the boy's father. How is this possible?

The solution to this problem, of course, is that the surgeon is the boy's mother. Yet in a 2014 study by Boston University Psychology Professor

Deborah Belle, only 15 percent of the 197 psychology students and 103 children studied could successfully pose the "surgeon is the mother" possibility. Even among the self-identified "feminists" in the study, 78 percent were unable to envision this possibility.

Belle expressed surprise at her results, given the high income and highly educated backgrounds of most of the participants. "These are two populations that we would expect, if anything, would be in the avant-garde," she wrote.[67] But we should not find these results surprising in the least—it is precisely the most privileged who are least able to think outside the box, because the box has been so thoroughly designed to suit them.

Developing that out-of-the-box thinking is the responsibility of all teachers, but math teachers in particular have an opportunity here simply because their subject matter is so often presented as clear-cut, straightforward, and single-solution-oriented. Exploring how mathematical thinking can be embedded in, and influenced by, cultural perspectives is one way to help students think in more lateral terms. Thinking of the failing grades of those African American students in the bus pass problem, or the billions of dollars wasted by the crash of the Mars probe, can remind students that the real-world stakes of critiquing these cultural blinders can be quite high.

There is also both an opportunity and a duty for social-justice-minded mathematics teachers to expose white, privileged students to mathematicians of color. It has become best practice in the STEM education of students of color to provide examples of mathematicians and scientists who look like them as a means of increasing engagement and STEM self-concepts; as the adage says, "If you can see it, you can be it." This works for gender as well: featuring female scientists and engineers can lead to improved STEM achievement for girls.[68]

However, as with so many trends in social justice education, this is usually presented as a set of strategies solely intended for the marginalized, forgetting that white, privileged students' stereotypes also need to be challenged. "If I see it, I know *they* can be it," is as important a lesson. To fail to do so risks generating comments like that of the white student mentioned in the Cambridge Rindge and Latin video, that essentially, there "is no such thing as Black history." If we do not teach white students of the existence of great and influential individuals in all fields who happen to be of color, how can we expect them to think otherwise?

Such figures should be presented without any particular fanfare—"Hey, listen up class, now we're going to learn about a *Vietnamese* mathematician!"—but rather as a normal part of the curricular diet. After all, how often do we jump up and introduce Shakespeare as "white, British playwright!" or Sir Isaac Newton as a "white, European physicist!" Students will be able to see color for themselves.

Also, such figures should be presented *in large quantity*. It naturally reads to students as tokenism if your classroom has posters of five white male mathematicians, and then one dutifully selected from each "marginalized category." Resources like the Minneapolis-based Mathematics Project's "Mathematicians Are Not Just White Dudes"[69] website offer literally hundreds of figures of multiple national, racial, ethnic, gender, and sexual identities from throughout history up into contemporary times. A daily five-minute "meet the mathematician of the day" routine could introduce students to 180 such figures over the course of the year.

Going deeper to look at some of the various traditions of mathematical development in various parts of Africa, Asia, or the Middle East, as well as the non-European (Chinese, Vedic, Persian, Arab, etc.) origins of so many elements of Western mathematics, from our numeral set to the processes of algebra, could be wonderful ways of engaging humanities-leaning students with the stories behind the math they use, yielding a kind of "diversity dividend" in the process.

Science, too, is a subject ripe for such approaches. As the UK-based nonprofit, The Company of Biologists, suggests, teachers could begin a genetics unit not with Gregor Mendel, but perhaps start earlier with "the Native Americans [who] have been doing experiments on corn for thousands of years but didn't write down their findings because they followed an oral tradition," or frame such a unit not just around Mendeleev but also

> Priya Moorjani, a geneticist who has used genomic data to understand the origins of the Indian caste system; Kono Yasui, a biologist who researched the genetics of several plant species; or Rick Kittles, who used genetics to trace the ancestry of African Americans. Or you might choose a woman like Barbara McClintock who was not encouraged personally or professionally to study science, but who still went on to win the Nobel Prize for her work in genetics.[70]

Ultimately, as Gutiérrez and others caution, just trotting out diversity on display is insufficient for the goals of social justice education. It is also important to address the question of *why and how* so much of the diverse historical origins, and more contemporary practice, of science and math has been occluded. The next chapter will spend more time on those ideas.

Before that, it must be pointed out that life sciences teachers have one of the biggest and most obvious opportunities to engage in social justice through challenging the core notion of race as rooted in biology. Yet according to *UnDark* writer Michael Schulson, despite what should be fertile ground for such lessons,

> [m]ost biology textbooks and curricula don't discuss race at all . . . to a growing number of academics, that's a problem, and the omissions represent

glaring intellectual lacunae—a sort of sanitized approach to biology that ignores the political and cultural veins that have historically run through it. After
all, the history of racial, sexual, and gender classification is very much a story
of scientific debate. And biological concepts—and misperceptions—continue
to exert profound influence on national conversations about diversity and human difference.[71]

As a result, biology teachers often need to look beyond textbooks in order to
find material to fuel such lessons. One potential starting point could be the
1998 statement on race from the American Anthropological Society:

> In the United States both scholars and the general public have been condi-
> tioned to viewing human races as natural and separate divisions within the
> human species based on visible physical differences. With the vast expansion
> of scientific knowledge in this century, however, it has become clear that
> human populations are not unambiguous, clearly demarcated, biologically dis-
> tinct groups. Evidence from the analysis of genetics (e.g., DNA) indicates that
> most physical variation, about 94%, lies within so-called racial groups. Con-
> ventional geographic "racial" groupings differ from one another only in about
> 6% of their genes. This means that there is greater variation within "racial"
> groups than between them. In neighboring populations there is much overlap-
> ping of genes and their phenotypic (physical) expressions. Throughout history
> whenever different groups have come into contact, they have interbred. The
> continued sharing of genetic materials has maintained all of humankind as a
> single species. . . . It is a basic tenet of anthropological knowledge that all
> normal human beings have the capacity to learn any cultural behavior.[72]

As just one example of such a study, a 2003 article published in the
Proceedings of the National Academy of Sciences described the findings of
two teams of researchers, in Brazil and in Portugal: determining the genetic
background of a person based on physical characteristics normally associated
with race, including skin color, facial features, and hair texture, was not
reliably possible.[73]

One could conceive of a science lesson that asked students to participate
in a similar kind of study, seeing if their own conclusions about the "race" of
certain individuals in photos wound up matching those individuals' actual
genetic records. Due to the potential for stereotyping, damaging comments,
and general volatility, however, such a lesson requires some very clear norm-
setting first, and much effort to lay the groundwork for conversations about
race (see chapter 2). A potential alternative, if the teacher is comfortable with
this, is to ask students to anonymously "guess" their (the teacher's) "race"
from physical characteristics, and then show the students the results of one of
several popular and relatively inexpensive genetic ancestry tests, especially if
the teacher knows ahead of time that the results might be surprising to the
students.

A unit on taxonomy is another place where a critique of race, and the past role of the scientific establishment of propagating unscientific definitions of it, could be broached. After all, the ways in which we sort organisms into kingdom, phylum, class, order, family, genus, and species depends upon conscious selection of certain traits, and not others, as distinguishing. Students could examine how previous taxonomies, like the Medieval European "Great Chain of Being," chose different attributes around which to classify species. In this particular case, animals that flew through the air were considered to be more "advanced" and "morally superior" to animals that lived in water, because air itself was positioned physically above water in nature.

Students could, in a lesson, be tasked with developing their own taxonomies for organisms (or food, or clothing), with a condition that they be organized along some internally consistent logic, and then shared with the rest of the class so everyone could see how this process is influenced not just by the inherent characteristics of those organisms or, but also by the value-laden choices of individual human classifiers.

The website Facing History and Ourselves has a robust (and free!) curriculum on race and eugenics, which includes a lesson along those very lines. The takeaway is that:

> while students' choices in this exercise are relatively inconsequential, we make similar choices with great consequence in the ways that we define and categorize people in society. While there are many categories we might use to describe differences between people, society has given more meaning to some types of difference (such as skin color and gender) and less meaning to others (such as eye and hair color).[74]

Another resource is the Illusion of Race series from the American Association for the Advancement of Science (AAAS), more overtly grounded in the language and examples of the life sciences.[75] The 2003 PBS film series, *Race: The Power of an Illusion*, is a robust resource (complete with its own curriculum on the PBS website[76]), and the Discovery Channel's *The Real Eve*, also from 2003, both provide an engaging presentation of the evidence we have of "mitochondrial Eve" and the theories of common human origin in Africa. A more recent book, Spencer Wells's *The Journey of Man: A Genetic Odyssey* (updated in 2017) provides much more detail.

Even outside of the contexts of evolution, genetics, and taxonomy, lessons about blood types, for example, or bone marrow donation, could help students understand that if they were ever in need of a transfusion, it is very possible that they might find a more compatible donor in someone with a different, versus similar, skin color to their own.

CONTESTING THE POSTINTEGRATION NARRATIVE

With desegregation and the end of the Negro schools, African American students lost an academic environment that celebrated black identity, that situated it within a historical frame of achievement.[77] Integration also resulted in the firing of hundreds of black teachers, depriving not only African American students of classroom role models,[78] but also depriving white students of the opportunity to see, and learn from, educated, knowledgeable, and powerful black teachers. America's ever-increasing de facto school segregation ensures that, "particularly for young white children, interaction with people of color is likely to be a *virtual* reality rather than an *actual* one, with media images (often negative ones) most clearly shaping their attitudes and perceived knowledge of communities of color."[79]

Theresa Perry chronicles how, in schools where white and black students did learn side-by-side, the racist reactions of white teachers transmitted continual messages of inferiority to black students and superiority to white students, leading both groups to internalize those values.[80] Combine that with the well-documented ways in which tracking and other forms of so-called ability grouping lead to students of color being overrepresented in "low-ability" classes and underrepresented in programs for the gifted and talented,[81] and it becomes incredibly easy for white students and teachers alike to buy into the narrative of black inferiority. Claude Steele's studies of stereotype threat demonstrate that even when African American students do gain entry into high-level classes, pressures on them to disprove these inferiority narratives ironically lead to disabling anxiety and poorer performance,[82] which of course only confirms the inferiority narrative in the minds of white students.

Whether in ELA, history, math, or science courses, a teacher has the power to offer alternatives to this narrative. A curriculum rich in examples and achievements of individuals of color, in sufficient quantity and integrated so thoroughly that it seems less a series of remarkable exceptions and more a reflection of how greatness is a phenomenon found among all cultures, can potentially erode or at least complicate that narrative. Cognitive/behavioral science calls this process "stereotype replacement," and it has been shown to improve participants' outcomes on tests of implicit bias.[83] It is no substitute for actual long-term, meaningful interactions with the "Other," but in today's highly segregated school environments it is easier to enact, and to scaffold.

The goal of this stereotype replacement, of what Gutiérrez calls "raising consciousness," is not, she says, to produce people "without prejudice, even though this goal is commonly embraced by those enacting a multicultural . . . curriculum." Instead, she says, such efforts are intended to make [white, privileged people] aware of their (dominant) positions in society, of the taken-for-granted practices, values and frames of reference from within a white, Eurocentric tradition so that they can better understand that such a position is just one among many possible—and one that continues to oppress others. [84]

Sleeter, in her review of the research, similarly found that "simply infusing representation of racially and ethnically diverse people into curriculum only marginally affects students' attitudes because racial attitudes are acquired actively rather than passively. Curricula that teach directly about racism have a stronger positive impact than curricula that portray diverse groups but ignore racism."[85]

Ultimately, it seems, exposing white, privileged students to a more diverse set of perspectives from and about people of color only goes so far. We need to go beyond Goodman's Competency 2: Understanding and valuing others' social identities, cultures, and perspectives—to Competency 3: Knowledge of societal inequities—understanding how social identities and forms of oppression affect people' experiences and access to power, resources, and opportunities. But it is no accident that Goodman places the competencies in this order. Because if we return to the introduction and to Evan, upset and indignant at having to read Martin Luther King Jr.'s writings on social and racial justice because he doesn't see what they have to do with his own lived experience, we now see that a bridge needed to be made. White, privileged students first need to see both the commonalities between their experiences and those of people whose skin color, religion, or economic circumstances seem so very different, and also to see the value and benefit to their own intellectual growth and critical thinking toolbox that come from exploring those differences.

Besides, if white students spend enough time delving into those perspectives, the injustices and inequities so inextricably entwined into those narratives become impossible to ignore. They become the natural extension of learning about, and from, the "Other," and with luck, the next natural extension beyond that is the self-evident need to do something to address those injustices. The tricky part, of course, is navigating the problematic waters of one's own culpability in and benefit from those injustices—quite literally, "what injustice *does* have to do with me."

NOTES

1. Freire, 1974/1998, 45.
2. de Waal-Lucas, 2007.
3. Ibid.
4. Jablon, 2014, 10.
5. Freire, 1974/1998, 34.

6. The appropriate English teacher buzzphrase is "making text-to-self-connections."

7. A student-moderated discussion; I will explain about this technique, and other tools of a democratic classroom, in chapter 7.

8. Swalwell, 2013, 42.

9. Ibid.

10. DiAngelo, interviewed by Courtney Martin, 2018.

11. Once again: You Know Your Students—Your Mileage May Vary.

12. The Anti-Defamation League (www.adl.org) has many resources to help with creating and running such activities.

13. Such bridges are the very stuff that Lev Vygotsky was talking about with his theory of the zone of proximal development (if you're interested in getting deep into Constructivist learning theory, check out some of Vygotsky's writings).

14. Quoted in Martin, 2018.

15. Hobson, 2014.

16. This is a fact I usually reveal along with the coda, "the best decision Lucas ever made, which almost—almost—makes up for *The Phantom Menace*."

17. Hobson, 2014.

18. "Racial and Ethnic Achievement Gaps," 2015.

19. Hobson, 2014.

20. Gutiérrez, 2013, 208.

21. Nguyen, 2017; see also Ahmed, 2007.

22. Nguyen, 2017.

23. If you're unfamiliar or need a refresher, Plato tells a story in *The Republic* of prisoners who have lived their entire life in a cave, chained to a chair and only able to see the shadows of objects that a fire behind them casts on the wall. When one prisoner escapes, he is baffled by the "real" objects of the "real world," since his whole life he has misunderstood the shadows to be the objects themselves. For Plato, there really was an objective truth, just beyond our access. Subsequent schools of Western philosophy, including postmodernism, posit all reality to some degree as being dependent on/limited by perspective, with any attempts to impose an arbitrating standard producing a privileging of one particular point of view, usually the perspective of whomever is in power (Lee, 2003).

24. Miner, 1956.

25. Depending on how the teacher handles it, it might be useful to show students excerpts from such pieces, although steps should be taken to prevent the casual racism of such texts inadvertently reinforcing students' existing prejudices. For example, I usually wait until after students have already read Chinua Achebe's *Things Fall Apart* (1958/1994) before showing them passages from Rudyard Kipling and Joseph Conrad that depict Africans as savages, so that my students can see the distance between the three-dimensional characters Achebe creates in his novel and these absurd caricatures created by white authors.

26. Thomas, 2017, 401.

27. Adichie, 2009.

28. Ibid.

29. As a huge Kurosawa fan, I might take a moment to recommend the use of *Rashomon* as well, although some prep work in studying Japanese history and culture might be advisable before viewing the film.

30. Tyson and Woodward, 1989.

31. Swartz, 1992, 341.

32. Ibid.

33. Bishop, 1990.

34. Stotsky, 1995, 605.

35. Applebee, 1990.

36. "What Kids Are Reading," 2019.

37. Ladson-Billings, 1998, 13.

38. Delgado, quoted in Ladson-Billings, 1998, 13.

39. de Bono, 1994.

40. Nishi, Shirado, Rand, and Christakis, 2015, 426.

41. Olsen, 2018.
42. Hammond, 2016.
43. Tatum, 2008, 34.
44. Stotsky, 1994, 29–30.
45. Bishop, 1990.
46. Delgado and Stefancic, 1992, 1258.
47. Massachusetts Department of Elementary and Secondary Education, 2017.
48. Black Student Union, Cambridge Rindge and Latin School, n.d.
49. Ibid.
50. Tyson and Woodward, 1989.
51. Yacovone, quoted in Benz, 2017.
52. Fernandez and Hauser, 2015. In response to public pressure, a company spokesperson wrote, "we conducted a close review of the content and agree that our language in that caption did not adequately convey that Africans were both forced into migration and to labor against their will as slaves. . . . We believe we can do better." McGraw Hill issued a new printing, and pointed out that other chapters did attest to the brutality of forced relocation and servitude.
53. Krehbiel, 2015.
54. Quoted by Van Susteren, 2010.
55. Sleeter, 2011.
56. Ibid.
57. Urist, 2015.
58. Conway, 2015.
59. Loewen, 2010, 3.
60. Conway, 2015.
61. Ukpokodu, 2011; see also D'Ambrosio, 1997.
62. Tate, 1994.
63. Ukpokodu, 2011 (emphasis mine).
64. Gutstein, 2013, 62–63.
65. "Lateral Thinking in Maths: Why You Cannot Cram for a Maths Exam," 2018.
66. For an extended version of this example, see https://psychology.wikia.org/wiki/Lateral_thinking.
67. Quoted in Barlow, 2014.
68. See Stinson, 2013, and Gutiérrez, 2013.
69. Perkins, 2016,
70. Butler, 2017.
71. Schulson, 2018.
72. "AAA Statement on Race," 1998.
73. Parra, Amado, Lambertucci, Rocha, Antunes, and Pena, 2003.
74. "Which One of These Things Is Not Like the Other?" n.d.
75. "The Illusion of Race," n.d.
76. California Newsreel, 2003.
77. Perry, 2004.
78. Tatum, 2008.
79. Ibid., 14.
80. Perry, 2004.
81. The correlation between placement, social class, and ethnicity is present regardless of the basis for placement (test scores, counselor and teacher recommendations, or student and parent choice). This, too, was supported by subsequent studies—see Gamoran, 1992; Hyland, 2006; Van Houtte and Stevens, 2008.
82. Steele, 2011.
83. Devine, Forscher, Austin, and Cox, 2012.
84. Gutiérrez, 2013, 214.
85. Sleeter, 2011, viii.

Chapter Four

What Does Injustice Have to Do with Me?

This chapter will address the third competency in Diane Goodman's "Cultural Competencies for Social Justice":
Competency 3: Knowledge of societal inequities—understanding of how social identities and forms of oppression affect people' experiences and access to power, resources, and opportunities.

One cold March morning, the affluent suburban Shady Point[1] school made statewide headlines, not for the usual reasons of students winning athletic victories or prestigious scholarships, but because an unknown student or students had scrawled a giant "N-word" on the school library wall. Administrators, faculty, and students alike responded with condemnation, but there was a sharp divide between the reactions of the African American students and the reactions of most of the white majority. Many white students, initially united in outrage with their counterparts of color, began to differ sharply in how they interpreted the incident. In their analysis, the graffiti was an anomaly, the work of an ill-intentioned individual or individuals, in whom lay sole culpability and responsibility. They acknowledged it was upsetting, but since the guilty party's anonymity made following up with consequences impossible, there was nothing to do but move on. Some began to grow frustrated with how the African American students refused to let the issue go.

In the minds of many of those African American students, this incident was no aberration. It seemed to them entirely consistent with the racism they experienced daily in the form of aggressions on both the micro and macro level. "I think this happens a lot," one African American student told the press, "but it just isn't as public."

Several white students reacted with outrage of their own when they became aware of these perspectives. Even some students who were initially sympathetic began to feel unfairly blamed for what they saw as the rogue actions of a single malcontent, so much so that they expressed their anger openly at the assembly convened in response to the graffiti incident. Some said they resented being called racist; others argued that to implicate all white students at the school was itself an act of racism. What had been meant to be a show of community solidarity quickly devolved into mutual accusations.

It became clear that most white students at the school did not possess an understanding of the daily injustices that many students of color had to deal with: The feeling of outsider status that came from being bused for up to 90 minutes to and from school each day (most, although not all, African American and Latinx students attended through a voluntary busing program from the city), and the extra hurdles that commute posed for participating in after-school and community life. The fact that students and teachers alike routinely confused and mispronounced their names (something I have also been guilty of, and had to develop conscious routines to change). The suspicious gazes cast in their direction whenever personal property was reported stolen. The sharper words of rebuke that white teachers used with them when they misbehaved, versus the more collegial way they spoke to white students for similar behaviors. The assumptions white students and teachers made that they were intellectually inferior, that their home neighborhoods were places of squalor and violence, that their college admission was assured because of affirmative action. The white student who had honestly expected her African American classmate could translate the Ibo words from Chinua Achebe's *Things Fall Apart* for her, the white student who had "jokingly" suggested that his Latinx classmate probably knew all about what "life in jail" was like.

Without the understanding or appreciation of the ongoing psychological, emotional, and physiological impact of this reality, many white students couldn't help but see their African American classmates as massively overreacting. After all, this was a "liberal" town. The police officer investigating assured reporters that this was "an isolated incident." The town's human rights council chair, the district superintendent, and the school principal all made public declarations that theirs was not a community that tolerated racism. And hiding in one article, among the many published statewide about the incident, was a mention that "some white students" argued that if African American students felt unwelcomed at the school, it was because they self-segregated at lunchtime.

Such disconnects are not unique to schools, of course. Roy Wood Jr., a reporter for the comedy news program, *The Daily Show*, once hosted a segment in response to surveys that alleged Boston to be one of the most racist cities in the United States. While the African American residents he interviewed agreed with that assessment, all of the white interviewees insisted they didn't see racism around them. Wood joked bitterly that, "if you want to find out if Jurassic Park is safe, you don't ask the dinosaurs."[2]

If you don't experience the effects of something directly, it's hard to understand that it exists, especially when your own education has reinforced the idea that it doesn't. The way I learned about U.S. history in school, and the way it is still taught in most schools, paints a linear and triumphalist narrative from slavery to Emancipation, from Jim Crow to the civil rights era to Barack Obama. White teachers teach white students from books written by white authors the story of how structural racism existed once, and then through a series of heroic actions was ended. "Racism" is an artifact of an ancient world, a series of long-ago practices like slave auctions and lynchings and poll taxes, as opposed to a force presently acting on our own society.

The elite, almost entirely white Pinnacle School exemplified this narrative with one of its "cultural awareness" assemblies. Taking advantage of a local one-man show in which an actor impersonated Thurgood Marshall, the school administration brought that actor in to perform his recap of the life of the first African American Supreme Court Justice for the entire school community. It was a wonderful performance, and the actor's charisma proved strong enough to draw (most) students' attentions away from their phones for a full hour—no mean feat.

But the play itself, as well as the preshow PowerPoint that teachers were given to prepare their students, tracked Marshall's life from childhood all the way up to the climax when he writes the majority opinion for *Brown v. Board of Education* in 1954. Cue lights, take a bow, applause.

Then the bell rang, and students just went on to biology or gym or wherever. The community could have used the assembly as a jumping-off point for a larger learning opportunity about the present state of racial injustice in our country (for example, by asking why there has only been one other African American on the Supreme Court in the 60 years since Marshall's appointment). Instead, it just became, despite what were surely the administration's good intentions, yet another reinforcement of the narrative of "things were bad once, but then they all got fixed."

If this is the narrative whites like me are taught, and if our segregated life experiences insulate us from any evidence to the contrary, then of course we are going to view something like the Shady Point graffiti incident as an isolated act of individual racism, and feel bewildered when told it's just one part of a larger pattern. If we are sure that structural racism is a thing of the past, solved long ago, then any allegations to the contrary sound absurd, manipulative, even "ungrateful" for the equal status the people of color now hold. Any structural racism that people of color see in such incidents must be the paranoid insertion of their own minds.

This is an old formulation. The majority decision in *Plessy v. Ferguson* in 1896 called out African Americans for the same kind of "paranoia":

> We consider the underlying fallacy of the plaintiff's argument to consist in the assumption that the enforced separation of the two races stamps the colored race with a badge of inferiority. . . . If this be so, it is not by reason of anything found in the act, but solely because the colored race chooses to put that construction upon it.[3]

After all, slavery was over, so now the only structural racism remaining existed in the minds of African Americans like Plessy, right?

If the first step in the social justice education of privileged white students is to consider the dimensions of their own identity, and the second is to gain a deeper and more nuanced understanding of and appreciation for the identities of those whom they might otherwise dismiss as irrelevantly alien, then the third step, according to Goodman, is to help them gain an appreciation for how these identities are inextricably connected with differential access to power, resources, and opportunities due to structural inequities in our society.[4] Even more so, privileged white students need to see this is a constellation that already includes *them* as well; the question is, do they want to be included as beneficiaries of injustice, or as those who work to remove it?

UNDERSTANDING STRUCTURAL RACISM AND WHITE PRIVILEGE

Eduardo Bonilla-Silva's seminal work, *Racism without Racists* (2003), outlines the same challenge the graffiti incident posed for engaging white people in an examination of racism: "Whereas for most whites racism is prejudice, for most people of color racism is systemic or institutionalized."[5] Peggy McIntosh describes how, "I did not see myself as a racist because I was taught to recognize racism only in individual acts of meanness by members of my group, never in invisible systems conferring unsought racial dominance on my group from birth."[6]

For many whites, the definition of racism begins and ends with racial slurs, or in black-and-white videos of policemen setting dogs on African American children. Furthermore, racism tends to be constructed in the contemporary white mind via the "fundamental attribution error": if someone delivers a racial slur, this is prima facie evidence that he is a racist. The converse also holds: if someone does not sling racial slurs, then that person is not a racist. For this reason, the idea of structural racism remains a challenging one for many white people to entertain, and students are no exception.

Nevertheless, one cannot have meaningful conversations about justice without addressing structural injustice, and its concomitant concept of *privilege*—particularly and especially in a racial context—because of its potential to draw white people into the story of racism as participants and not merely outside observers.

Sadly, there is no short supply of intersectional injustices in the United States, and as such it is quite common for white Americans' discussions to steer toward any other form of inequity besides race: sexism, heterosexism, ableism, prejudice along the lines of gender identity, or along the lines of class and economic status. Nevertheless, educators have a responsibility to bring the conversation back to race, not because those other forms of oppression are unimportant, but simply because those other forms of oppression are more conversationally "permitted" in discourse among whites.

Far too often, white people seem to want to relegate sole responsibility (or at least, leadership responsibility) for talking about race to persons of color. But for white people like me there is a thin line between giving our colleagues of color voice, and making excuses to exempt ourselves from difficult conversations. So we must keep the focus on race because there is such pressure to focus anywhere but, and that is also why it takes up so much of the focus of this book.

Previous chapters have emphasized the need to start gradually with white, privileged students when it comes to introducing a concept as potentially volatile as structural racism, lest this trigger the usual "shutdown" responses of white fragility. In constructivist tradition, a teacher can have their students begin with creating their own definition of racism, and then comparing it to a dictionary definition: "Prejudice, discrimination, or antagonism directed against someone of a different race based on the belief that one's own race is superior."[7]

Then, the teacher can shift into something more immediately personal by asking the following three questions, revealing them one at a time and allowing a good bit of discussion on each before introducing the next:

1. If I tell you, "your opinion doesn't matter because you're young," is this an example of age prejudice?
2. Is the law that says you cannot vote until you are 18 years old an example of age prejudice?
3. Is adults' general unwillingness to change the laws to lower the voting age an example of age prejudice?

Students' responses tend to vary widely. Nearly all will agree that statement #1 is ageist somehow, but on #2 and #3 they will likely not reach consensus. Some might maintain that voting laws need to discriminate based on age due to the comparatively limited reasoning faculties and life experience of younger people versus their elders, while others might counter that it is quite possible for, say, a 15-year-old to have a deeper grasp of political issues, or perhaps even more relevant life experience, than some adult voters might possess, so why make age the determining factor of civic participation?

Eventually, if the conversation hasn't moved there on its own, the teacher should bring up the question of whether there is a different quality to an individual expression of ageism (i.e., statement #1) versus one that is enumerated and enforced by a larger system (i.e., statements #2 and #3). In other words, even if no adult ever says the first statement to their faces, are they still, as teenagers, facing ageism as a result of statements #2 and #3?

* * *

Parking Permit Plight

Another avenue I've sometimes used, ever since it arose one year entirely by accident, was a discussion of structural injustice that began with my eleventh graders complaining about how they had to compete for a scarce number of on-campus parking permits, unlike the seniors, who were generally guaranteed spaces. Here, in a form they could not only name but also experience, was an example of structuralized inequity.

Now, one might balk at the idea that I'd mention frustration about parking permits anywhere within the same zip code as race-based discrimination, but remember, without a personal entry point, many of my white students would just avoid the zip code entirely, in much the same way that their parents may have literally done so when they moved to the suburbs. Remember the reaction of white students at Shady Point to the racist graffiti at their school, how so many were unmoved, or hurt, or resentful, when their classmates of color tried to link this incident with a larger pattern? For many of my white students—for many whites in America, period—it is the very discussion of race that perpetuates racism, that creates divisions where none need exist. I doubt any of my white students would disagree that racism is a bad thing, but too many of them, ultimately, feel it doesn't have anything to do with them.

* * *

Structural racism is what creates systems of privilege, and it is through studying privilege that many whites can not only start to see the operations of structural racism, but also see where they themselves are included in those operations. That's why Peggy McIntosh's article, "White Privilege: Unpacking the Invisible Knapsack," was so brilliant, couching inequity as a series of "assurances, tools, maps, guides, codebooks, passports, visas, clothes, compass, emergency gear, and blank checks"[8] that white people possess. Despite the article's continued popularity and, with some modifications, continued general acceptance in liberal American academic discourse about race,[9] for many white students at the high school, undergraduate, and even graduate levels, reading this article is the first time they encounter the concept. The teacher should present it the same as any social theory—as an argument. The students' job is to break it down, try to understand its component parts, and try to analyze the effects of presenting oppression through this apparently counterintuitive lens.

It seldom takes white, privileged students long to come up with the idea that presenting racism not as "some people are disadvantaged" but rather as "some people have *too much* advantage" makes people like them (like me, like white people across the country) into an obvious part of the equation. Another equation can then follow: *If racism is now not just a phenomenon that is relevant to racial minorities, if white Americans are both included and implicated in the system as well, then it demands a responsibility and a role for us whites in doing something about it.*

This is not an easy discussion to have. It may be wise to have students do a lot of private, personal journaling, to which the teacher offers nonjudgmental feedback and poses questions, before having them take on this topic in small group and finally full-class conversation. But before even touching McIntosh's article, there are ways to introduce white, privileged students to the concept of privilege that are more immediately tangible, and perhaps less immediately threatening.

Lesson: Wastepaper Basket Toss

Goal: Students will gain insight into the concept of privilege before they learn the actual term and social/racial context.

Time: 5–10 minutes.

Materials: Wastepaper basket/recycling bin. Three crumpled pieces of paper.

Step 1

Announce that the class will be undertaking a challenge, a test of skill and coordination. Either ask for three volunteers, or select three students whom you trust will handle the activity well.

Step 2

Place the wastepaper basket in a centralized spot in the room. Give each of the three students a crumpled piece of paper, and ask them to stand in three particular spots:

- One spot should be extremely close to the wastepaper basket, to make for a laughably easy, impossible-to-miss shot.
- One spot should be a moderate distance away, maybe three or four feet, to make for a moderately easy shot.
- One spot should be very far away, a not-impossible but still very difficult shot.

Step 3

Announce, with much pomp and fanfare, that each of the three students will, in turn, face this test of skill. Emphasize that they are all being asked to do the exact same task: toss the crumpled paper into the basket. Allow the students, one at a time, to toss their paper. Give dramatic congratulations for those who make the shot successfully.

Step 4

Bring the class back together and ask what they thought of that contest. Was it fair? Remind them that you were asking all three students to do the exact same task. Doesn't that make it fair? It should not take long for students to respond that while the instruction was the same, the three students' relative positions were not. While the students may characterize this as some of the contestants being at an unfair disadvantage, the teacher should remind them that they could also look at the situation as some of the contestants having an unfair *advantage*.

Step 5

Ask the students to journal their thoughts about this contest—how it made them feel, either as one of the three participants or as observers. Tell them to keep this activity in mind as we pursue our lessons this week, because we'll be referring back to it.

Having completed this activity, the students now have a very visible, tangible reference they can return to in order to try and comprehend the more abstract idea of privilege. This is a cut-and-dried case in which it is almost impossible to argue that privilege was not a valid frame through which to interpret what happened. Later references to people who have privilege as "the people who start closer to the basket" can serve as a helpful scaffold.

Another, similar activity—this one a little more emotionally fraught be-cause of its personal implications—can be used later on. You may not wish to attempt it with all of your classes, because, as you will see, it involves a certain level of trust and faith in the teacher. You can only successfully employ this lesson if your relationship with the students (and the students' relationship with one another) is positive, clear, and strong. Here more than usual, YKYS-YMMV applies.

Lesson: Donuts, Crackers, and Chairs

Goal: Students will gain firsthand insight into the rhetoric versus the reality of segregation's "separate but equal" claims. They will also explore the implications of a system of privilege that involves them, and their actions, personally.

Time: 20–50 minutes.

Materials: Donuts or a similar treat, enough for the entire class. Stale crackers or a similar unappealing food, enough for half the class.

Step 1

Begin by announcing that the class will be in a "special configuration" for today's lesson. Ask half the class (or a sizable minority) to sit on the floor, and not in their chairs.

Choose the floor-sitters carefully—pick self-confident, well-adjusted students whom you know will be able to "roll" with what will follow. Try to pick the students with whom you have the strongest personal relationship, and, if they also match the above criteria, students whom the class knows are habitual high achievers. You could even give these students prior warning the day before, and enlist them as "accomplices." Never put a student of color, or students marginalized for other reasons, in this group.

To the best of your ability, postpone and defer student questions about and reactions to the activity as you are conducting it, and emphasize the need to push forward and go on with the lesson. Remember, you are embodying a "character" here (and could do so in an exaggerated way that provides a certain level of "wink wink" to reassure the class).

Step 2

Announce that, because this class has been performing/behaving so well lately (or because research demonstrates well-fed students learn better), you will be providing everyone with food (make sure you are in compliance with your school's policies regarding allergens, etc.). Then pass out the donuts to the students in the chairs, and the crackers to the students on the floor. Again, deflect concerns and protest with something reassuring like, "everyone is getting food. Everyone has a place to sit. Even though it might look different, that's not important. Let's move on."

Again, say these things, and especially what follows, with a small bit of humor so as to let the students know that all is not necessarily as it seems.

Step 3

Proceed with a lesson. Any lesson. The content is irrelevant—the key is to lavish praise and positive attention on the students in the chairs, regardless of what they do, and to be curt and disapproving of the students on the floor. Again, keeping this somewhat tongue-in-cheek is important.

Step 4

Now, unbeknown to the students, your attitude regarding student protest is going to change slightly. If students on the floor raise objections to the differential treatment, dismiss or ignore them. However, if a student in the seats raises objections, stop the activity immediately. If no student in the seats raises objections, stop the activity on your own after a few minutes.

Step 5

Explain that this was all a simulation, and bring everyone back into the seats. Thank the students who were on the floor for being willing to run with this and deliver an apology on the chance that, even in jest, you wound up hurting anyone's feelings.

Step 6

Ask the students to journal about what they were feeling during the simulation—what they thought about their own situation, but also what they thought about the people in the opposite group.

Step 7

Invite students to share their responses, in pairs, groups and as a class. At some point, ask the following questions:

- Did you think I as the teacher owe the students whom I made to sit on the floor an apology? Why or why not?
- Do you think I as the teacher should give the students whom I made to sit on the floor a donut now? Why or why not?
- Do you think that they deserve *two* donuts for what they went through? Why or why not?

Eventually reveal, if it didn't come up naturally, that you would have stopped the simulation if someone in the chairs had spoken out, which leads to the question:

- I, as the teacher, was initiating and perpetrating this injustice. The people sitting in the chairs didn't know about this special rule. Should they in any way be held responsible for the situation?

With that question, and perhaps with all of the questions, offer the opportunity for students to deliver their perspectives anonymously (e.g., students can write their responses on a piece of paper, turn them in, and you then read them out loud). Very often, the answers to that last question will differ depending on whether a student was in a chair versus on the floor, and that is a trend you should mention if and when it happens.

Emphasize that you are not placing blame on any of the students in the chairs, and remind everyone that this was all a somewhat silly simulation, but that they should think about what this sort of situation might look like in the "real world," with stakes as high as people's lives, liberty, and prosperity.

You can also use this as an opportunity to introduce what will become perhaps the most provocative idea of this entire book:

- It was clear that the people in the chairs had certain advantages. Do you think that the people in the chairs suffered at all, or faced any disadvantages?

Step 8

At this point you can segue into a lesson about historical segregation in the Jim Crow era, or a more contemporary related topic. As with the wastebasket activity, this exercise gives students an immediately accessible experience that you and they can reference during later classes.

Organizations like the Anti-Defamation League (adl.org) or the Southern Poverty Law Center (splcenter.org) can provide many similar sorts of activities that can serve as preparation for the eventual time-to-name-it discussion about present-day racism and privilege.

At some point you will want to engage your students with McIntosh's "Invisible Knapsack" article. It generally prints out to between four and eight pages, making for a manageable homework assignment or even an in-class read. Students can, with teacher guidance, create a Frayer chart, Venn diagram, or other structure to compare/contrast the traditional definitions of "privilege" they may have heard before with the one McIntosh creates, eventually resulting in something like table 4.1.

Even with the "preparation" activities, this article tends to provoke a great deal of resistance among some white students, especially (and perhaps not accidentally, given gender privilege) among boys. Therefore, before a teacher even gets started with asking the class to identify where they might have

Table 4.1.   Definitions of "privilege"

Traditional definition	McIntosh's definition
A special benefit or advantage that a person has, which others do not	A special benefit or advantage that a person has, which others do not
Something that everyone is consciously aware of	Something that is often "invisible" to you if you possess it, but very visible to those who do not have it
Conferred by an authority figure	Can be conferred by an authority figure, or can just be in place because of larger societal structures
A potential source of pride	A potential source of guilt, shame, or discomfort
Can be a stand-alone benefit or part of a suite of benefits	Inherently intersectional with other advantages and disadvantages
It is clear and self-evident how to lose or remove this privilege	It is not always clear or self-evident how to lose or remove this privilege

privilege, she may wish to invite them to begin instead with incidences—no matter how seemingly minor, like the aforementioned junior parking permit situation—in which they are *not* the privileged party, but someone else is. Because privilege is not just something that applies to race, as it is often both contextual and intersectional, then you can begin this conversation with privileges that provoke less discomfort when discussed.

* * *

Set the Stage with Age

Once again, age privilege is a pretty reliable place to start, because the lack of it affects all students. I ask my white students if any of them were ever "tailed," monitored closely, or even harassed by sales staff in a store, even if they were not engaging in any overtly suspicious behavior like stuffing items into their coat. Inevitably some report yes. Given my students' affluence, they tend to shop at high-end stores where merchants might place them under especial scrutiny, but sometimes they also report it happening at convenience stores or supermarkets.

I invite them to tell their stories, and they often need little encouragement to declare how humiliating it was to be asked to turn out their pockets, or how unfair it was when they were suspected of crimes they were not committing.

After we've heard several of these stories, I will say, "Hmm. That's odd. I'm pretty confident—I'd bet money, even—that if I was in that store with you, doing nothing different from what you were doing, no one would have hassled me. Why is that?"

Because I'm an adult, they will say. I sometimes add, "Because I'm a white, male adult," since adulthood alone doesn't necessarily account for all of it, but age is what I focus on with them at that moment.

"Did I earn my age?" I ask. Although once a student did quip, "Well, you managed not to die all these years, that takes some work," generally we agree that the year of my birth was not something in my control.

"Could you say, then, in that situation, that I possessed an unfair and unearned advantage over you?" I then add, "Furthermore, I bet that unless I'm really paying attention, which I'm probably not since I'm usually pretty spacey, I won't even be aware that you're being treated differently. But I'm pretty sure it's crystal clear to you, when you see it's your pockets that are being turned out and not mine."

Helping white, privileged students explore the idea of privilege when they lack it, where they can identify as a sympathetic victim, lowers the affective barrier and lets them consider the potential validity of McIntosh's construct more readily. On the other hand, I need to be careful to keep these examples "light" and not to put my white students who might be lacking privilege in significant areas like gender identity, sexual identity, or able-ness in the position of having to "testify."

* * *

TURNING STUDENT RESISTANCE INTO
TEACHABLE MOMENTS

Eventually, however, students and their teacher do have to face the racial elephant in the room, and if it hasn't happened yet, this is the time when white students will often express discomfort and resistance. Their pushback will likely revolve around some version of one of the following seven basic lines of argument, and for each argument, this book offers some advice for turning it into a teachable moment that involves use of evidence as opposed to just rhetoric.

Teach*able*, emphasis on its conditional sense. In none of these activities, in none of your discussion of privilege, should you ever require students to acknowledge the construct of privilege as the only valid lens through which one can view systems of power in our country and in the world at large. However, those students who contest the construct of privilege should be expected to provide specific evidence to support their challenges, the same as you should require for any argument.

The sample responses below to each of the following avenues of student resistance are designed to model and encourage such use of evidence. They are not designed to "parry" resistant students' arguments, but rather to use those arguments as a launching point to pursue additional avenues of inquiry. Whatever position students hold, you will want them to unpack it and support it. A student who passionately disagrees with the theory of privilege, and studies it hard in order to find excellent evidence to counter it, in part or as a whole, should be able to earn a higher grade than a student who repeats McIntosh without evidence of detailed exploration.

That all said, here are the seven basic "pushback" arguments.

Argument 1

They/their parents/white people in general have worked for everything they have—they've earned it.

This is a great place to refer back to the wastepaper basket activity. Did everyone in that activity work to earn their successful basket? Yes. Did everyone start from the same place, and therefore have to do the same amount of work to reach the same goal? Not remotely. This activity can also lead to a discussion and/or research project regarding the inequitable funding of public schools, how redlining and restrictive covenants governed both school attendance (and therefore college preparation and admission, and therefore adult earnings) and the amount of wealth one can earn from real estate value . . . in other words, *structural* inequity that has long since outlasted the racist laws and policies that created it.

A popular misunderstanding of the theory of white privilege is that it claims white people have never suffered or had to work hard, or that white privilege automatically negates other ways besides race in which a white person might not be privileged. Correcting this notion presents a great opportunity to introduce the concept of *intersectionality,* the idea that, in the words of author Gina Crosley-Corcoran,

> people can be privileged in some ways and definitely not privileged in others. There are many different types of privilege, not just skin-color privilege, that impact the way people can move through the world or are discriminated against. [10]

As a class, students can make a list of various ways a person might be born into advantage: age, sex, gender, sexual orientation, able-ness, family wealth, religious affiliation at birth, country of birth, various life experiences that were not under our control. The teacher could ask students to (privately!) make a checklist wherein they see where they do, and do not, identify with a privileged category. Nearly all of us have privilege in some ways, and lack it in others. However, this is not to imply that any form of privilege is exactly the same as another, or that people lacking in one area of privilege understand what it's like to be lacking in other areas. Race discrimination is not equal to sex discrimination and so forth.[11]

Retreating to the more "comfortable" topics outside of race, you can ask students to make another private list, this one of all the challenges they have overcome in their life. Then ask them to make a list of the challenges overcame by someone from the usual pantheon of figures whose struggles against oppression are commonly studied in school curricula, with whom you could reasonably expect students to be familiar (Ruby Bridges, Rosa Parks, Elie Wiesel, Malala Yousafzai). White students can do their own comparisons and contrasts, and see that it is quite possible to work hard to overcome real obstacles in our life, yet by dint of the time period and other circumstances in which we live, be privileged enough to escape far more difficult challenges.

You could then segue from those more extreme examples to texts like Deborah Foster's 2014 article, "A Guide to White Privilege for White People Who Think They've Never Had Any," wherein a white woman who grew up struggling with the depravations of poverty, foster care, and prejudice from her African American neighbors nevertheless came to recognize certain advantages and "lucky breaks" that still conferred upon her some degree of preferential treatment when compared with those neighbors of color.

Giving students the tools to examine structural privilege is not just the purview of humanities teachers. Mathematics class can provide a forum for students to, in the course of learning how to calculate property appreciation, discover just how much of an economic impact that generations of redlining had on the ability for many Americans of color to accumulate household wealth, for example. There are many such phenomena that math can explore, according to Dr. Thomas Shapiro, author of *The hidden cost of being African American* (1998):

> That gap, a 10-fold ratio, is exemplified by . . . "transformative assets"—gifts, from parents and others, that work to lift succeeding generations economically and socially beyond their own achievements . . . most [whites] don't recognize [these advantages], while middle-class blacks report far more issues with needy parents, relatives and friends . . . discrimination in credit, higher interest rates (whites have more capacity to pay "points") and depressed home values caused by residential segregation.[12]

Science teachers can engage students in an exploration of how, regardless of their socioeconomic situation, men still reap greater benefit than women from most medical experimentation and drug development (in which, among other things, medicines intended for both sexes are tested mainly on men), or how eugenics was used as a frame for discriminating against African

Americans and homosexuals of all races, creating barriers to immigration, medical care, and even basic human rights to reproduction. These are disruptions whose echoes are still being experienced by those people's descendants today. From the Tuskegee syphilis experiments to the story of Henrietta Lacks, whose cells were used without permission to further cancer research, marginalized peoples have been victims or unwilling sacrifices in the name of "scientific progress" in ways that, regardless of their other challenges, people from more privileged groups never would have been at risk for . . . and never were in danger of not being the beneficiaries of whatever "progress" resulted.

Argument 2

Privilege is just a simple function of demographics—there are more white people in our country, so of course society is set up to provide advantages to them.

Assign students some research questions to explore in groups using the internet. These questions should focus on the racial demographics of our country as a whole, and then the racial demographics of positions of power in our country. Depending on the state of their research skills, you might steer students toward certain reliable sites in a "WebQuest"[13] model, or else dovetail this lesson with a lesson in finding and evaluating reliable online sources.

While the specifics may change from year to year, here is a representative sample of the sorts of data students will discover: the "White, non-Hispanic or Latino" percentage of the U.S. population, according to the 2017 U.S. Census, is 61.3 percent. Yet 82.5 percent of business owners in America are white,[14] and so are 90 percent of Fortune 500 CEOs. As of this writing, the 116th Congress is the most diverse one in American history, and yet 70 percent of the legislative branch remains white. Eighty percent of teachers are white.[15] Black Americans make up over 13 percent of the population, yet the tech industry is only 7 percent black.[16] After a day or two of comparing notes, the students may start to see that privilege is not a simple function of population demographics.

Furthermore, it is easy to find stories from and about societies like apartheid-era South Africa, or pretty much anywhere in the European-colonized world, where a small minority of white occupiers held a vastly disproportionate amount of political and economic power over the native, nonwhite majority.

Argument 3

But people of color have the privilege! Thanks to affirmative action/political correctness/a mandate to "seek diversity," whites are now at a disadvantage when applying to college or to a job.

In keeping with Norm #4, try to respond with questions. "Is it unjust to use race as a potential factor in such situations? And if we're asking that, can we make sure the question includes, 'Is it unjust to have advantage due to whiteness?'"

White racial advantage is baked into American public schooling, in a cycle that begins with how local property tax dollars fund the lion's share of school expenses. Redlining historically barred African American and Latinx families from buying houses in areas with high property values, and since schools are funded mainly via local property taxes, these policies restricted them to those districts with the worst-resourced schools. Laws that (with just a few exceptions) restrict student attendance to their local school districts ensure that these students remain in inadequate institutions, unprepared for admission to the kind of postsecondary education that could best equip them to enter high-paying jobs (where, even if they are prepared, they face extensively documented impediments in the form of discriminatory hiring practices) that would then allow them to purchase property in wealthier communities with better schools to serve their own children. The cycle continues, and it is a cycle that many white people never need to worry about. White students might still need to work hard in school, but the contract—that hard work will lead to an economically prosperous life—is far more likely to be honored.

The insidiousness of a history education that ends the story of school segregation with the "victory" of *Brown v. Board of Education* is that it ignores subsequent developments, like 1974's *Milken v. Bradley* (desegregation cannot cross district lines) and *Board of Ed of Oklahoma City v. Dowell* (the federal courts cannot order or enforce desegregation), as well as the twenty-first-century Supreme Court decisions mentioned in the introduction, all of which essentially undid what *Brown* sought to accomplish.

Schools remain highly segregated today, yet the myth of *Brown* leads many white people to attribute the academic and economic challenges faced by many students of color to be the result of nothing more now than those people's own poor efforts and bad decisions. By extension, this also tempts whites to attribute their own success solely to their own efforts, and not to the systemic advantages they possess. As coach Barry Switzer famously put it, such individuals start life's baseball game "born on third base, but believe they hit a triple."

Even in the same schools, research has demonstrated that white students enjoy greater than double the chances of African American students that

teachers will recommend them for gifted and talented programs, [17] even holding constant such variables as standardized test scores, income, and the age at
which they entered kindergarten. Regardless of the type of school or level of
poverty involved, white boys remain about three times less likely to be
suspended or expelled for the same disruptive behaviors as black boys, and
white girls are six times safer from such punishments than their African
American counterparts. [18] These are powerful advantages. Students could discover this information through WebQuests/research assignments, which
could also reveal that these advantages persist well beyond K–12 education
as the following examples show:

- According to the Georgetown University Center for Education and the
  Workforce, [19] the student body in the 468 best-funded and most selective
  four-year institutions is 77 percent white. By contrast, enrollment at the
  3,250 worst-funded, least selective institutions is 43 percent African
  American and Latinx, and these are the schools where we see the most
  dramatic rise in the last 20 years among nonwhite enrollment.
- Students may argue that the above statistics merely reflect that African
  American and Latinx students simply don't earn good-enough grades to
  attend selective colleges. But the disparities persist even with grade-point
  average held constant: Only 22 percent of "high-performing" (those with a
  high school GPA of 3.5 or higher) white students end up at community
  colleges, versus one-third of African American and Latinx students with
  similar grades. [20]

The job world paints a similar picture. *Forbes* magazine reported on an
series of 28 studies over the last 30 years from Northwestern and Harvard
Universities that found that white job applicants receive on average 36 percent more callbacks than black applicants, and 24 percent more callbacks
than Latinx applicants, with "no change in the level of hiring discrimination
against African Americans over the past 25 years, although we find modest
evidence of a decline in discrimination against Latinos." [21] The *Forbes* author
concludes: "The truth, based on lots of data over years, is that if you're Black
or Latino in the U.S., you get far from an equal shake [let alone a preferential
one!]. Your efforts have to be longer, stronger, and chances are you still will
be treated worse." [22]

Whether it is the college admissions legacy system, or merely the legacy
of segregation and redlining and other institutionalized discrimination, it
would indeed seem like race plays a disproportionate role in such decisions.
Usually, however, it is to the advantage of white applicants, not applicants of
color. As described earlier, there is much potential here for math and science
teachers to help students acquire and apply the skills of STEM disciplines

through the study of persistent, present-day advantages whites have in personal finance, health care, and more.

Argument 4

People of color dominate in the sports and entertainment worlds, so that's a place where white privilege doesn't seem to apply.

Once again, it's a job for a research assignment, one that is particularly well suited to student athletes and pop-culture superfans. Spoilers: The National Football League is indeed 65 percent black, and the National Basketball Association is 75 percent black (let's not talk about baseball). But of the 153 major league professional sports franchises in the United States and Canada, as of 2014 there was only one—yes, one—black majority owner.[23] Even some of the highest paid African American athletes still face angry media backlash when they attempt to protest injustice, such as when LeBron James, Derrick Rose, Reggie Bush, and others wore "I Can't Breathe" T-shirts to protest the police slaying of Eric Garner, or when several St. Louis Rams players took to the field in a "hands up, don't shoot" pose in support of the Ferguson protestors, or when Colin Kaepernick famously knelt rather than stood for the National Anthem to protest racial discrimination.

And although Oprah Winfrey, Jay-Z, and P. Diddy are among the country's richest celebrities, they constitute half of the only six people of color in a 2018 ranking of the 25 celebrities with the highest net worth.[24] And once again, the people off-screen who control what happens on camera remain white: Of Hollywood's 779 directors in 2017, only 5.8 percent were black and 2.4 percent were Asian.[25] The majority of music company executives are white, even those labels which specialize in hip-hop and R&B.[26]

Argument 5

This isn't about privilege, it's about culture. There is something about the culture of marginalized peoples, especially African Americans, that is to blame for disparities in education, economics, health, opportunity, and treatment by the justice system. It's not that whites have an advantage—it's that minorities are shooting themselves in the foot.

Dealing with this one is fraught in all sorts of ways, but it is almost certain to come up sooner or later. This kind of argument tends to sound something along the lines of how Jason Reilly, a senior fellow at the Manhattan Institute and *Wall Street Journal* columnist (who is, incidentally, African American) articulates it: "We can't hope to address effectively the social pathology on display in so many black ghettos by playing down the role of culture and personal responsibility so as to keep the focus on white racism."[27]

Or, put more bluntly, by *Washington Times* columnist L. Todd Wood: "Too many black youth are being left behind. And it is no one but black America's fault. No one can solve this problem but black America. . . . Black America needs to look in the mirror and stop blaming others, especially white people."[28] In this analysis, a "self-destructive, urban culture of gangs, drugs, crime, single-parent households, welfare dependency and the objectification of women," in the words of a user commenting on Wood's article, is what hinders African Americans from taking full advantage of a playing field where opportunity is not in fact restricted by racism.

This view is not the sole province of political conservatives. There is a liberal version of this argument as well, which *Atlantic* writer Phillip Bump exemplifies when he explains the idea of a "culture of poverty," namely that

> there is something about the culture of being poor that prevents the poor, regardless of race, from escaping poverty . . . parents who have been out of work take refuge in the welfare state, living on food stamps and government services, and their children learn that this is a viable means of survival.[29]

This position, like the one espoused by Reilly and by Wood, allows for the possibility that institutional racism no longer restricts opportunities, but adds that its legacy has so seriously impacted the economics of many African American communities that somehow those people got "stuck." The problem only looks racial because the financial situation was rooted in racism's legacy, but now somehow continues independent of it.

Various versions of these "blame the marginalized themselves" explanations are appealing not only because they absolve present-day whites of responsibility for addressing inequities, but also because a great deal of data is available to point to proportionally higher levels of crime, unemployment, single parenthood, economic distress, or other negative attributes among black and Latinx Americans versus whites. Yet a wealth of data also demonstrates that America's systems of criminal justice and employment (just to pick two examples) treat whites and people of color very differently, even in the present era, when it comes to very similar situations.

Criminal Justice

Statistics from the Department of Justice and the FBI indeed reveal that African Americans commit proportionately more crimes than do white Americans, although contrary to the fearmongering tone of some white pundits who quote these figures to claim victimization, the majority of the victims of these crimes are also African American.[30] According to the Department of Justice, the rate of white-on-white violent crime is about four times the rate of black-on-white crime.[31] But even if one uses this data to support some sort of "culpability" narrative for social inequities, one must also acknowledge the data about the dramatic difference in the way the justice system arrests and sentences black and white offenders disproportionally by race.

For example, according to a 2017 report from the U.S. Sentencing Commission, black men who commit the same crimes as white men receive federal prison sentences that are, on average, nearly 20 percent longer, and these disparities were observed "after controlling for a wide variety of sentencing factors," including "age, education, citizenship, weapon possession and prior criminal history."[32] These disparities have in fact been growing ever since the 2005 *United States v. Booker* Supreme Court decision, which "gave federal judges significantly more discretion on sentencing by making it easier to impose harsher or more lenient sentences than the USSC's sentencing guidelines called for."[33]

FBI data also indicates that in every year from 1980 to 2007, African Americans were arrested nationwide on drug charges 2.8 to 5.5 times more often than white Americans—and state by state, 2 to 11 times more, yet "the higher rates of black drug arrests do not reflect higher rates of black drug offending . . . blacks and whites engage in drug offenses—possession and sales—at roughly comparable rates."[34]

Employment

The "culture of poverty" explanation for inequality tends to rely on data such as the U.S. Census Bureau's Current Population Survey and Annual Social and Economic Supplements, which record black family poverty as hovering around 30 percent from the 1960s through the present day, with the exception of a drop to 19 percent during the economic boom times of the 1990s, while white poverty has been on a steady decline.[35]

But a strict "stuck in the habits of poverty" reading neglects facts like the demonstrated race-based barriers to employment; in addition to the *Forbes* data mentioned earlier in this chapter, one could also look at a recent study of 1,300 résumés sent to 5,000 employers, in which applicants with identical résumés but "whiter" sounding names receive 50 percent more callbacks than those with "black" or "Latinx" sounding names. Even when the "black-named" résumé was designed to be better than that of the "white-named" résumé, the white-named candidates still had a 30 percent advantage.[36]

In another study of 59 applications sent to 1,600 employers in 16 cities, black and Asian job applicants who "whitened" their name received 10 percent or more callbacks.[37] Once hired, the data shows that, even accounting for differences in education and workforce experience, race-based pay gaps favoring white workers still exist.

The point of sending students in search of data like this is to introduce them to evidence that at the very least complicates blame-the-underprivileged explanations for white advantages. The fact remains, though, that these issues are complex and demand more than just a quick teacher response. A more in-depth exploration could involve, for example, the teacher engaging students in a scaffolded comparison and contrast of passages from the Moynihan Report[38] (perhaps the most famous "culture is to blame" treatise) with its critics, like Daniel Geary's *Beyond Civil Rights: The Moynihan Report and Its Legacy* (2015).

* * *

Supporting Your Students of Color

Before moving on to the last two common oppositional responses to the idea of white privilege, we need to back up and remember that serious regard must be taken, in conversations that involve these kinds of arguments and statistics, to the feelings of any students of color in the classroom, especially this last one about "whether or not some marginalized peoples are to blame for their own situation." Here is where the practices for supporting your students of color described in chapter 2 are especially vital.

The inescapable fact is that discussions about white privilege and advantage will inherently include the many ways in which people of color are disadvantaged. The more you can precede, and follow, discussions of deficit narratives like these with narratives that demonstrate pride, success, and resilience of people of color, the better. Doing so at least provides some small degree of cushioning for what can, even under the best of circumstances, become highly uncomfortable conversations for many of your nonwhite students.

* * *

Argument 6

None of this is my fault. Neither I nor my ancestors created any of these conditions.

Privilege isn't about blame, it's about benefit. Students whose ancestors immigrated to the United States long after the end of slavery, or even after the Civil Rights Act of 1964, are absolutely correct when they say that neither they nor their forebears are responsible for the historical oppressions for which they were not present. However, the moment a white person takes part in American society, they begin enjoying the benefits, in much the same way that a consumer does not need to have been a part of the founding of the Mastercard corporation in order to get the benefits of using its credit cards. Being white gives a person automatic access to the "credit" accrued by previous white generations' oppression of people of color, whether or not that person's specific ancestors were among them, and this credit is automatically used unless one consciously takes action not to do so.

A version of the following metaphor may be useful: imagine a house, under which some people are slowly being crushed. I may not have built the house. Perhaps my ancestors weren't involved in building the house, either. But the fact remains that I moved into and now live in this house underneath which people are being crushed. Don't I have some responsibility to do something about that?

Privileged white students, however naive they might appear at times, are by no means stupid. Many might actually realize, or at least suspect, that their privilege comes at the *expense* of those whose voices accuse people who look like them of unjust conduct. They can, for example, recognize without much prompting that much of their clothing is made in sweatshops, and the inexpensive price they bought it for came at the expense of foreign workers' human rights. Often the same students who rail against Affirmative Action will sheepishly admit that they are eligible for legacy admissions at various schools, and their acceptance could deny a slot to another, equally or even more-well qualified candidate. Dwelling on this can provoke either denial (a healthy mind's first impulse is to resist such cognitive dissonance) or feelings of shame, guilt, and culpability.

* * *

Get Off the Bench

One of the most uncomfortable parent conferences I've had involved a mother who talked about how her daughter, Jill, had suffered emotional distress as a reaction to the material and discussions in my class still had become convinced her every word was somehow revealing to others some racist undertone. "Jill thinks what you're saying is that she's evil because she's white."

My heart broke. This was not at all the message I intended to propagate, but at the same time I could understand how some white students' minds might have ended up there. In Jill's case, it led to her near-total shutdown for the rest of the course, and forced me into yet another round of soul-searching, research, and rethinking my approach. I took a great deal from Jill's own final exam essay, in which she wrote:

> *Maybe . . . the reason why people who benefit from a system that awards them privilege don't often "get off the bench"[39] is for fear of being attacked or shamed for being there at all. And maybe the way to truly get people off the bench is to remind them that the option is there, but not fault them for being on it in the first place.*

* * *

While social justice scholars have discussed and debated the legitimacy of universal white culpability, responsibility, and/or blame, whether this is right or wrong, such a message is not necessarily *pedagogically useful*. While educational theorists such as Piaget consider a certain amount of "disequilibrium" to be a necessary component for learning and evolution, research is also very clear that students cannot learn effectively if they are suffering psychological harm, nor would it be morally defensible to inflict it. Even from a pragmatically activist point of view, encouraging privileged white students to feel sadness and angst does not in and of itself produce a more just society; indeed, it might risk disabling the very people with the most potential to be effective white allies if given the tools (e.g., Jill), creating what Swalwell calls the aware yet "resigned" mode of thinking. [40]

The more a teacher can do to help students draw distinctions between blame and benefit here, the better. On the other hand, lack of blame does not mean lack of responsibility for doing something to change the situation. Besides, as we will explore shortly, the binary between "beneficiary" and "victim" may in some particular ways be a false one, and it is in troubling this binary that there lies great potential to engage privileged white students in the work of social justice.

Argument 7

The world is just unfair. There will always be winners and losers, injustice is a part of human nature, so what's the point in obsessing about it?

Despite what it might sound like, this can actually be a very encouraging question to take up, because it includes an acknowledgment of injustice, and opens up the conversation about whether in fact anything can be done—or, to rewrite that phrase from out of the passive voice, *whether people with privilege can do anything*—to help change that system.

It is an interesting paradox that privileged white students can claim agency and credit for "earning" their privileged position in life, yet simultaneously seem so assured of their powerlessness to change social injustices that seem like the product of larger forces. For some, this paradox is resolved through the belief in the inevitability not so much of injustice, but of *hierarchies*. Shamus Khan describes the belief of the privileged white students he studied at St. Paul's that, "unlike the past where [high-status] positions were ascribed through inheritance, today they are achieved"—in other words,

> Whereas elites of the past were entitled—building their worlds around the "right" breeding, connections and culture . . . the new elites think of them-

selves as far more individualized, supposing that their position is a product of what they have done. . . . The story that the new elite tell is built on America's deeply held belief that merit and hard work will pay off. [41]

Someone's got to be on the bottom, the idea goes, but hard work and savvy decision-making allows one to get to the top. Seen from this point of view, says Khan, hierarchies themselves only become dangerous when "too fixed or present—when society is closed and work and talent don't matter."[42]

When and if privileged students see flaws in the narrative of meritocracy, the nature of their resignation might shift instead to the inevitability of a corrupted system. Although Swalwell creates four separate categories of attitudes students adopt once they acknowledge the reality of inequity and privilege, two of those categories—the "meritocrat" and the "resigned"—share a theme of powerlessness, as evidenced in these responses from some of the students in the classes she studied:

- "I don't think it's possible there's ever going to be a world where everyone will care and everyone will want to help and no one will be, like, selfish."
- "Sometimes I feel sort of helpless . . . it makes me sad, but I've accepted these are things that have been happening and will be happening when I'm dead, too . . . for me to go out of my way to rewire human nature is completely impossible."
- "I see myself as someone who's just detaching because there's nothing that can be done."[43]

Paolo Freire noted how his *under*privileged students were plagued by a kind of fatalistic determinism, "the position of those who consider themselves to be totally powerless in the face of the omnipotence of the facts,"[44] but this plague afflicts the privileged as well. To be sure, the roots of some of their fatalism may lie in an attempt to avoid cognitive dissonance, to escape the responsibility for having to do something to change this state of affairs.

But there may be something deeper, something simultaneously more pitiable and more hopeful at work. This feeling of powerlessness may be just the edge of a larger phenomenon, one that indicates that privilege, in addition to advantaging its possessors, can also bring with it some substantial costs. And if this is the case, it can present a real opportunity for a social-justice minded teacher of white, privileged students to make a significant difference in those students' lives.

NOTES

1. All school names are pseudonyms.

2. "How Racist Is Boston?" 2018.
3. *Plessy v. Ferguson* (1896), Digital History, 2019.
4. Goodman, 2013.
5. Bonilla-Silva, 2017.
6. McIntosh, 1989.
7. Merriam Webster online, https://www.merriam-webster.com/dictionary/racism.
8. Ibid.
9. See Edmondson and Nkomo, 2003; American Mosaic Project, 2003.
10. Crosley-Corcoran, 2014.
11. Ibid.
12. Shapiro, 2004.
13. "What Are the Essential Parts of a Webquest," 2004.
14. Soergel, 2016.
15. Loewus, 2017.
16. Heer, 2016.
17. Brasher, 2016.
18. Lopez, 2018; Crenshaw, Ocen, and Nanda, 2015.
19. Marcus, 2018.
20. Ibid.
21. Sherman, 2017.
22. Ibid.
23. Hoenig, 2014.
24. Ingolfsland, 2019.
25. Cole, 2017.
26. Mitchell, 2018.
27. Riley, 2018.
28. Wood, 2017.
29. Bump, 2014.
30. Cooper and Smith, 2011; "Uniform Crime Reporting (UCR) Program," n.d.
31. Neiwert, 2017; Morgan, 2017.
32. Schmitt, 2017.
33. Ingraham, 2017.
34. Fellner, 2009.
35. "Poverty in Black America," 2014; Gould and Schieder, 2018.
36. Francis, 2003.
37. Kang, DeCelles, Tilcsik, and Jun, 2016.
38. Moynihan, 1965.
39. A reference to Athol Fugard's *Master Harold . . . and the Boys*, where choosing to get off a "whites-only bench" is used as a metaphor for white people giving up their own privilege as a part of creating a more just society.
40. Swalwell, 2013.
41. Khan, 2012, 14–15.
42. Ibid., 15.
43. Swalwell, 2013, 92; 96–97.
44. Freire, 1974/1998, 102.

Chapter Five

Privileged Victims

There is of course a moral argument for reshaping a system that advantages some at the expense of others, but if that were the sole argument, then discussions of privilege among whites would only be relevant to a few die-hard altruists. Small wonder, then, that creating a more just society seems impossible to so many white, privileged students: doing so would seem to require them to work against their own self-interest. In the words of one of my own students: "To make things better for [the marginalized] would make things worse for us."

This principle can be seen at work in the negative reactions that some white people have to Black Lives Matter; instead of the emphasis on *matter*, they perceive emphasis on *black*, reading the name (incorrectly so, in the eyes of the movement's originators[1]) to be exclusionary—that is, it is black lives, and not white lives, that matter—giving rise to the "All Lives Matter" countermeme.[2] This adversarial interpretation echoes the misperception of feminism as a philosophy not of equality between the sexes, but of "flipping" gendered power disparities to make women superior to men. Such interpretations see social justice as a zero-sum game, and to give their proponents their due, they correctly perceive that, in an equitable society, the privileged would lose their institutionalized advantage.

Fortunately, this "see-saw" picture of justice is too simple a metaphor. The counterintuitive notion that privilege can harm its possessors is of enormous import in conversations with privileged white students about social justice, especially discussions involving structural racism and other institutionalized prejudice. It opens the door to the possibility that privilege, once we acknowledge we possess it, might actually be something we wish to rid ourselves of—not in the name of martyrdom or for the benefit of some marginalized "Other," but out of rational self-interest. If this interest is urgent enough, then fighting for change becomes less of an "option" that can be abandoned once the path seems too difficult, and more of a necessity, to be pursued by any means necessary until success is achieved.

While Paolo Freire does not spend much time discussing the privileged, he does argue that, "as the oppressed, fighting to be human, take away the oppressors' power to dominate and suppress, they restore to the oppressors the humanity they had lost in the exercise of oppression" and that "this, thus, is the great humanistic and historical task of the oppressed: to liberate themselves and their oppressors as well."[3]

Perhaps, by assuming that only marginalized people are harmed by systems of oppression, educators and students alike could be making a mistake. We may be missing opportunities for authentic engagement that involve exploring feelings of victimization, and *anger* about that victimization, among the privileged.

HISTORICAL PRECEDENT

It is a safe assumption that all or nearly all students in the United States will be taught at least a few lessons about Martin Luther King, Jr. and Rosa Parks, perhaps even with a little bit of Malcolm X thrown in the mix. Students will watch footage of Ruby Bridges being escorted into a white school with her head held high, and of black children in Birmingham marching bravely into the spray of firehoses. Perhaps they will watch films of Selma, or the March on Washington. Such lessons are both necessary and inspiring, but when they constitute the sum total of civil rights content in humanities classes, it sends a clear message to students of all racial backgrounds: the fight for equality is one that people of color are responsible for taking on alone, with whites in the picture only either as oppressors or bystanders.

Of course, the vast majority of whites during this era did serve in one or the other of these roles, and all still benefitted from white privilege. But there were also whites who did their best to either open up that system to be more inclusive, or even to actively work to dismantle it. Their absence from most history curricula not only does their memory a disservice, it robs privileged white students of a chance to explore the enormously important question: "Why?"

Why did Birmingham lawyer David Vann put his professional and political reputation at risk to aid the Southern Christian Leadership Conference's (SCLC) campaign of civil disobedience in "Project C," promoting the successful civil reforms that led to the ousting of racist sheriff "Bull" Connor? Why did Vann mediate the 1963 "Accord of Conscience" between Martin Luther King and the leaders of city businesses, that led to the repeal of lunch-counter segregation? Vann appears in both the PBS series' *Eyes on the Prize* and in Spike Lee's *Four Little Girls*, but does not appear in any history curriculum standards I was able to find.

It is worth studying both how and why Vann used the privilege he had, racially and politically, to help bring about a reduction of that privilege. For indeed, Vann's was more than just a "white savior" act of charity that left the overall system of privilege fundamentally unchanged: Vann actively helped end a system where only people with his skin color could freely choose where to eat and which merchants to patronize. Nor was his role one of a white person dictating from on high, but instead one of brokering and mediating meetings to enable the SCLC leaders to engage in dialogue with white business owners.

Other white people chose to part with the privilege of their own safety. Fifty percent of the Freedom Riders were white, and some, like Andrew Goodman and Michael Schwermer, gave their lives for the sake of that struggle for justice. So did Viola Liuzzo, a white Michigan housewife who was aiding black activists in the Selma-to-Montgomery march when she was murdered by members of the Ku Klux Klan.

That such whites were the minority does not change the fact that there were still a great many of them: James Reeb, Jonathan Daniels, Jim Letherer, Anne Braden, Peter Norman, Juliette Morgan, William Moore . . . not to mention white activists in other countries, like Donald Woods, Jeremy Cronin, and Athol Fugard in South Africa who were, respectively, exiled and jailed for publicly opposing the racist apartheid regime.

Social studies teachers might not even know about such figures, let alone teach about them. But teaching privileged white students about them serves at least two important functions:

1. "If you can see it, you can be it" applies as much to white students considering resisting systems of oppression as it does to students of color seeking professional careers. Sociologist Elise Boulding noted that "no one can work seriously for an outcome that seems inherently impossible."[4] The trap of the "resigned" student Swalwell observed is reinforced as long as white people see no actual examples of people who made alternate choices besides embracing their privilege.

2. It demands an exploration and discussion of *how* and *why* so many white people decided to make these choices. What events shaped their beliefs and actions, and what were the key decision points in their lives? Such exploration can reveal a certain syllogism: If rational human beings generally try to choose the things that benefit them and to reject things that cause them harm, *and* if some individuals—too many to write off as somehow unique in either their moral purity or their irrationality—choose to work against the system that brings them privilege, even to risk freedom and life itself in order to do so—then

something about privilege must have the potential to harm those who possess it.

These discussions can create an on-ramp for white students of privilege. Suddenly, the cause of racial or social justice is not just something espoused by people of color (plus Abraham Lincoln), and the role in the story for people who look like them is not just that of oppressor or bystander, not just of unconscious or guilt-ridden beneficiary. Now there are two new possibilities: covictim, and coagent of change.

HOW DOES PRIVILEGE HURT THE PRIVILEGED?

The remainder of this chapter will list, then suggest teaching ideas for, the following five arguments that privilege harms its possessors:

1. Privilege may confer societal power, but at the cost of individual powerlessness. A life lived absent serious barriers to overcome will not equip a person for the inevitable time when true challenges come.
2. Privilege can transform its possessors into people they do not want to be, can threaten the psychically necessary sense of oneself as an essentially good person.
3. Privilege can impair one's free agency at the cost of maintaining power.
4. Privilege can isolate and therefore disadvantage its possessors at a time when diverse teams are needed to solve complex problems, with negative consequences at the individual and global levels.
5. Privilege, perhaps due to all of the above conditions, can amplify anxiety. There is an epidemic of teen emotional distress in the very environments that are safest and best provisioned. This epidemic is seriously eroding teaching and learning, lowering the quality of education—as well as the quality of life—for many privileged students and families.

Although these phenomena are interconnected, the remainder of this chapter will explore these arguments separately for clarity's sake, looking at the first three through the lens of the humanities and the last two through the lens of STEM fields.

1. Privilege May Confer Societal Power, but Individual Powerlessness

The damaging effects of having an external locus of control—a belief that your fate is determined by powers beyond you—have been well documented, especially with young people.[5] On the one hand, research provides evidence that wealthier, more privileged people are likely have an internal locus of control, believing their advantages to be the product of their own efforts as opposed to good fortune.[6] On the other hand, among those born into privilege, this belief in self-agency can be a surprisingly thin veneer. Summarizing more than a hundred studies of affluent adolescents, psychologist Madeline Levine describes how

> while many privileged kids project confidence and know how to make a good impression . . . they lack practical skills for navigating the world; they can be easily frustrated . . . [they] are overly dependent on the opinions of parents, teachers, coaches and peers and frequently rely on others, not only to pave the way on difficult tasks but to grease the wheels of everyday life . . . modest setbacks frequently send them into a tailspin.[7]

In her book, *The Price of Privilege* (2006), Levine documents how the overinvolved practices now popularly labeled as "snowplow" parenting give affluent children few practical tools for developing their own solutions to problems. Teachers of such children see this all the time: when privileged students are faced with a challenging task, a sense of perceived helplessness can set in. Even the academic superstars among them, who may have worked hard to earn their success, have usually done so within the well-defined contours of a system that has been created for them and in whose rules they have been explicitly instructed by parents, teachers, test-prep classes, and hired consultants. When faced with problems whose solutions lie outside of these carefully crafted structures, they often panic. For Levine, this explains cases like when a "talented 13-year-old seriously considers hacking his way into the school computer system to raise his math grade. An academically outstanding 16-year-old thinks about suicide when her SAT scores come back marginally lower than she had expected. A 14-year-old boy cut from his high school junior varsity basketball team is afraid to go home."[8]

As is often the case, psychology rushes to catch up with what art and literature have already revealed. Composer Lin-Manuel Miranda captured the phenomenon of "privileged-induced helplessness" beautifully with his characterization of the Revolutionary-era American politician Aaron Burr in his musical, *Hamilton*. Miranda's Burr is a brooding aristocrat who finds himself at a loss with how to compete with the "hunger" that leads his rival, Alexander Hamilton, a "bastard orphan" from "a forgotten spot in the Caribbean . . . impoverished, in squalor,"[9] to heights of fame and political influence that Burr envies.

Burr, like Hamilton, is an orphan, but one who has grown up with such wealth and privilege that he, unlike Hamilton, has never had to develop strategies for self-advancement. He laments how his wealthy parents died having "left [him] no instructions, just a legacy to protect." Burr's signature song, entitled "Wait for it," reveals his philosophy of a universe governed by incomprehensible powers where he is "the one thing in life [he] can control," and the decision he keeps making is to simply wait for the day when his own success and advancement will inevitably, somehow, happen. Teachers of white, privileged adolescents can see this phenomenon at work in their students, this external locus of control that often lies beneath their arguments about individuals being largely responsible for their own positions in socioeconomic hierarchies.

Centuries earlier, Shakespeare described a similar dynamic in *King Lear*, with the titular king blaming his fall from power—a fall in many ways a product of his own arrogance and caprice, as well as his failure to see past the flattery he has always been accustomed to—on cosmic forces, calling himself "the natural fool of fortune."[10] Lear, a man accustomed to vast wealth and power, simply wanders the woods helplessly raving once deposed.

By contrast, Edmund, the illegitimate son of Lear's aristocratic friend, Gloucester, works tirelessly (and, for much of the play, quite successfully) to change his circumstances, all along mocking Lear's and Burr's kind of determinism:

> This is the excellent foppery of the world, that,
> when we are sick in fortune,—often the surfeit
> of our own behavior,—we make guilty of our
> disasters the sun, the moon, and the stars[11]

Edmund, like Hamilton, is a child born out of wedlock and without certain privileges, who rises above his station through wits and willingness to seize opportunities. It is perhaps a telling change in the professed attitudes of our times that Edmund is cast as the villain of his play,[12] while in *Hamilton* the self-made man, for all his flaws, is presented as a hero.

What provokes the rage of these characters' aristocratic counterparts in both plays is the audacity of those who would seek to upset the perceived natural order of things. It is an outrage echoed in privileged white students' complaints about affirmative action candidates somehow robbing them of their own "rightful" college admission slots.

But such frustration may reveal more than just a sense of entitlement. It may reveal anxiety among whites like me about our privilege making us weaker and less adept, less in touch with our own sense of agency, than those who have had to sharpen their skills in order to survive and combat marginalization.

The next two disadvantages of privilege often go hand in hand.

2. Privilege Can Transform Its Possessors into People They Do Not Want to Be, and 3. Privilege Can Impair Free Agency

Social science experiments consistently provide evidence that the more wealth and power an individual has, the less likely that person will act in ethical, charitable, and empathic ways.[13] Yet cognitive science reveals that considering ourselves as essentially good, decent people is vital to our sense of psychic stability. In 2018, "being a better person" topped out all other New Year's resolutions, even weight loss, in nationwide polling.[14]

Part of the resistance some privileged white students might feel toward narratives written by marginalized people may stem from how they see people like themselves reflected in these stories. That reflection is not pretty, morally speaking. A white student may well flounder for a point of reference when asked to identify not only with an African American child growing up under segregation, but also with the often irredeemably cruel, privileged white characters found in books like Toni Morrison's *The Bluest Eye* or Jeanne Wakatsuki Houston's *Farewell to Manzanar*.[15]

Sandra Stotsky cautions that

> an overdose of "white guilt" . . . in the curriculum . . . may cause students to associate "multicultural" literature with white-guilt literature and to develop a negative reaction either to "white" America or to the [non-white] authors and the groups featured in them.[16]

The results, respectively, can be Jill, the girl whose takeaway was that her whiteness made her evil, or Evan, who felt that Martin Luther King, Jr. was spouting irrelevant nonsense. We who are privileged either feel shame at the ugly reflection of our privileged selves in the mirror, or else activate the defense mechanisms of denial and reaction formation.

The problem with reading these kinds of books isn't that the white, privileged characters are exaggerations—such cruelty as they display was and is all too real—but in most of those texts such privilege is presented as *uncomplicated*. The takeaway for a privileged white reader cannot help but be mixed. If they were to be transported into the world of such novels and allowed to inhabit the body of any of the characters, how many would choose the white ones, despite their villainy, simply because their lot in life seems so much more comfortable?

But there are also texts that feature white characters who not only recognize the horrible moral transformations privilege demands of them, but question and struggle against it. Helping students engage with these texts can raise the question of how it may actually be in the rational best interest of the privileged to *not* become the kind of person who gains material comfort at the expense of others, by showing examples of characters who feel some measure of psychic discomfort with their unfair advantages.

The literature of colonialism, perhaps the most naked manifestation of global white privilege and oppression of peoples of color, also sometimes reveals white discomfort with that same situation. Joseph Conrad's the *Heart of Darkness* offers the iconic example of the white man corrupted by colonialism, but Kurtz is so grotesque and grandiose that students may be tempted to dismiss him as mere caricature (not to mention how Conrad's critique of colonialism is too often undermined by his unceasingly racist depiction of Africans).

George Orwell's unnamed colonial-era policeman protagonist in "Shooting an Elephant" is somewhat more accessible: he begins his narration exhibiting liberal sensibilities: "I had already made up my mind that imperialism was an evil thing and the sooner I chucked up my job and got out of it the better," and "Secretly, of course—I was all for the Burmese and all against their oppressors, the British." But within the same paragraph he admits that "with another part [of my mind] I thought that the greatest joy in the world would be to drive a bayonet into a Buddhist priest's guts. Feelings like these are the normal by-products of imperialism."[17]

As the story progresses, Orwell portrays the policeman, too, as a kind of victim of the Raj, ironically *because* of the power that colonialism invests him with. Despite his moral revulsion at killing a "grandmotherly" escaped elephant, an act that he feels "would be murder," he does so anyway because of his need to appear superior in front of the native Burmese. "A sahib has got to act like a sahib," he laments.[18]

> He has got to appear resolute, to know his own mind and do definite things. To come all that way, rifle in hand, with two thousand [Burmese] people marching at my heels, and then to trail feebly away, having done nothing—no, that was impossible. The crowd would laugh at me. And my whole life, every white man's life in the East, was one long struggle not to be laughed at.[19]

The policeman concludes that "when the white man turns tyrant, it is his own freedom he destroys." That is a frightening lesson for those of us with privilege—that the chains of the slave, in an admittedly very different way, also enslave the master. Once you don the mantle of oppressive power, the need to maintain that power dictates your actions from there on in. "He wears a mask," Orwell says of the white man in the Colonies, "and his face grows to fit it."[20]

Such an analysis does not so much forward an idea of white *guilt* as one of white *victimization* by the very system that gives them privilege. Such privilege, for Orwell, is a source not of guilt but of horror, a force that impairs not just one's ability to be a moral human being, but one's free agency in general.

Orwell's story provides an opportunity to engage students in authentic conversations about times when they perceived that, ironically, a position of power actually limited their freedom. A teacher can invite students to share stories of their surprise at how being a camp counselor or babysitter, invested with institutional authority, made them act meaner than they had planned to, made them seek to impose limits on younger children that they would have resented having been imposed on them.

Of course, young children at an American sleepaway camp and adult Burmese under military occupation are hardly equivalent. This exercise in analogy is not the end goal in the conversation, but rather a potential on-ramp to those more difficult conversations that the students would otherwise shut down before engaging.

White South African writer Athol Fugard also argues for a self-interested approach to dismantling privilege, through his character of Hally from the one-act play, *Master Harold . . . and the Boys*. Hally, as a teenager, may prove a more readily accessible character with whom white high school students can identify. Like many privileged white teenagers, he expresses distaste for conditions of racial and social injustice while simultaneously resigning himself to their inevitability. "I oscillate between hope and despair for this world," he says, decrying the unfair conditions of apartheid. But after a phone call that reminds him of the power his openly racist, alcoholic father has over him, he declares, "We've had the pretty dream, it's time to wake up and have a good long look at the way things really are."[21]

Hally struggles with his anger and shame over his father, perhaps serving as a symbol for the young generation who did not construct the unjust apartheid system, but who now inherit and benefit from its fruits, nonetheless. Thanks to apartheid, the mantle of the oppressor, the "mask" Orwell describes, is always waiting for Hally should he, in a moment of weakness, decide to claim it.

And claim it he does, most overtly in the latter half of the play when he takes out his anger at his father on Sam, the adult black employee of the family store who has been a father figure to Hally since Hally's childhood. From barking orders to hurling insults to actually spitting in Sam's face, Hally demonstrates that he has the power to abuse Sam, at any time, without fear of any obvious consequences.

Before reading these scenes, the teacher can conduct an exercise in class where students ponder and then debate whether it would be a good thing to have the power to overrule their parents and teachers if they wanted to. After some initial enthusiasm, the class consensus will likely gel around the answer, "no." Students will probably be able to recognize, however grudgingly, the need to have limits, to benefit from voices of experience.

By wielding his privilege unchecked, Hally cuts himself off from all of this. With the exception of one near-explosion, Fugard's (almost unrealistically) patient Sam endures the abuse and responds with pity for Hally: "You've hurt yourself, Master Harold. I saw it coming. I warned you, but you wouldn't listen. You've just hurt yourself *bad.*" Sam laments that he, Sam, has failed in his mission to "save" Hally: "You love [your father] and you're ashamed of him. You're ashamed of so much! . . . And now that's going to include yourself. That was the promise I made to myself: to try and keep that from happening."[22]

It is not just that Sam doesn't want Hally to become the face of apartheid, although he clearly doesn't. He also knows that *Hally* does not want to become the face of apartheid, does not want to turn into a teenage version of Conrad's Kurtz. By exerting his unfair power, Hally becomes the very monster he loathes in his father, and thus has a clear *self-interest* in resisting that process.

Furthermore, without the voice of Sam, Hally cannot even recognize this problem with his own privilege because that privilege blinds him to it— hence Fugard's own argument for "multicultural/social justice education," and another potential on-ramp for white, privileged students to see that, yes, there may well be value for them in reading works by marginalized authors. Those voices, contrary to Evan's argument, might really have something to offer them.

Hally's story can be seen as thinly veiled explanation of Athol Fugard's own decision to, as his character Sam says, "get off the whites-only bench" and challenge apartheid. In doing so, the author himself can become an alternate model of white behavior, to be paired or contrasted with the unrelentingly negative (although not necessarily inaccurate) images of white characters in a great deal of "multicultural literature."

As David Foster Wallace once wrote, the privileged should engage in social justice work not only for marginalized people's sake, "but for our own; i.e., we should share what we have in order to become less narrow and frightened and lonely and self-centered people. No one ever seems willing to acknowledge aloud the thoroughgoing *self-interest* that underlies all impulses toward . . . equality."[23]

4. Privilege Can Isolate

Privilege can isolate and therefore disadvantage its possessors at a time when diverse teams are needed to solve complex problems, with negative consequences at the individual and global levels. Since diverse teams have an advantage tackling complex challenges, those raised without the skills to interact with unfamiliar "Others" may be left behind. On a much larger level, if society's reins are in the hands of those who cannot draw upon the full spectrum of ideas from a diverse populace, everyone will suffer.

Dr. Joseph Graves of North Carolina State University's Joint School of Nanoscience and Neuroengineering argues that

> science as an enterprise has always been more than working out the various principles of nature; it has always been imbedded in a social milieu, and therefore has always been tasked to addressing particular socially defined priorities. Some of these priorities have been neutral to or even in rare cases supported notions of social justice . . . [or] has aided and abetted social injustice.[24]

Those "rare cases" are actually pretty numerous. For example, the March 4, 1969, "research strike" when scientists at the Massachusetts Institute of Technology, one of the most respected scientific institutions in the world, stopped the normal course of research and held a "teach-in" to examine the role that scientists were playing in enabling and advancing the lethal technologies employed in the Vietnam War. "The feeling in 1969 was that scientists were complicit in a great evil," recalls physicist Alan Chodos, "and the thrust of March 4 was how to change it."[25]

This was neither the first such moment in the history of American science (Robert Oppenheimer, for example, sacrificed career and reputation for his public opposition to the nuclear weapons he had helped create), nor was it the last (for example, the May 3, 1981, "Scientists Against Reagan's War" march against U.S. intervention in El Salvador, or the Union of Concerned Scientists' ongoing advocacy for global denuclearization). Nor is antiwar activism the only social justice activity in which scientists have taken part: William Montague Cobb played a key role in debunking the racist underpinnings of anatomy and genetics in the early twentieth century, Albert Einstein bravely signed a public petition for gay rights in an increasingly fascist Germany, and to be a climate scientist in contemporary America almost necessitates a role in political activism.

What motivated all of these (mostly white) scientists who held such privileged positions to step out of the lab and into public debate, forwarding positions that often cost them dearly? Altruism may play a role, but also self-interest: phenomena like global nuclear war, human-made pandemics, or destructive climate change threaten to claim the lives of scientists as well as lay people. Social justice in the long term, if not the political short term, can be synonymous with the realization that you, too, are a potential victim when science is used for oppressive or irresponsible purposes.

There is also the self-interest inherent in the idea that examining the way scientific questions are framed and applied makes you a better scientist. The Union of Concerned Scientists suggest that scientists and engineers should always ask:

- *Who* identifies the problems and asks the research questions?

- *Which* questions do they ask and how are they framed?
- *What* is the important context for the study?
- *What* methods do they use?
- *How* will the results be reported and applied?[26]

These are good questions for students to learn how to ask as well. Teaching students to do so teaches them the tools of critical thinking, and is thus more in keeping with the disciplinary practices of science—the constant examination and reexamination and testing—than simply treating scientific knowledge as a series of facts to be memorized, as too often happens in classrooms. To neglect exploration and application of these questions threatens to put even the privileged at a competitive disadvantage versus those who have done so.

So too does remaining socially and racially isolated. There is strong evidence from multiple studies that diverse teams have more success at complex problem solving than do homogenous ones.[27] A math or science teacher can help students to understand this phenomenon through experience by creating a problem to solve: Each student is only given access to some of the necessary information. Place some students in groups that contain only individuals with the same information, and others in groups that, between all their members, have the necessary pieces of the puzzle. The teacher can then help lead the whole class in a discussion of how this in-class lesson could serve as a metaphor for research in the real world. As the Union of Concerned Scientist reminds us,

> The scale of the problems threatening our health, security, and environment demands the best minds. We are more likely to develop effective solutions to these problems by tapping into the skills, talents, and experience that people of different races, ethnicities, and economic classes can bring to bear . . . we cannot hope to solve problems that threaten *all* people by working only with *some* people.[28]

If we value science because of its potential for addressing some of the most serious issues facing humanity, then working in an isolated, all-white, privileged environment is not going to get us the results we need. There is, once again, a harm that done to the privileged by their very privileged status, as well as harm done to the well-being of humanity as a whole.

The University of Michigan, the University of Vermont, and the University of Washington have all added programs that study climate change specifically through multiethnic lenses. In addition to increasing efforts to recruit students from a wide variety of backgrounds, these institutions also now explicitly teach skills in cultural competency. "We need perspectives from every angle possible, from every type of worldview, from every type of religious and spiritual background, and gender orientation," says Xavier Brown of the University of Michigan's Master of Science in Leadership,

> because everybody is oriented to the Earth differently . . . ideas to [curb] climate change are going to manifest themselves differently. . . . Ecosystems lacking in diversity experience more problems than those rich with it. If we continue down the same, homogeneous path, we'll only get the same troubling results.[29]

A science teacher could have students experience this firsthand through a project where the class reads climate science narratives from around the world, from multiple ethnic and social groups. "When we think of environmental science," says Adam Pearson of Pomona College,

> we may think of someone like Al Gore or a whole slew of other prominent environmentalists who may be white and who are more likely to be male. We may be less likely to think of someone like [Mexican-American chemist] Mario Molina, who's responsible for galvanizing support for international measures to combat ozone depletion.[30]

Students could read articles from or about such scientists, or draw on resources like Anna Lau's "People of Colour in the Story of Climate Change" project, which provides access to writings by indigenous and other marginalized peoples, to "jigsaw together" a more comprehensive picture of both the effects of, and possible solutions to, the global climate crisis.[31]

5. Privilege Can Amplify Anxiety

Anxiety among the most privileged students in the United States is rampant, and it erodes the quality of their education as well as their overall quality of life. Questioning, and even disabling, one's position of privilege may even be a genuine life-and-death issue for some privileged adolescents. The news media routinely reports on rising rates of disabling anxiety in teenagers—a 20 percent increase since the mid-2000s, by some counts.[32] Various culprits have been identified, from phones and social media, to the increasing competitiveness of highly selective colleges, to anxiety about their generation's political, economic and ecological future. This epidemic of anxiety is most pronounced (or at least, most diagnosed) in the wealthy white echelons. Affluent adolescents' rates of anxiety, depression, and substance abuse are higher than those of any other socioeconomic group of young people in the country.[33]

The response of many privileged schools and communities toward this problem is questionable. Programs like Challenge Success have gained traction in high-powered school communities across the country. Challenge Success, with its almost entirely white leadership staff[34] and website full of photos of predominantly white, preppy-looking children, advertises its consultancy services in "areas such as curriculum, assessment, homework, school schedule, and a healthy school climate."[35]

Whether under the auspices of a program like Challenge Success or on their own, suburban and independent schools across the country are scaling back homework (at Oak Hills, I have seen expected reading pace in ELA classes literally halved over the last two decades, and each year brings more mandated "no homework" nights and "no assessment" days) and offering all manner of attempted emotional supports. In the words of one suburban district's newsletter, this has included providing "Hershey's kisses on Valentine's Day and Smarties for [standardized test days], as well as organizing seasonal events including hot chocolate by the digital fire, bubble soccer, and Barn Babies," a traveling petting zoo.[36]

The students' anxiety, and that of their parents and teachers, is real, which only makes it more unsettling. The American success narrative for the marginalized has always included an "up-by-one's-bootstraps" struggle against the nigh-insurmountable odds of poverty, community violence, and racism. By contrast, when students with tremendous privilege nevertheless perceive themselves as unable to cope with daily life without the intervention of soap bubbles and small animals to cuddle, it speaks of some catastrophic failure of the system in which they have been given every possible advantage to thrive.

At a time when schools that serve low-income, majority-minority students fight for more challenging curriculum and more instructional time, privileged schools with unparalleled resources for students to learn are rushing to ask less and less of those students academically, to limit learning because those young people aren't seen as resilient enough to handle its demands. What on Earth is wrong with this picture?

Maybe, just maybe, America's stratified and unjust systems are failing *everyone*. Maybe the privileged really do have just as much at stake in reshaping these systems as the marginalized, and that is a task which, as the next chapter will explore, the privileged cannot accomplish alone.

NOTES

1. Grant, 2016.
2. This brings to mind one of the best counter-countermemes I've seen on social media: "Save the whales doesn't mean fuck the seals."
3. Freire 1970/2000, 24; 28.
4. Boulding, 1990, 112.
5. For more information, start with Joelson, 2017.
6. Battle and Rotter, 1963; Muoio, 2015; Whitbourne, 2019.
7. Levine, 2006.
8. Ibid.
9. Miranda, 2016.

10. Open Source Shakespeare, *King Lear,* IV.vi. 2797.

11. Ibid., I.ii. 442–45.

12. Edmund, to be fair, *does* frame his brother for murder, although by his brother's own admission the scheme only works because their aristocratic father is laughably gullible.

13. Piff, Stancato, Côté, Mendoza-Denton, and Keltner, 2012. In addition to the authors' own study in this article, they also provide a comprehensive literature review of previous studies that found similar results.

14. Miringoff, Carvalho, and Griffith, 2017.

15. Noted in Stotsky, 1995, 605.

16. Stotsky, 1994, 30.

17. Orwell, 1936.

18. Ibid.

19. Ibid.

20. Ibid.

21. Fugard, 1984, 51.

22. Ibid., 56; 58.

23. Wallace, 2006, 113.

24. Graves, 2016.

25. Chodos, 2019.

26. "The Role of Science in Advancing Racial Equity," 2016.

27. Hong and Page, 2004; Richard, McMillan, Chadwick, and Dwyer, 2003; Phillips, Northcraft, and Neale, 2006.

28. "The Role of Science in Advancing Racial Equity," 2016.

29. Quoted in Vollman, 2017.

30. Ibid.

31. https://www.indiegogo.com/projects/people-of-colour-in-the-story-of-climate-change#/.

32. Nutt, 2018.

33. Levine, 2006.

34. Based on photos on their website as of May 2019. I do recognize the possibility that not everyone on that leadership team with Caucasian-seeming features identifies as white.

35. "Our Approach," Challenge Success, n.d.

36. "District Progress Report," Wellesley Public Schools, 2018.

Chapter Six

Struggling to "Be the Change"

Allyship, Activism, and the Dangers of the "Savior" Trap

This chapter will address the fourth and fifth competencies in Diane Goodman's "Cultural Competencies for Social Justice":
Competency 4: Skills to interact effectively with diverse people in different contexts—ability to adapt to and work collaboratively with different cultural groups.
Competency 5: Skills to foster equity and inclusion—ability to identify and address inequities and create environments, policies, and practices to ensure diversity and fairness.

ALLIES, NOT SAVIORS

Previous chapters have attempted to provide teachers with opportunities to engage white, privileged students in the study of inequities, particularly privilege itself, because the narrative of privilege is one that includes, and therefore engages, these students. Issues of justice cannot be relegated to the realm of the abstract, to the pitiable plight of "someone else," when the privileged themselves are included in the story. In that story they are the beneficiaries, but also the victims, of privilege's double-edged sword.

A classroom where privileged white students reach this stage of understanding risks producing one of three equally unhelpful reactions: paralyzing guilt, exculpatory relief ("whew, thank heaven I won the birth lottery"), or well-intentioned but highly problematic altruism. This last outcome is what Katy Swalwell calls the "benevolent benefactor" mind-set where, "rather than working *with* marginalized people . . . the emphasis is on doing things

121

for marginalized people that will improve their situation rather than transform society."[1]

This chapter will explore in more detail how to help privileged white students—and any of their white teachers!—channel their desire to do good into methods that do not unintentionally replicate or reinforce patterns of oppression.

Matthew Kay advises that efforts to teach social justice set the following two goals: to help students locate their sphere of influence and find solutions, and to encourage new lines of inquiry. For Swalwell, both of those goals require asking the questions:

- What power do we have?
- When and where do we have it?
- What do we do with that power?
- In what ways should that power be justly distributed?

"In and of themselves," she writes, "such conversations are an example of the Educating Activist Allies model in action."[2]

Swalwell's definition of an Activist Ally is someone who has a "sophisticated understanding of injustice as current and local, systemic and individual, and negatively affecting both the oppressed and the oppressor," someone whose "sense of agency" stems from "feel[ing] complicit in systems of injustice" and who therefore feels "obligated to interrupt it," and, importantly, is "strategic and cooperative . . . mobiliz[ing their] resources in concert with marginalized people."[3]

For Swalwell, it is both the sense of personal involvement (simultaneously complicit and also covictim) and of realizing the need to strategically work with, and not just for the benefit of, marginalized peoples that separates the Activist Ally from the well-meaning but highly problematic "Benevolent Benefactor."

What Swalwell calls the "Benevolent Benefactor" position, and what others call "white savior" syndrome, is captured in a quotation from one of the students in her study: "It's sort of your responsibility to understand you're very fortunate, very lucky for this to happen to you, and that you can take that power that's been given to you and help someone who's not as lucky."[4] This is not to say that such helping acts are never beneficial. Privileged white people have historically devoted, and continue to devote, a great deal of financial investment and volunteer hours that directly benefit social justice movements. However, sometimes such actions involve "framing of problems and solutions that are more likely to reproduce inequality than interrupt it."[5]

For example, charitable donations from the privileged can draw attention away from efforts to change the system that maintains their position of privilege, a phenomenon that African American novelist Teju Cole's viral series of tweets once described as follows:

> The white savior supports brutal policies in the morning, founds charities in the afternoon, and receives awards in the evening . . . the world is nothing but a problem to be solved by enthusiasm. . . . The White Savior Industrial Complex is not about justice. It is about having a big emotional experience that validates privilege.[6]

* * *

Benevolent Benefactors?

In the summer of 2017 my family and I traveled to Poland to take part in a reunion of Holocaust survivors and their descendants. At one time, 3.5 million Jews lived in Poland, 3 million of whom were systematically murdered during the Nazi occupation, including nearly all of my wife's paternal family.

One of the most surreal and disturbing moments of the trip came not during our visits to the sites of ghettos or concentration camps, but during an attempted visit to the mass graves of Jews at the Okopowa Street Cemetery in Warsaw. Despite having made an appointment, our group was turned away at the gate. There we were, a crowd not only of relatives and descendants of the people buried there, but also survivors whose living memory included those victims, and we were kept out.

Why? We were told apologetically that the cemetery was temporarily closed to the public, because a group of Polish Christian college students dedicated to the preservation of Jewish history were busy cleaning and beautifying the place. We could see the cheery teenagers in the distance, clearing fallen tree branches and dusting around grave markers.

This is the kind of painful irony that can arise from Benevolent Benefactors operating according to their own well-intentioned but ignorant perspective, and it can easily provide cover for oppression. Just a few months after those well-meaning, idealistic Polish teenagers kept us out of the Warsaw cemetery, the Polish government passed a bill that made it a crime, punishable by fines and up to three years in prison, to make any mention of the Polish state or people's culpability in the extermination of Jews during the Holocaust. Deputy Justice Minister Patryk Jaki declared, "We have to send a clear signal to the world that we won't allow for Poland to continue being insulted."[7]

* * *

Swalwell reminds us, however, of the need to be understanding and supportive to students with "Benevolent Benefactor" mind-sets. She feels that it is

> crucial to note that students thinking within these frames care about the world and believe the best way to advance justice is by maximizing their monetary donations, engaging in charitable acts, or living the most conscientious life they can. These are core beliefs with which any good social justice teacher can connect . . . [and use as] a reflective tool to think about the very different conceptions of what it means to be a "justice-oriented" privileged person and to more effectively . . . acknowledge their complicity in these systems, feel a sense of empowered agency to make a change, and mobilize their resources as a way to act in concert with others to further justice. [8]

Just as part of social justice education is to design learning experiences that help privileged white students recognize and understand inequities and injustices, an equally important part is helping well-meaning white students who *do* recognize and who *do* want to address these issues to do so in a way that is respectful, and that does not merely reinforce the inequities they seek to help repair.

Compounding this challenge is the fact that white, privileged teachers are no less vulnerable to these pitfalls. Such teachers, in designing experiences aimed at giving privileged white students genuine opportunities to make a difference in issues of social justice, must think extremely carefully about how to structure those opportunities.

THE TRICKY TERRAIN OF SERVICE LEARNING

Indiana University professor Robert Bringle defines service learning as an "educational experience" in which students

> (a) participate in an organized service activity that meets identified community needs and (b) reflect on the service activity in such a way as to gain further understanding of course content, a broader appreciation of the discipline, and an enhanced sense of civic responsibility. [9]

Service learning of some form or other is a staple at American universities, and increasingly in K–12 education as well. Service learning is designed to offer students the opportunity to simultaneously broaden their own knowledge and skill base, build personal character and empathy, and be of assistance to a larger community. When service learning is a feature at schools with affluent and privileged student populations, it tends to take the form of service not to one's own community of peers, but instead for the benefit of others with less socioeconomic privilege.

It is in these cases that service learning tends to draw criticism, as summarized by Professor Dan Butin of Gettysburg College, because it "privileges volunteer activities done by individual students with high cultural capital for the sake of individuals with low cultural capital within the context of an academic class." Butin cautions that such projects make privileged students "necessarily involved in asymmetrical and static power relations, a dichotomy between teaching and learning and the essentialization of who 'we' and 'they' are."[10]

Butin's analysis of the literature offers the following standards for teachers looking to create service learning opportunities for privileged students:

1. A commitment to learn about and respect the "circumstances, outlooks, and ways of life of those being served. . . . The server is not a white knight riding in to save anyone, but just another human being who must respect the situation he or she is coming into."
2. The actual service done must not only provide "meaningful and relevant" service to the people being served (as opposed to just existing to educate the privileged server), but also "the members of the community being served should be the ones responsible for articulating what the service should be in the first place."
3. The service activity must somehow be used to help the privileged students engage with larger issues/questions related to academic content.
4. Students must engage in continual reflection "to provide context and meaning" for their actions.[11]

In keeping with these principles, Nadinne Cruz and Dwight Giles, authors of *Service Learning: A Movement's Pioneers Reflect on Its Origins, Practice and Future* (2000), recommend that service learning activities not be assessed just in terms of individual outcomes for the students doing the service activities, but on the quality of the partnership between the student (and by extension the student's school) and the individuals for whom they are pursuing this activity in order to help.[12]

Applying Butin's Four Standards to Service Learning Projects

LearnServe International, a nongovernmental organization based in Washington, DC, presents several scenarios designed to help teachers prepare for and intervene successfully in the kinds of potential missteps that they or their privileged students might unintentionally make when designing or executing service learning activities, such as seeking to tackle the issue of students of color in a nearby urban school "not appreciating their education enough," trying to help foreign kids get an American education because it's superior, or asking well-meaning but wholly inappropriate questions of sexual assault victims. Visit learn-serve.org for more information. For each scenario, the teacher and/or students should explore:

- What (possibly incorrect) assumptions is the student in the scenario making?
- In what possible ways could you support this student in making the project more in keeping with Butin's standards?

This chapter does not recommend against designing, or having students design, service learning activities—only that said activities must be designed very carefully and consciously. Privileged white students will almost certainly need their teacher's active assistance in constructing and executing such activities, and best practice is to codesign projects *with* the members of the community the students seek to serve, acting as full partners in the process.

* * *

The Justice Project

A regular feature of my junior Honors English class is "the justice project," a six-week unit in which students learn skills in research and evidence-based argumentation by picking an issue of social justice that they care about, then composing an argument on how to address it, and taking part in an "act of activism." In this manner, students make the transition from scholar to scholar-activist.

The project's definitions of "addressing" the issue and "act of activism" are left intentionally vague, as exploring the nuances of these processes is one of the students' learning goals. Students have free reign to pick whatever issues and focus areas they wish, but when their choice involves populations with whom they do not identify as a member themselves, I require that they conduct an interview, preferably on-site, with a local organization or group of people directly affected by the issue, who are working to change it. Often this results in the student's act of activism being to volunteer for, or raise money to support, the organization they visit.

I do not require helping the organization to be their form of activism. Logistically this is not always possible for the students, and not always desired by the organization. However, when it does happen, there is at least the potential for students to learn from people who are directly experiencing and resisting the injustice (rather than through some sort of detached "observation from on high"), and the nature of their service then is guided, and sometimes entirely determined, by those people. The students are then expected to reflect upon and critically examine the experience afterward.

> Incidentally, the justice project does not require that students exclusively deal in issues traditionally aligned with liberal or progressive causes. Over the years some self-identified conservative students have used their projects to highlight what they perceived of as lack of respect for American soldiers, to try and encourage Evangelical Christian students and teachers to express their religious views in schools, and to end what they see as the injustice of affirmative action in college admissions.

* * *

COGNITIVE WORK ON REDUCING IMPLICIT BIAS

For the Activist Ally, guilt may be "an important aspect of learning about injustice," but guilt in and of itself is "not considered to be a productive emotion." Activist Allies instead spend their energies "consider[ing] how best to enter in the matrix of efforts to end injustice at both the structural and individual levels."[13]

To this end, before and while undertaking projects aimed at addressing and repairing issues of social injustice, would-be Activist Allies—students and teachers alike—would do well to work on addressing their own implicit bias, with the goal of taking steps to reduce it. Ohio State University's Kirwan Institute for the Study of Race and Ethnicity defines implicit bias as the "attitudes or stereotypes that affect our understanding, actions, and decisions in an unconscious manner."[14] The concept was forwarded in 1995 by psychologists Mahzarin Banaji and Anthony Greenwald in their book, *Blindspot*, and has since been a guiding tool for understanding how individuals can perpetuate racist structures even without consciously intending to do so. That concept is uncomfortable for many whites like me, as it posits a disconnect between our conscious desires to be equitable and anti-racist with deeper, socially instilled motivations that may run counter to what seem like our fundamental beliefs.

Greenwald went on to codevelop the Implicit Association Test three years later, and the IAT and its cousins can be useful and engaging learning tools. Although not without its critics, the original IAT, and its later modifications, have been cited over 4,000 times, making it one of the most referenced concepts in the psychological literature.[15] The computer-based test requires its users to rapidly categorize certain visual stimuli as "good" or "bad" and, in most cases, images of marginalized or "out" groups (in terms of race, ethnicity, body type, and more) prompt an unfavorable categorization.

The IAT can be an effective tool for use with students; it takes only about fifteen minutes and is very engaging. Some white students may balk at the results of the test, claiming that it has "declared them" to be "racist." The teacher needs to emphasize that the IAT is not the Implicit Racism Test; it focuses on associations. As Las Vegas police officer Brett Bosnahan put it,

> having a bias isn't being racist . . . biased is, you know, maybe I've stopped three or four guys that look exactly like this man. And every time I've stopped them, I found guns or dope on them. So you just put the trait from the person that was guilty onto the person that's innocent. . . . It's scary because it's not fair. It's not fair for me to assume that this guy's going to have the same background. I mean, he might be the CEO of a company, just out for a walk, and didn't want to walk to the crosswalk. I don't know.[16]

Addressing bias as "pattern recognition gone berserk" can make it a less threatening and volatile idea for white students to consider. Doing so has the potential to move them away from an understanding of racism as a deeply embedded aspect of one's character or identity (where their only options are to either deny it or feel guilty about it), and toward an understanding of racism as being embodied in a series of ordinary practices that one can change.

Implicit bias is by no means limited to adolescents; their teachers are just as susceptible, and even social justice–minded educators prove no exception. Zaretta Hammond, author of *Culturally Responsive Teaching and the Brain*, describes a three-year study in which white

> student teachers who self-identified as social justice or anti-racist educators but when actually in physical proximity of a diverse group (especially when they were in the minority) they experienced classic signs of implicit bias— irrational nervousness, anxiety, and fear—[even] when they were in no immediate danger.[17]

The good news is that "our brains are incredibly complex, and the implicit associations that we have formed can be gradually unlearned through a variety of debiasing techniques."[18] Cognitive-behavioral science, which informs so many schools of psychotherapy, child-rearing and classroom management, can also be applied to eroding implicit bias.

Hammond is clear about what the research says does *not* help the debiasing process, at least for teachers: large-group "diversity trainings" (which may increase knowledge about historical and present injustices but are not correlated with significant behavior change in participants), cross-racial dialogue (which often results in increased anxiety and "shut down" for whites), or looking at student achievement data (which can activate confirmation bias in white teachers, reinforcing the notion that African American or Latinx students are inferior to their white counterparts). It is likely that versions of these approaches that a teacher might use with their students would similarly fail.

Hammond instead relates University of Wisconsin professor Patricia Devine's process of successfully eroding one's implicit bias:

> Intention: Acknowledging the existence of your unconscious biases and making an active decision to try and change them.
> Attention: Learning to recognize your triggers and how your stereotypes tend to get activated.
> Time: Make time to deliberately do activities designed to "break your automatic associations that link a negative judgment to behavior that is culturally different from yours."[19]

Devine's own study subjects[20] engaged in the following three activities on a weekly basis:

- Reassociation (stereotype replacement): When you catch yourself responding to a person or situation with a stereotype, consciously think about why you are thinking this, and try to replace your response with an unbiased one.
- Refuting (counter-stereotypic imagining): Come up with examples that contest or challenge the stereotype.
- Perspective-taking: Try and use empathy to put yourself in the position of the person you are having the stereotypical reaction about.
- Make the effort to put yourself in environments where you have many opportunities to challenge stereotypes.

These are the practices that research indicates are necessary to move privileged white people toward a place where they are not held captive by their unconscious biases. Ultimately, teachers of white, privileged students need to design ways for those students to undertake such practices themselves. This is fraught territory for a whole host of reasons, but that is not necessarily a reason to not attempt it.

Lesson: Kangaroos and Bears, Oh My

Goal: Students will understand the deceptive ease with which we can unintentionally ascribe negative stereotypes about the "Other."

Step 1

Teacher randomly divides the class in two, telling one group of students that they are now bears, and the other group that they are now kangaroos. Teacher sends the groups to opposite sides of the room.

Step 2

The teacher assigns (or the students in each group select) a "scribe" from each group to write down the contributions of all group members, and a "spokesbear"/"spokesroo" to share those contributions with the class at a later point.

Step 3

The teacher asks each group to assemble a list of qualities and characteristics of their animal, "Hey bears, what are bears like?" and "Hey, kangaroos, tell us the essential qualities of kangaroos." Allow five minutes or so, and remind the scribes to write down what their groupmates say. Students who are hesitant to speak up, even in their group, can write their contributions on a card and hand it to their group's spokesperson. Alternatively, or in addition, the teacher can enlist a student in each group to be an "encourager" to solicit, in a friendly way, contributions from quieter members.

Step 4

The teacher then asks each group of students, in a slightly leading, edgy voice, "Hey, bears, what are kangaroos like?" chucking a disdainful thumb in the kangaroos' direction, and repeats the gesture the other way, "Hey, kangaroos, what should we know about bears, eh?" with a suspicious face. Once again, the students in each group contribute to their scribe's list.

Step 5

After five more minutes, the teacher calls time again, then asks each spokesperson to say aloud the qualities of their animal, as assembled by their group. The teacher, or a selected student or students, writes these words on the board. Then the teacher asks for a list of the qualities each group ascribed to the *other* animal.

Step 6

The teacher asks the students to look at the board and see if they can detect any patterns. Almost inevitably (especially if the teacher was egging them on earlier), the qualities each group comes up with for themselves tend to be positive images, while those that describe the other group tend to be negative stereotypes. See table 6.1 for examples.

Step 7

The teacher tells the students they are all human beings again, and gives them the mission of trying, through discussion, to come up with possible explana-

Table 6.1.   Sample student responses for "Bears and Kangaroos" exercise

Bears, according to bears	*Bears, according to kangaroos*
Fierce	Vicious
Brave	Mean
Good mothers	Quick to anger
Great climbers	Lazy
Love fish	
Cute	
Furry	
Strong	

Kangaroos, according to kangaroos	*Kangaroos, according to bears*
Energetic	Hyperactive
Fun-loving	Silly looking
Fast	Weird
Good mothers	Goofy
Cute	Exotic
Bouncy	
Playful	
Good boxers	

tions for why this pattern emerged. If the students need prompting, the teacher could ask something like, "Hmm, do you think *all* bears are mean? What about the Care Bears?" or "Why do you think both sides considered their animal to be a good mother, but never suggested that quality about the other side?" Eventually, students may come up with something to the effect of how it can be easy, even the default, to view those whom we consider to be unlike us through a negative lens.

Step 8

At some point, if a student doesn't come up with this connection on their own, the teacher should ask the students to make the leap (no kangaroo pun intended!) from animals to humans. Where and how might we unintentionally, but easily, ascribe to negative stereotypes about whole groups of other people?

If none of the students remarked on it earlier, the teacher can also ask if anyone noticed the "agitating voice" the teacher was using when asking them to describe the other side. Who might be some of those "agitating voices" in the real world, encouraging us to think negatively about the "Other," and why might they want to do this?

This activity could make for a great lead-in to the "Danger of a Single Story" activity, based on Chimamanda Adichie's TED talk, described in chapter 3. Either through that activity or a similar one, students can then brainstorm what sorts of experiences *challenge* their stereotypes and make them rethink their single stories. Students can write about any such experiences they've had, and turn them in to the teacher, who can then evaluate whether it is appropriate, with the student's permission, to share anonymously with the class the next day as an example.

Lesson: Challenging Stereotypes Through Experience

Goal: Students will examine and challenge an existing stereotype through direct experience.

This lesson assumes that students already have at least a surface-level understanding of the definition of *stereotype*: "a standardized mental picture that is held in common by members of a group and that represents an over-simplified opinion, prejudiced attitude, or uncritical judgment."[21] If not, there are a host of lessons available on the internet that engage students with that basic understanding, particularly from sources like Facing History and Ourselves (facinghistory.org) or Teaching Tolerance (tolerance.org).

Step 1

Students should make a list of groups of people that they are aware of, but don't really know personally. In other words, most of the knowledge they have about these people comes from secondhand reports, images, and stereo-types. These groups need not be racial or ethnic groups. Some examples could be:

- Kids from a different clique who eat at the same table at lunchtime
- Elderly residents of an assisted living home
- People who ascribe to a political affiliation different from your own

Step 2

Each student should then make an "honest inventory" of the stereotypes they have about this group, to remain private—even the teacher doesn't need to look at it.

Step 3

The student's mission from here is to obtain a narrative, in person or through an established primary source, from someone from one of these groups. Examples:

- Reading a memoir written by someone from this group
- Unobtrusively but closely observing and listening to people from that group (e.g., sitting at that unfamiliar lunchroom table and eavesdropping

on conversation; attending an open-to-the-public event that caters to an interest group you are not very familiar with, like a school club meeting, sporting event, or concert; open-house day at a church, synagogue, or mosque). Always be respectful of the people you observe and/or interact with—no one likes to be treated as the subject of an experiment.

• Having a conversation or interview with someone from this group, *if there is an intermediary who knows a person from this group and can obtain their consent* (these are important "ifs"—the teacher may wish to take an active hand in this). The teacher will want to work with the student ahead of time to make sure their interview questions are respectful and appropriate.

A parent or guardian should approve each proposed activity, especially where off-campus activities are being planned.

Before and afterward, students engage in reflection, including reflecting on the idea that there is far more to this person/group than they could observe or experience directly. Help students avoid emerging from their brief experience thinking they now can draw conclusions about a certain group (especially a group as large and varied as a racial, ethnic, national, or religious group), or even that they now understand some fundamental truths about the particular individuals they have read/observed/spoken with. Explain that the goal of this assignment is to take small steps to challenge or expand one's existing ideas of an "Other," as opposed to considering this as some sort of comprehensive research project from which major inferences can or should be made.

Ideally, the students would pursue more than one encounter/observation, but it all depends on how much space the teacher can carve out of the curriculum, and the students can carve out of their out-of-school time.

Sustained Interaction

Ultimately, however, working past bias requires more than simulation or momentary observation. It demands sustained interaction, with very specific scaffolds. Gordon Allport's Contact Hypothesis posits, among other things, that

> under appropriate conditions interpersonal contact is one of the most effective ways to reduce prejudice between majority and minority group members. If one has the opportunity to communicate with others, they are able to understand and appreciate different points of views involving their way of life. As a result of new appreciation and understanding, prejudice should diminish. [22]

Mere contact alone, however, does not accomplish these goals: "Contact fails to cure conflict when contact situations create anxiety for those who take part," says Allport,[23] and contact is of little benefit if the groups involved use the contact situation as a grounds for exchanging insults and discrimination, intended or unintended.

The contact hypothesis states that the kind of contact that erodes prejudice depends upon four vital elements:

1. Contact needs to happen for long enough that initial anxiety between the two groups can decrease and dissipate.
2. The two groups must have equal status, and be interacting on more or less equal terms.
3. The two groups need to have a common goal, a shared problem or task (what Allport calls a "superordinate goal") that neither group is able to accomplish without the help of the other group.
4. The two groups must interact personally (as opposed to asynchronously or remotely in parallel), and it really helps to have the support of some outside authority whose auspices both groups recognize and respect.

Educating Activist Allies (to coin the term from Swalwell's book title) requires events and activities that accomplish the above, which is a tall order for traditional pedagogies and classroom structures. At least one pedagogy, however, is ideal for contact situations, and has many benefits for higher order thinking and student engagement as well: project-based learning.

THE POWER OF PROJECT-BASED LEARNING

What is a "project?" While project-based learning (PBL) comes in many flavors and varieties, most agree that a project is not just "any long assignment that's not a paper or a test." The Buck Institute of Education (BIE), contemporary standard-bearers for PBL, defines a project as something students work on "over an extended period of time—from a week up to a semester—that engages them in solving a real-world problem or answering a complex question. They demonstrate their knowledge and skills by developing a public product or presentation for a real audience."[24] Some definitions of PBL present projects as a more authentic assessment of learning, a way for students to apply knowledge and skills to a new, preferably "real-world" contexts.

For others, PBL is the use of projects as pedagogy, "a teaching method in which students gain knowledge and skills by working . . . to investigate and respond to an authentic, engaging, and complex question, problem, or challenge."[25] In other words, more than just a summative assessment, the project *is the means and context* through which the students learn required content.

Examples could be a unit in which students learn research skills specifically so that they can accomplish a real-world task like making an argument before the school committee (and then do so), or learning about the principles of drama specifically so they can put on a play (and then do so), or learning about ecology through the act of examining pond samples and presenting their data to a local conservation group. Technical/vocational schools operate in this manner as a rule, but the concept of learning-through-doing is comparatively new and unfamiliar to the "academic" school environment.

Since truly complex problems have no one singular solution, students should be able to create divergent products, perhaps even pursue divergent processes, in order to complete the project. Rather than ending up with 25 identical dioramas, a PBL unit could result in a variety of different plans for addressing the issue of invasive species, a variety of different proposed constitutions for student government, a variety of different poems to illustrate the concept of irony, and so forth. In each case, though, the students would need to learn, and demonstrate competency in, the skills and content they have been studying. While there is not one single correct answer, there could be many products that fail to demonstrate understanding—it's never a case of "just anything goes."

Regular formative checks need to happen during all stages of the project, or else students risk wasting weeks of time barking up the wrong tree, or ending up with a product that is way off from the assignment's guidelines with no time left to go back and revise. Given that the learning goals of projects tend to be complex, and that student products are likely to diverge, the teacher must design and employ sophisticated and adaptable rubrics in order to assess learning.

The size and complexity of many projects demand more time and resources than most students are capable of by themselves, so most PBL utilizes some form of cooperative group work, not only for the purpose of dividing up labor but also to achieve the kind of "clash of ideas" necessary for solving complex challenges. The ability to leverage multiple students' different skills, interests, strengths, and points of view is vital to effective PBL; revisit chapter 2's tools for formally instructing students in the skills of collaborative work, to avoid the kind of disasters that ensue when untrained students are told to "do a group project" together. Finally, student reflection is a key part of PBL. Teachers can use student reflection as a tool to check up on student learning, to evaluate their own project design and implementation, and to encourage student metacognition and intellectual/personal growth. Katy Farber, author of *Real and Relevant: A Guide For Service and Project-Based Learning* (2018), says such reflection invites students to ask, "Look at how the perspective has changed: this exercise is all about you."[26]

In sum, project-based learning is well-suited for engaging students in the process of tackling as complex an issue as systems of privilege and oppression. PBL demands real-world involvement and impact, personal reflection, and being able to work with, respect, and synthesize ideas from people who have different perspectives. These are the very skills this book argues that privileged white students, and their teachers, need to hone and employ in order to teach, learn, and practice social justice.

What follows are profiles of three PBL units that attempted that exact mission. One project comes from the author's own practice, one from a pair of high school ELA educators in two Ohio schools, and one from a pair of humanities teachers in an affluent, majority white Massachusetts school. They are all presented as exemplars, but not paragons; examining both their successes and their shortcomings may be useful to you.

All three projects brought privileged white students together with comparatively less-affluent students of color for a joint project, in which all of the students would work as partners to solve a problem. These setups gave the white students the opportunity to serve as allies and partners (but importantly, not sole directors) in social justice work.

Unlike the previously described justice project, none of these three projects would match the usual definition of service learning, as neither group of students was positioned to be "helping" the other as anything other than coequal partners in a learning task. Although only the first two programs explicitly cited Allport's standards for successful contact learning scenarios, all three featured elements of those standards in action.

All three programs suffered from similar limitations, including selectivity of the student participants and, ironically for programs designed to create partnerships between privileged and marginalized students, a suite of instructors who were either all white (the first two projects) or all African American (the third project).

Case Study #1: "Green Technology: What Will It Take?" (The G.L.O.B.E. Consortium)

Project Description

This after-school, interdisciplinary PBL course was funded by a grant from the National Science Foundation for the purpose of providing opportunities for students to learn about "green" technology like solar panels, fuel cells, and wind turbines. I codesigned and cotaught the course with a professor in MIT's Materials Science and Engineering Department and one of his graduate assistants. The curriculum spanned the subject areas of chemistry, physics, and engineering as applied to green technology, along with social studies perspectives of politics and economics, plus the ELA skills of argumentation, rhetoric, and persuasion.

Guided by the instructors, the students worked together weekly in mixed-school cooperative groups as they took part in class activities that were part lecture, part discussion, and part hands-on experiments, culminating in a student-designed research presentation for which each group chose an environmental problem, assessed the role of current technology in it, and proposed a better solution both in terms of technology and policy.

The project was funded for three consecutive years (2015–2016, 2016–2017, 2017–2018) and involved the joint participation of students from both urban and suburban schools in more or less equal numbers. The course offered students detailed feedback on their work, but no grades. Depending on the participating school, students either did or did not have the option to earn academic credit for their participation. All students received a personalized recommendation letter for their college application file upon successful completion of the course.

The course content was not framed as addressing issues of social justice or racial equity, but such issues inevitably arose when examining the impact of environmental catastrophes, patterns of who uses and benefits from different energy technologies, inequities between developed and developing countries and between more or less well-off Americans, and more. For example, one topic that surfaced each year involved the economic impact of green technology adoption on coal miners, and the mutual social (mis)perceptions that could arise between blue-collar fossil fuel industry workers and more well-off "techno-elites" in the green technology sector.

Over three years the program enrolled 36 students from four urban and two suburban schools. We had taken conscious effort with the liaisons at the participating schools to recruit a diverse student body. Racial demographics, based on student self-identification, were approximately 20 percent African American, 30 percent East Asian, 5 percent South Asian, 5 percent Latinx, and 30 percent white, and 10 percent other or who did not respond with a self-identification.

Even though the course did not explicitly address issues of racial and economic segregation, it was very much our intention as the instructors to erode that segregation by bringing urban and suburban students together, both white students and those of color. We believe the course successfully addressed three of Gordon Allport's requirements for transformative contact—sustained in-person contact, a common goal, and the backing of a mutually respected authority.

That the two groups must have equal status, and be interacting on more or less equal terms, was the most challenging requirement for us to meet, as not only racial but socioeconomic differences existed between the students. In addition, the wide range of ages of the students (14–19) and, more importantly, the wide range of students' command of science concepts and writing/presentation skills, created differences in the ability to contribute that were difficult to mask, and these differences could manifest themselves as tied to racial and socioeconomic markers. We attempted several measures to create conditions that would establish as equal a footing between students as we could, including:

- All students worked in mixed groups that included members from all participating schools, and representing a range of ages, which was designed to at least equalize the capabilities and resources of every *group*, if not every individual student.
- We met at the MIT campus, which was more or less equidistant, timewise, from all participating schools, and easily accessible via public transportation.
- A free dinner was provided each week, and students were reimbursed for all travel-related costs.

A major obstacle to our goal of "equal footing" was that MIT, as an institution, may constitute what Elijah Anderson, a Yale University professor of sociology, calls a "white space," defined as a setting that "reinforces a normative sensibility in settings in which black people are typically absent, not expected, or marginalized when present."[27]

While MIT's student population is only about one-third white, and has been steadily growing less white since 2005 (trending mainly in the direction of East and South Asian students), in that same time span the African American student population has remained at between 3 percent and 6 percent, and the Latinx student population has also failed to break out of the single digits. The MIT faculty is about 50 percent white at the lower ranks, and 78 percent white at the rank of full professor; African Americans constitute about 4 percent of the faculty.[28] On top of the fact that all three of our course instructors, myself included, were white, this meant that the odds that students would see African American or Latinx faces while roaming campus were minimal.

We had at one point planned to have our class meet on a rotating basis at each of the participating schools, so as to balance out the racial demographics of the surrounding student population, but since the suburban schools were very difficult to access on public transportation, we abandoned this idea. Similarly, we looked for but were unable to find faculty of color who could participate, although we did find guest speakers of color for some sessions.

In an attempt to erode some of the traditional elements of the white academic power structure (not to mention to enact good constructivist practices of cooperative learning), the class was about evenly split between instructor guided activities and student coteaching. In the words of one of the students' postcourse evaluations, "the class was a really good mix of you guys [the instructors] teaching us, and kind of like us teaching you."

In addition, the final project presentations were delivered to a panel of industry experts that, depending on the year, included other MIT faculty and graduate students, local green tech entrepreneurs, local politicians, and members of environmental groups like the Sierra Club. This panel was another attempt to not only give the students an authentic audience for their products, but one that was designed to be a mutually respected outside authority.

Outcomes

We had three primary means of evaluating course outcomes: student attendance, written end-of-course evaluations completed by the participating students, and recorded video interviews with student participants.

Our course evaluations did not ask any specific questions about racial or social justice, but did ask for feedback about what it was like to "work with students from other schools." Responses to these questions were generally positive, as evidenced by comments like this one:

> I learned a lot in this class, not just about global warming, but also how to communicate with people who you don't know, and it doesn't matter where they're from, if they're from other schools and stuff . . . if you have a good attitude toward them, they will respond back very good to you.

A pattern of concerns did arise in student feedback, however, about the difficulty of working on the projects outside of class, since the working groups, by design, were composed of students who attended different schools and thus could not easily meet in person during the intervening time between class sessions. Every year, a majority of students suggested that, for this reason, the groups be constructed only of students who attended the same school. Some students, in this context, expressed upset feelings at classmates whom they perceived "did not take the work as seriously" or whose commitment they questioned.

We did not employ any means of following up with the students to see if their cross-race or cross-school interactions, either with the particular classmates from this project or with others, persisted or increased. As stated earlier, the grant-funded resources available to us focused primarily on assessing science content knowledge.

Informal observations, however, revealed the students' final projects, self-chosen and self-researched, inevitably focused on issues of equity, even if those issues were usually articulated in socioeconomic or location-based terms as opposed to racial ones. One particularly memorable student project attempted to address the problem of disproportionately high asthma rates in a certain Boston neighborhood near a transport hub constantly full of idling buses. The suburban students in that group reported not being aware of that problem before, and were eager to learn about so serious an issue affecting an area so physically close to their own homes. In many ways the urban (and in this case, entirely African American) students in that group took the lead as experts in defining the problem's parameters and guiding the inquiry and research, and the white and Asian suburban students often deferred to their leadership here.

We employed no formal means of measuring whether and how members of each demographic (racial or urban or suburban) may have changed their stereotypes or perceptions of the other, or what "bumps," misunderstandings, and microaggressions may have happened along the way; we are considering building in such structures for future iterations of the course.

Limitations

Given that this was an optional (and for the majority of the students, entirely extracurricular and non-credit-bearing) endeavor, those who attended were a self-selected group with strong academic skills and motivation, as well as some degree of economic privilege regardless of the community the students came from (the fact that all but one of the urban schools participating were selective "exam schools" added to this likelihood). Although we did not collect data on this, it seems probable that the students who attended were not shuffling demanding after-school jobs or significant family responsibilities at home. We recognize that our course was accessible only to students with a certain level of privilege, regardless of their race or school of attendance, and we have not yet developed an adequate solution to this issue.

A larger and more systemic limitation was that the purpose of the grant that funded the program was science instruction, and we did not wish to subvert that mandate. Only one of the three instructors had any training in equity, identity work, and/or anti-racist pedagogy. For all of these reasons, issues of social justice were not placed front-and-center in the content of the course; instead, we attempted to incorporate them into the structure of how the course operated, as described earlier.

Case Study #2: Erase the Space

Project Description

Erase the Space is a nonprofit organization formed by two Ohio public school English teachers, one working in an affluent suburban school with an 82.9 percent white student population, and one working in an urban school with a 69.6 percent African American population. Their program began as a partnership between their two freshman English classrooms that took the form of a year-long writing exchange with the stated mission of "fostering public discourse." In the teachers' own words:

Students wrote letters and opinion pieces, communicated via Twitter and gChat, and ultimately met in person. Working in teams (two students from each school), students developed an idea to get teenagers from different backgrounds and areas of our city together authentically to have a discourse on problems facing their community.

The goals of their program include "teach[ing] students to interact with people from different backgrounds and with different life experiences with empathy and respect," "bring[ing] teachers from different districts together to work collaboratively," and getting "people living in the same metropolitan area to bridge the divide between disparate communities and foster the idea of a larger community."[29]

Erase the Space has been operating for three years as an integrated part of the normal ninth-grade English curriculum in both teachers' classes, totaling 15–20 hours "sprinkled" throughout the school year between October and early May. Assignments would be given out between major units of study, or on the days before school vacations (later iterations of the program with eleventh graders, however, were strictly extracurricular). Eventually the program expanded in 2019–2020 to include 177 students and 8 teachers from 8 classrooms. In all three years, the racial demographics of the classrooms were representative of their respective schools.

Each student would be paired with a counterpart at the partner school and begin corresponding, starting with mutual introductions but eventually cooperatively participating in a joint research project to study the history, and contemporary manifestations of, segregation in the Columbus area. Students worked together to examine the history of how certain neighborhoods were formed, the practices of redlining and racially restrictive covenants, and the role schooling played in that process. The learning process proceeded from student inquiry, and student research rather than teacher lecture was the primary mode of instruction.

"By making it about examining your community," stated one of the organizers, "you can look up and research facts that are grounded in a place that is personal, but [that is] not all about you as an individual, and so it's a little less threatening."

The culmination of the project brings students together in person to draft a proposal for how to get young people from different segregated neighborhoods in the region to meet authentically. Student proposals included youth-oriented festivals, a more inclusive sports league, a week-long "Amazing Race" type of experience across the city, and a summer camp for students interested in increasing their cultural competency.

Like the Green Technology course, Erase the Space was designed to address Allport's requirements for transformative contact. Sustained, in-person contact was their biggest challenge. Although the actual face-to-face meeting between the groups only happened at the end of the program in May, students did spend eight hours together on that day.

While most of the interaction between the students at the two different schools was both remote and asynchronous, the organizing teachers challenged Allport's assertion that "personal" interaction can only happen in person. "Part of what we were trying to do," said one of the teachers, was "transform the role of the Internet as public space."

Teachers gave the students little information on the partner school beyond basic demographic and neighborhood info, leaving the students to craft descriptions of their community in their own ways that felt authentic to them; this process was explicitly tied to curricular goals in learning the principles of narrative and storytelling. Students exchanged four written pieces and, if they chose, photos, before taking on the research project.

Regarding interaction on equal terms, the culminating student meeting took place in neither class's school or neighborhood, but in a mutually unfamiliar space (e.g., a city museum). In this way, said one of the organizers, "there were no issues of 'we're hosting, you're coming in, I'm feeling defensive about my space, I'm opening myself up for judgment.'"

Outcomes

The original goal was to target students' implicit bias, but a consulting researcher cautioned that such deep-seated preconceptions were too difficult to change within such a short period of time.

The target goal eventually became students feeling comfortable coming to different neighborhoods, students actively investigating (or expressing desire to investigate) events and initiating conversations outside of their racial and economic comfort zones. Until they develop a more systematized way to measure and track this process (they have recently acquired a grant to do so), the teacher organizers rely on anecdotes and observations, such as:

- Six or seven of the suburban white students voluntarily attending an after-school anti-racist book club for educators that meets in the evenings at a library in the inner city.
- Suburban students "voluntarily investigating whiteness openly" in conversations and written assignments.

Survey data showed that 100 percent of the 150 student participants responded that the project should be repeated with next year's students.

As the program continues to expand, both organizers consider their ongoing internal struggles to shape a fully inclusive and just program to be a necessary and positive element of their work: "Actually, seeing both of us still uncomfortable after three years looks like success."

Limitations

As with the Green Technology course, there was the limitation in that all instructors involved in the program were white. However, the instructors had both undergone substantial identity work and anti-racism training, and secured grant funding to hold at least two sessions of such training for new teachers who were eventually brought into the project.

Even though this program included a far wider range and number of students than the Green Technology course, there was still an element of curation involved to select those students who would seem most receptive from the outset. Participating students might be selected based on who had the best attendance, or based on who, in the teachers' judgment, seemed "ready" for conversations about race and privilege.

Organizing teachers also faced social obstacles in dealing with parental concerns about a "political agenda" to the program, with one suburban family using this as grounds to remove their son from the program and require that he be given alternative assignments.

While working with students from the majority-minority urban community, the organizers grappled with the fact that their project was still the sole construct of white teachers, even though one had seven years of experience working in the local school environment. "We always keep asking ourselves," said one of the organizers, "is it our place to do this?"

To try and make the project more of a collaboration than an "intervention," the organizers attempted to host focus groups in the city community, providing food and drink and inviting both parents and community activists to come give input and help them shape the program. "We wanted to engage with the community, to involve them more in the planning, rather than just asking for their blessing on work we're already doing."

When only two people came to their focus groups, it prompted the organizers to do some soul-searching. "People [in this community] are very busy, they have a lot going on," said one of the teachers. "We didn't want this to be yet another task . . . we didn't want to be essentially saying, "I need you to co-sign on this so I can keep doing what I'm doing, so you can legitimate it' . . . it just feels wrong."

Case Study #3: The Colors Forums

Project Description

The Colors Forums, which ran from the late 1980s to the early 2000s at a mostly white, largely affluent Massachusetts public high school, was a student-led, faculty-advised project in which a racially diverse core group of students met weekly as a club with the goal of focusing community attention on issues of race and multiculturalism through various means, including

inviting guest speakers, organizing school forums, publishing students'
thoughts through "broadsides," and exposing the school community to the art
of different cultures through guest performers. The Colors Club met every
other week during a daily activity block.

One or two of these meetings per year would be public forums, open to
the school community, in which a panel of five to seven speakers, plus a
moderator, would educate the audience about the issue through a combination of video, images, and speech, provide multiple perspectives on it, and
facilitate a discussion among all attendees. Forum topics included affirmative
action, immigrant stories, "playing the race card," political correctness, and
the killing of Trayvon Martin.

The issues were student-chosen; the two teacher advisors would help
guide the process of their research and give advice for framing the subsequent discussion for the larger audience, and ensure that students were backing up their words with facts and evidence.

At its height, about 15–20 students were involved, though a smaller core
did the bulk of the organizing and leadership. Although the organizers did
not keep records of racial demographics, anecdotally they describe the population as about "50/50" white students and students of color. The students of
color were predominantly East Asian and South Asian, with somewhat
smaller African American and Latinx representation. Most student members
were residents of the town, but some students from Boston were enrolled at
the school via the voluntary busing program, METCO. The big Colors Forums tended to draw attendance in the hundreds, sufficient to fill the auditor-
ium and place some would-be attendees on a waiting list. Reflecting school
demographics, those audiences were majority white.

Both instructors identified as African American. No other faculty were
involved with the advising and organizing of the Colors Club or the Colors
Forums, although many chose to support it by bringing their classes to the
events.

While not explicitly designed to address Allport's contact hypothesis, the
Colors Forums nevertheless appear to have met many of those standards:
Students who regularly attended the club met for 35–45 minutes each week,
and met more frequently as the dates of the forums drew closer. The full-
community forums met for 60 minutes.

The advisors took several deliberate steps to ensure "equal footing" for all
participants: the Colors Club, by design, had no officers and no hierarchy.
Teacher advisors sat among the students and only spoke to try and facilitate
equal participation in discussions (for more on the important role of democratic classroom structures in social justice work, see chapter 7). "We did not
want whites, or any group, or any person, to dominate the meetings," said
one of the advisors, "so we worked hard to make that happen."

Outcomes

The program successfully produced at least one large-scale forum, usually two, per year for the duration of its existence. While no formal system was implemented to track outcomes, anecdotal evidence speaks to classroom discussions and assignments that followed up on issues raised by the forums. The school newspaper frequently featured coverage of the forums, and provided a public space in which students, through letters and opinion pieces, continued to discuss the issues.

Limitations

Garnering participation from the minority students from Boston was an ongoing challenge, which the advisors blame primarily on the logistical difficulties. Gender diversity was also an issue, as the club members were overwhelmingly female. The advisors said this was true of most of the "academic" type clubs on campus.

One of the two forms of resistance the Colors Forums had to face stemmed from its "academic" focus. Some faculty and students expressed criticism that the club was too academically demanding for an extracurricular activity. "We didn't do lectures," says one of the organizers, "but . . . we had a lot of kids coming [to the forums] with no background, no idea what we were talking about," so an explicitly educational focus was deemed necessary.

The other primary form of resistance came through expressions of discomfort from some white students and faculty. According to one of the advisors,

> We let people speak their mind—and sometimes they would say things that others didn't really want to hear, or that some of the adults didn't particularly care for . . . they would say, "That's not how students should talk," but we didn't think it was horrible or abusive. It was open and direct . . . that's kind of the point.

One year's forum caused something of a stir among the student body when a student panelist included, in his response to the question, "At lunch do you feel any racial tension in terms of where people sit?" the sentence, "all of my friends are rich white kids." This provoked a series of passionate editorials and letters in the student newspaper, in which white students expressed their offense and outrage at being "stereotyped." Many repeated the sentiment, so common among whites, that calling attention to issues of race and class was by its very nature divisive and dehumanizing. The student who made the comment eventually felt compelled to publish a lengthy apology.

"We didn't think any students [on the forum panels] said anything personally insulting," said one of the advisors. "The whole point was speaking candidly, [voicing] strong opinions. If others felt uncomfortable, so be it. The goal wasn't for us all to come out feeling good and holding hands. . . . Having said that—to be honest—we haven't done this in a few years, I don't know how this would go over in 2019—things are a little more tense now, our admin is a little different, so I'm not sure." The Club became defunct in the mid-2000s, following the retirement of one of the advisors and increasingly dwindling membership.

None of the three exemplar programs described in this chapter represent perfect models for fostering equitable cooperation among students, from across lines of race and privilege, for the purposes of solving societal problems in which all parties share a joint interest. All three miss a major opportunity to model such cooperation through a racially diverse teaching staff, and because of this, the first two programs may unintentionally reinforce the "benevolent benefactor" archetype. The next section, on establishing cross-race friendships, is particularly relevant in this context. Nevertheless, all three of these programs can serve as models on which future educators can build and adapt.

ESTABLISHING CROSS-RACE FRIENDSHIPS, AND RECOGNIZING AND AVOIDING MICROAGGRESSIONS

The exemplar programs described above considered the facilitation of equitable contact between privileged white students and students of color from less privileged environments to be, in itself, a social justice goal. However, with contact, especially with contact that hopefully leads to the development of friendships, there remain significant hurdles for adolescents (and adults!) to overcome in order to share meaningful cross-race relationships.

While research demonstrates the power of cross-cultural contact and interactions to help people of all groups erode stereotypes and develop new and more accurate schema, cross-race *friendships* do not develop simply as a function of contact. *New York Times* columnist John Eligon writes that "building meaningful relationships across the color line can be difficult, in large part because race remains a touchy subject. Many white people are uncomfortable talking about race or defensive against accusations of racism, according to academics. Oftentimes, they're just not equipped to do it."[30]

Here is yet another place where privilege harms the privileged, particularly during the teenage years. As Beverly Tatum, author of *Why Are All the Black Kids Sitting Together in the Cafeteria?* (1997) and *Can We Talk about Race?* (2008) writes,

Black teenagers and other youth of color typically begin to explore their racial identity during adolescence, but White youth may wait a long time before they think about what it means to be White. Sometimes they never do. Whether such reflection begins at all is certainly a function of social circumstance and context, and if the context doesn't require it, may never occur. [31]

Tatum cites examples of cross-race friendships of hers that encountered difficulty for the reason that, at some point, a moment would arise that "require[d] my White friend to think about his or her own Whiteness, an act of self-examination that may be uncomfortable to undertake," and quotes poet and playwright David Mura, who spoke of how a part of him always "remained beyond the view" of a white friend of his "because if she truly saw it, she would have to change." [32]

Without such self-examination and changes, white friends of people of color continually run the risk of unintentionally committing racist acts, as in the anecdote Tatum cites from the experience that University of Vermont Professor Emily Bernard had with a close white friend of hers:

Susan asked me what "the black community" really thought about names like Sheniqua and Tyronda, because the "white community" thought they were just bizarre. As she asked me the question, I watched myself turn, in Susan's eyes, from Emily into "the black community," and I watched her transform . . . it was just a moment, but it changed everything. [33]

In the words of Kimberly Norwood, a Washington University professor of law, unless a white person "increases their conscious awareness of U.S. racist history and connects the historical dots to the continued, present-day effects of our societal order, [they] cannot even begin to understand, much less address, the issues of racism in America." [34]

One of the ways that teachers of white, privileged students have an opportunity to help their charges "increase this conscious awareness" is to engage them in the study of *microaggressions.*

Not every venture into allyship need be the product of a large-scale project. Sometimes one of the most powerful actions a white, privileged person can take as an Activist Ally is to be aware of, and avoid committing, micro-aggressive actions. If a project is going to bring white students who have had little experience around people of color into sustained contact with them, conscious preparation for avoiding microaggressions seems prerequisite.

However, the concept of microaggressions is a very challenging one for many white people to wrap their heads around. Columbia University Professor Derald Wing Sue defines microaggressions as

the everyday verbal, nonverbal, and environmental slights, snubs, or insults, whether intentional or unintentional, which communicate hostile, derogatory, or negative messages to target persons based solely upon their marginalized group membership. In many cases, these hidden messages may invalidate the group identity or experiential reality of target persons, demean them on a personal or group level, communicate they are lesser human beings, suggest they do not belong with the majority group, threaten and intimidate, or relegate them to inferior status and treatment. [35]

The most alarming portion of that definition for many white people is "intentional or unintentional," the idea that somehow a well-meaning statement or action may be construed as derogatory without the speaker ever intending or realizing it. The very idea can seem like an invisible minefield, a hidden "gotcha" trap.

Canadian blogger Spencer Fernando represents this view when he describes microaggressions as "a way for someone . . . to pull something out of thin air and accuse those who disagree with them of being racist—shutting down conversation and debate. It's about deliberately looking for, and then making up racist and offensive remarks, comments, or even looks, and then attributing that to someone else." [36] Fernando's flaw lies in his assumption that the same set of words has one and only one meaning to all people, a position Lewis Carroll lampoons through the character of Humpty Dumpty in *Through the Looking Glass:* "When I use a word, it means just what I choose it to mean—neither more nor less." If one ascribes to this view, then indeed the only explanation for two people having a differing reaction to the same remarks is that one party is misunderstanding, deliberately lying for manipulative reasons, or is in some other way wrong.

The study of microaggressions then has dual value, both in teaching social justice (in helping white, privileged students to identify and avoid committing them to such actions), and in teaching the higher-order thinking skill of perspective taking, useful across all academic disciplines. Romeo and Juliet see their romance in a very different light than their families do. People in the U.S. North and South viewed, and continue to view, the Civil War through very different lenses. Even in the sciences, Einstein's theory of relativity posits that under some circumstances two parties observing the same physical phenomenon from different perspectives and making conflicting observations can simultaneously be correct, while Heisenberg theorized that the mere act of observing a phenomenon can alter its definition.

The following three lessons attempt to introduce students to the idea of microaggressions in a gradual way that is tangible and, at least at first, less potentially threatening, for white, privileged students.

Rebas and Amblers

(Adapted from *Conflict Resolution in the Middle School: A Curriculum and Teaching Guide* [37])

Goal: Students will understand, through experience, the effect of perspective, bias, and misunderstanding.

Time: One or two class periods.

Step 1

Write the words "Reba" and "Ambler" on the board. Explain that students are going to have an opportunity to take on the role of an alien creature for a short time. They will either be Rebas or Amblers. First they will learn about their own role.

Step 2

Distribute Reba handouts to half the class and Ambler handouts to the rest of the class. Ask the students to make sure they don't share their description with the other "aliens" just yet! Note: Kriedler's activity includes gender differences in Ambler culture, but assumes a gender binary of "girls" and "boys" that a teacher may wish to expand or even discard. For example, the teacher can pass out purple armbands, and sentences about Ambler boys could refer to "Ambler people clothed in purple," etc.

> *Rebas:* You are a Reba. Rebas are friendly and outgoing. Rebas love to meet new aliens. When Reba meets a new alien, he or she always gets up very close to that new alien so as to better look him or her in the eye. A Reba will shake that alien's hand. If the alien doesn't offer his or her hand, the Reba will grab it and shake it (Note: grab *hands*, and *only* hands.). This makes an alien feel welcome!
>
> Rebas don't tend to spend a very long time in one conversation—there are so many aliens to meet! The more aliens a Reba meets and shakes hands with, the better! Then he or she can sit back and say, "Wow, I have made so many aliens feel welcome!"
>
> Reba boys and Reba girls have no problems talking to one another. Reba boys especially like to talk to alien girls, and Reba girls especially like to talk to alien boys.

> *Amblers:* You are an Ambler. Amblers are very polite and peaceful. Amblers like to really get to know an alien for a while before saying much. To do anything else would be hasty and rude!
>
> Amblers like a sense of personal space. They do not like physical contact with aliens unless they have known them for years. Amblers always address strangers as "sir" and "miss." This makes strangers feel more respected.
>
> Ambler boys look to Ambler girls for protection, and if scared, they will hide behind them. Ambler boys do not make eye contact or speak with alien girls. Ambler boys will speak to alien boys but only if an Ambler girl is present, because they feel safer that way.

Step 3

Have students read their handouts, then meet with their fellow Rebas or fellow Amblers to make sure they understand how they are supposed to act. Questions for scaffolding this process could include:

- What does your alien like to do?
- How do you interact or relate to others?
- How do you speak? What is your body language like?
- If you had a motto, what would it be?

Step 4

When both groups feel they know their culture, present the following scenario:

> Guess what? This is a momentous day! We're about to have a historic first meeting between Rebas and Amblers. You are going to have the opportunity to meet people from a whole new planet. Mingle and get to know each other. As you mingle, remember to stick to the characteristics of your aliens.

Step 5

Give students three to five minutes to mingle, preferably in a space that allows for a lot of movement. The Amblers will probably stay still while the Rebas move quickly from their side of the room and rush the Ambler side, and Amblers will likely try and retreat or hide behind one another. A reminder of norms about physical contact and safety is advisable before embarking upon this stage of the lesson!

Step 6

Have everyone return to their seats. Ask the Rebas, then the Amblers, to explain how they felt they conducted themselves. The teacher, or a student scribe, will write those answers on the board. Typical Reba replies might be, "Friendly, outgoing, welcoming, etc." Typical Ambler replies might be, "Polite, respectful, dignified."

Step 7

Ask the Rebas, then the Amblers, what they thought of the *other* group. Again, the teacher, or a student scribe, will write those answers on the board. These answers will likely be different. The Rebas will probably regard the Amblers as "standoffish" or "scared," while the Amblers might call the Rebas "rude, pushy, or aggressive."

Step 8

A spokesperson from the Rebas, and then from the Amblers, should read aloud the handout they received in Step 2, after which the class should engage in a discussion, guided by such prompts as:

- What was different about the way you saw yourselves, vs. the other aliens?
- What do you think was the source of these differences?
- What *misunderstandings* did each side have about the other, and why?
- How could they have learned about each other and avoided misunderstandings?
- What things do you need to think about when you are talking to someone whose background and experience may differ from yours?
- What are some of the features of your own way of looking at the world that can be misinterpreted or imposed on others?

In the Rebas and Amblers exercise, the two groups are on more or less equal footing, mutually misinterpreting the other with similar results on both sides. To understand microaggressions, however, the issues of *power* and *history* must also be brought into play.

Consider this useful analogy to accompany the following two activities: "Microaggressions are like coming into a movie midway, or first opening a book to chapter 10. People who have been reading it from the beginning may very well take whatever you say or do in the context of all of those events that have happened in the earlier chapters, that you haven't read."

Lesson: Teachers, Students, and Homework

Goal: Students will examine how differences in power can influence misunderstandings.

Time: 30–40 minutes.

Step 1

The teacher asks students to think of a time when one of their teachers assigned a large and/or challenging homework assignment, one that required a very long time to complete. How might teachers and students sometimes view a situation like this differently? Make two columns, one for "teacher perspective" and one for "student perspective." For many students, and especially for students at "high-powered" schools, such anecdotes should come easily. Complaints about unmanageable workloads and unsympathetic teachers are near-universal.

Step 2

Students should share these anecdotes in groups and pairs, and—assuming the teacher earnestly commits to just listening and not weighing in with a personal opinion or with any defensive statements—with the class as a whole.

Step 3

The teacher should then ask the students to take up that same pattern with the question, *Why* do teachers and students sometimes see the situation of work-load differently? Putting themselves in the shoes of a teacher, seeing things from that perspective, might be very challenging for students. The teacher can prompt and scaffold with questions like:

- What might you be aware of, but teachers might not be aware of when assigning students work? (Answers might include the homework students have in other classes; responsibilities they might have at home such as jobs, chores, or taking care of younger siblings; health issues)
- What might the teacher be aware of, but students are not? (Answers might include what the principal or the state wants the class to cover, or theories of how students learn best). Even this might be a tough question for students to answer, so further scaffolding might be needed, with such questions as: "What do you think is the reason why teachers assign home-work?" or "How do you think a teacher attempts to determine how long an assignment will take a student to complete, or how challenging to make it?" or "What do you think would happen to a teacher who didn't assign any homework at all?"

Step 4

The teacher can now pose the additional question, "If a teacher said, 'Come on, you're blowing this homework/stress thing way out of proportion. I'm not doing anything wrong here as your teacher, or trying to be mean to you,' how would you respond?" There are a couple of important potential take-aways here. One is that even when a teacher, from their point of view, thinks they are treating students appropriately, the same assignment might seem very different from the student's point of view, given the student's own set of experiences and perspectives. Another is that teachers sometimes tend to assign homework in a "vacuum," in that they don't have knowledge, unless they ask, of the fact that their assignment is entering a pile with seven other assignments each night. What to them is an isolated encounter (i.e., assigning a student homework) is, to the student, just the latest of many incidents in an ongoing, accumulating, and already large tally of stresses.

Step 5

Ask the students, "So do both sides bear equal responsibility in addressing this issue? Isn't this just like Rebas and Amblers?" Of course, it's different. The teacher has much more power and privilege in this situation than the students do. That power and privilege are in fact part of what makes it difficult for the teacher to understand the students' perspective, and what makes it difficult for the students to successfully advocate for their point of view.

If the students feel that the teacher's privileged position makes it incumbent on them to try and understand and accommodate the students—or to at least more carefully regard the potential effects of their own actions—then the teacher can inform them that they have just taken a major step toward understanding microaggressions.

Lesson: Mosquito Bites and Microaggressions

(The first part of this lesson is adapted from a video created by Fusion Comedy, and the second part makes use of videos from MTV's "Think Different" campaign[38])

Goal: For students to understand microaggressions, including evaluating presentations of real-world examples of microaggressions in action.

Time: One or two class periods.

Step 1

The teacher asks the students if they have ever been stung by a mosquito. How did that make them feel? How did they react?

Step 2

The teacher then asks, "How would it be different if you were stung by mosquitos *every* day, dozens and dozens of times a day, for years? How would that make you feel? What would your reaction be when you saw a mosquito, and how might it be different than your reaction to only occasional bites?" While the intention here is to contrast an occasional annoyance with the sum total of dozens of daily annoyances, some students might respond with, "I guess I would get used to it and it wouldn't bother me as much." Research has actually been conducted on mosquito bite immunity: a few people develop it, but most never do.[39] Tell the students to assume that they are among the majority of people, for whom each new sting remains as itchy and annoying as ever. You may also wish to remind them that some mosquito bites, in the real world, can transmit life-threatening diseases and pose other threats that go far beyond mere inconvenience.

Step 3

Let's say a person who *did* have that immunity, though, came up to you, saw your reaction to being bitten, and told you that you were overreacting? How would you feel? What might you say to them?

Step 4

Play the videos from MTV's "Look Different" campaign: http://www.mtv. com/news/1871828/look-different-microaggression-videos/. There are seven videos, each of which presents a 30-second scene between students who seem to be friends, at least one of whom is a member of a minority group or person of color. At some point, however, one of the friends makes a comment that results in a cut-scene where we are treated to a sequence of glass panes breaking over the marginalized student's head, set to an internal monologue where the student explains how the comment hurt them. Then the action returns to the scene, and the marginalized student keeps quiet or laughs awkwardly and moves on. For each video, the teacher can ask their students:

- What do you think the offending students were thinking when they said what they said?
- What was the effect on their friend?
- Why did the comment have that effect on the friend? (replay the internal monologue if necessary, or provide a transcript)
- How is this like, and unlike, the mosquito bite scenario we talked about earlier?
- Why do you think the offended student remained silent?
- Was this in fact a microaggression? What responsibility, if any, did the student who made the comment have? What could/should that student have done differently?

Step 5

In the ensuing discussion, expect and allow for disagreement. Some students may well say that there was no microaggression committed, that the offended student was making too big a deal, that there was no way the friend could have known the comment would be offensive and that it is unfair to expect the friend to have known.

The teacher can gently prompt and refer back to the mosquito metaphor, the "coming in midway through a book or movie" metaphor, and/or the "one teacher's assignment adds to a pile of existing assignments" idea from the previous lessons. The examples that may seem least like microaggressions for many white students are those that appear to be compliments, such as "You're so articulate!" The problem with such statements, even if the speaker makes them in earnest, is that

> the meta-communication is . . . the person complimenting them is surprised that [the person of color] can be bright, intelligent because that's not the way black Americans are, and that you're an exception. And it allows a person to hold onto the stereotype that African Americans are unintelligent, inarticulate—and all the negatives that go with it.[40]

A teacher might try the example, with white teenage students, of the following microaggressive compliment: "Wow! You're so good at paying attention without glancing at your phones!"

Ultimately, though, it is important to not require the students to declare certain actions microaggressions. So long as the teacher helps ensure that the discussion adheres to the norms (see the introduction and chapter 2) of respectful discourse, students are free to come to what conclusions they will. As always, the students should be expected to explain their reasoning, and respond to possible alternate readings. This, incidentally, holds just as true for those students who identify the events as microaggressions—how do they respond to a devil's advocate argument that the offended students are just being oversensitive?

This is another one of those times when students of color in your class might feel particularly vulnerable. Such students may or may not feel comfortable sharing their personal experiences and perspectives with microaggressions (recalling chapter 2, remember never to put such students on the spot and invite them to speak unless they have taken the initiative). Once again, "bracketing" such discussions with more affirming and strengthening material is advisable.

Ultimately, as long as all of your students can come away with the understanding that the same words might be experienced differently, and furthermore might be experienced as either innocuous or oppressive by different people, then it may well prompt them to be more thoughtful in their own future interactions.

* * *

Names Matter

I've written earlier about the power of a teacher—especially a white teacher—modeling his, her, or their own ongoing learning process, and bringing up examples of one's own past microaggressions can provide fodder for this. For me, remembering student names is an ongoing challenge. Despite vari-

ous mnemonics and visual aids, I still inevitably call many students (and sometimes colleagues) by the wrong name.

With fellow white individuals, this is usually just an "oops" moment, or a chance to amusingly self-deprecate. But with students of color, mixing up names, especially when there are only two or three students of that race in the class, can awaken all sorts of emotional reactions that come from years of having white people think "all of you X-es" look alike. It certainly touches an annoyed chord in me when students call me "Mr. Goldberg," which happens several times a year, to which I often reply, "Nope, that's the other Jewish teacher here."

For that reason, I now try and take extra, above-and-beyond efforts to learn, and properly pronounce, the names of my students of color. When I screw up (and it still happens occasionally), I take the student aside at the first good opportunity, apologize for the error, and outright call that error what it is—racist—even if it arose out of internalized, subconscious racism. I have even on occasion stopped a class when I've called a student of color the wrong name during a whole-class discussion or other very public activity, apologized in front of all my students, and refer to that moment later on when we get to our formal study of microaggressions.

* * *

Stressing about Race

One of my white graduate students once related an anecdote of a time she spent sitting on a train next to an African American woman. "I loved her hair and wanted to compliment her on it," the student said, "but then I remembered that it's not PC to focus on black women's hair." She expressed her frustration that "these days it's just gotten so stressful [for white people]—everything's become so loaded. There's no way you can win."

An African American classmate then raised her hand and said, "Welcome to how people of color feel a thousand times a day, for their whole lives."

In other words, my white student's experience on that train gave her momentary insight into a world where she no longer had the privilege of immunity to the stress of considering how race can complicate even simple, ordinary interactions.

I have heard so many white people express sentiments to the effect that "if we all just didn't focus so much on race, it wouldn't be a problem." But if our society wasn't so inequitably structured around race, there would be no intrinsic discomfort in focusing on it.

* * *

Ultimately, to really understand microaggressions requires more than learning to avoid certain "landmine" phrases as a white person interacting with people of color. A thorough understanding of the historical and present forms of oppression that marginalized people face will better prepare more privileged people to understand what sorts of words and actions are likely to activate or intensify the trauma of that oppression. Claudia Rankine's 2014 book, *Citizen: An American Lyric*, is just one example of a text that helps readers connect that larger picture to the more mundane realm of daily interactions between white Americans and Americans of color.

In her book, *Can We Talk About Race*, Beverly Tatum describes a valuable and healthy friendship she maintains with a white friend who

> had thought about what it means to be white in a race-conscious society. She had spent a lot of time prior to our meeting examining her own whiteness, thinking about what it meant to have privilege, about what it meant to be in a relationship with those who might not have the same privileges. I did not feel, as a person of color, that I needed to teach her what you might call the first things about race. We both had things to learn in our friendship, and over the years we have taught each other many lessons, but we had both done internal work on understanding our racial identities, and the lessons learned were, I would say, in balance.[41]

"Ideally," writes Swalwell, "both privileged and marginalized people have much to learn from each other and will be mutually transformed in the process."[42] This is the end toward which social justice education with the privileged is aimed, the kind of work that erodes the very system of inequities and helps improve the lives of everyone.

As teachers and students working within a nested series of systems (a classroom, a school, society writ large) that are structured to be inequitable, there are obviously limits to what we can accomplish, but that is no reason to avoid taking whatever steps we can. It is also true, as Swalwell cautions, that "[g]iven the complexities and challenges for people privileged by oppression when they engage in social justice work, it is likely that even dedicated allies will find themselves at times operating within other frames and supporting the reproduction of hierarchies."[43]

This should remind those of us who are privileged, teachers and students alike, to practice continual reflectiveness and introspection, but it should not in and of itself dissuade us from action. The activities and examples in this chapter, however imperfect, represent attempts to educate and transform at the individual and small community level, and begin to touch upon that "larger picture."

Ultimately, developing competencies for social justice must aim toward initiating action. It is the ultimate answer to that student question, "Why are we learning this?" and perhaps also the teacher question, "Why should I even attempt to teach this?" We learn, so we can do. If we misstep, we learn to do better.

Or, drawing on the author's own cultural background, in the words attributed to the ancient Jewish sage Rabbi Tarfon, "It is not our responsibility to finish the work of repairing the world, but neither are we free to desist from it."

NOTES

1. Swalwell, 2013, 94–95.
2. Ibid., 124.
3. Ibid., 91.
4. Ibid., 108.
5. Ibid.
6. Cole, 2012.
7. Pawlak and Kelly, 2018.
8. Swalwell, 2013, 108.
9. Bringle and Hatcher, 1995, 112.
10. Butin, 2003, 1684.
11. Ibid., 1677.
12. Cruz and Giles, 2000.
13. Swalwell, 2013, 99.
14. "Understanding Implicit Bias," 2015.
15. Ortner and Van De Vijver, 2015.
16. Glass, 2015
17. Hammond, 2015.
18. "Understanding Implicit Bias," 2015.
19. Hammond, 2015.
20. Devine, Forscher, Austin, and Cox, 2012.
21. Merriam-Webster online, https://www.merriam-webster.com/dictionary/stereotype.
22. "Gordon Allport's Contact Hypothesis," n.d.
23. Ibid.
24. "What Is PBL?" n.d.
25. Ibid.
26. Farber, 2018.
27. Anderson, 2015, 10.
28. MIT Registrar, 2018.
29. Gordon and Burtch, n.d.
30. Eligon, 2019.
31. Tatum, 2008, 91.
32. Ibid., 90.
33. Ibid., 95.
34. Quoted in Eligon, 2019.
35. Sue, 2010.
36. Fernando, 2017
37. Kreidler, 1994. Used with permission.
38. Fusion Comedy, 2016; Walker, 2014.
39. Mitchell, 2013.
40. Martin, 2014.
41. Tatum, 2008, 93–94.
42. Swalwell, 2013, 103.
43. Ibid., 108.

Chapter Seven

Choosing Between What Is Easy and What Is Right

CONSIDERATIONS FOR SOCIAL JUSTICE EDUCATION BEYOND CURRICULUM, INSTRUCTION, AND CLASSROOM MANAGEMENT

The previous chapters have attempted to marry the author's experience with relevant research to provide aspiring social justice educators with a wide set of tools from which to choose—tools that they may adopt, modify, or reject as fits the needs of their school, students, and personal teaching style. They are presented in an order that tracks with what Diane Goodman saw as the evolution of a person's competencies in social justice: awareness of self, knowledge about and respect for others, awareness of injustice (and one's own possible roles as beneficiary and as victim), the ability to interact and ally effectively with marginalized peoples, and using those alliances to effectively work toward a more equitable world. If this book has been successful, the reader can now walk away with tangible "things to do" in curriculum, instruction, and classroom management.

Would that this were sufficient for successful social justice teaching with privileged white students, but it is not. Curriculum, instruction, and management do not exist in a vacuum; they are situated within the larger structures of classroom and school culture, which are in turn situated within a larger community. This final chapter aims to highlight the importance of a social justice educator considering those larger-scale factors, as well as some advice for doing so.

CHANGE BEGINS AT HOME: MODELING SOCIAL JUSTICE AND DEMOCRACY IN THE CLASSROOM

Ralph Waldo Emerson, another affluent, white privileged educator who focused on social justice, characterized teaching as an "involuntary" act: "What you are stands over you the while, and thunders so that I cannot hear what you say to the contrary."[1] In short, "talking the talk" of social justice means little without "walking the walk," not just "out there in the world" but also in the classroom itself.

Swalwell's studies of social justice education among the privileged concluded that classrooms that had

> emphasized intellectual and emotional personal connections to injustice require critical self-reflection, prioritized listening to each other as well as marginalized voices, and offered opportunities to build relationships with people from backgrounds different than them over time tended to produce more of the desired responses among privileged youth (awareness, agency and action).[2]

As we know, students learn any concept more readily and thoroughly when the teacher facilitates their making connections to their own lived experience. That is why Swalwell advises:

> [R]ather than presenting issues of injustice as primarily historical, abstract or attributable to individual actions, teachers [should] ask students to make connections between what they are learning and long-standing structural inequalities with contemporary issues and their daily lives . . . and critically reflect on this information in both intellectual and emotional ways.[3]

Freire used the injustices of the school system itself as context for his students' learning, but he did more than just have his students analyze the elements of school structure that limited their voice—he transformed his classroom in order to include and amplify their voice. "The democratic school that we need is not one in which only the teacher teaches, in which only the student learns, and in which the principal is the all-powerful commander,"[4] Freire wrote. Instead, learning must be "a process where knowledge is . . . shaped through understanding, discussion and reflection."[5] In other words, the social justice model extends to the very dynamics of power of the classroom.

This vision of schooling is at least as old in the West as Locke and Rousseau; the author/educators Leo Tolstoy and Janusz Korczak both taught students in an atmosphere of shared authority over community rules and curriculum alike. Various forms and degrees of this climate were later established in numerous "alternative" schools like the Summerhill School in England, the Hadera Democratic School in Israel, and the Sudbury Valley School in Massachusetts.

Few contemporary schools allow such environments to flourish, but within the bounds of a given classroom a teacher can cocreate a space where his or her role is facilitator and not dictator of the learning process. Here are some examples.

1. *Making a healthy space for disagreement and dissent between students*, encouraging explorations of many points of view for any issue and playing devil's advocate when needed.

2. *Allowing students a forum for respectful disagreement with the teacher*, and for giving the teacher evaluative feedback that the teacher then acts upon.

3. *Cocreating norms and rules for the classroom* (recall chapter 2's brief treatment on this subject). Soliciting student input when creating classroom management structures has the benefit of making the rules more culturally responsive, and framed in language the students find naturally accessible and comprehensible. For example, if a rule is, "We show each other respect," then the students get to specify in terms that make sense to them as to what respect specifically looks like, and what words and actions convey and signify "respect" in their view.

You as the teacher are still ultimately responsible for the safety and maintenance of your classroom; it is not as if you have to allow students to create ridiculously inappropriate norms. But generally students will wind up designing norms that create a sense of order and good treatment of one another, and having them create those rules increases the likelihood of their buy-in. When they violate those rules, the teacher—and their classmates!—can remind them that *they* were the ones who designed these norms of respect and safety, and agreed to abide by them.

Cocreation can extend to all manner of classroom procedures. Will we raise hands during discussion and the teacher will pick someone, or will the person who just spoke pick the next speaker? Will everyone just "jump in" when so inspired? Will more confident students be responsible for soliciting and supporting participation from the less confident? How might discussions develop means of participation that favor introverts as well as extroverts? It is important to establish, from the beginning, that these norms and rules will be open to critical examination and renegotiation. Some procedures may well turn out to be unworkable, or ineffective for accomplishing what the community wants them to. The idea that rules can be sent back to the drawing board and reshaped is a key element of democratic process, and both demands and sharpens critical thinking skills.

4. *Engaging in differentiated instruction*. This is the practice of, within a single classroom, "ensuring that what a student learns, how he or she learns

it, and how the student demonstrates what he or she has learned is a match for that student's readiness level, interests, and preferred mode of learning."[6]

For the same learning goal, different students might work alone or with others. They can choose to learn from a lecture (from the teacher, a classmate, or a video), or a discussion, or a hands-on activity. They can choose how they demonstrate mastery, from writing an essay to creating a poster, enacting a performance, or something else; the teacher's responsibility is to design rubrics that allow assessment of student understanding through all of these means. Students might be enlisted to employ or even codesign such rubrics themselves, using assessment as a *means of learning* as well as just a mechanism by which teachers measure their learning.[7]

5. *Enlisting students as partners in teaching*, or even as teachers-of-the-teacher. In *For White Folks Who Teach in the Hood and the Rest of Y'all Too* (2017), Christopher Emdin pitches what he calls "reality pedagogy" specifically to white teachers working with students of color—but the student-empowering strategies that he proposes as vital for serving traditionally oppressed populations can also work with privileged populations as a direct, living experience of what an alternate, more equitable kind of society can look like.

Emdin's strategies include "cogenerative dialogues" or "cogens," where students regularly work in small teams with the teacher to shape classroom curriculum and instruction, and "coteaching," where students play direct roles in the instruction of the entire class, their teacher included. Doing so encourages students to be the "expert[s] at pedagogy . . . while the teacher is positioned as a novice who is learning how to teach,"[8] insofar as the students, as more intimately familiar with how they and their agemates learn best, work with the teacher to develop processes for more effectively teaching whatever the required content is. Ultimately, the students should even have a say in choosing some of that content or knowledge they will be learning, as opposed to it being entirely dictated to them by the teacher or state standards.

Democratic classroom structures are rare because they can be difficult to employ, if for no other reason than the fact that neither most teachers nor most students have had much experience with them. The standards-based world of education accountability, with its emphasis on uniformity (supposedly in the name of equity) and narrowly defined measurement of learning via standardized tests, also presents a substantial obstacle.

Yet a wealth of research connects the pedagogies and structures described in this chapter to the very learning goals enshrined by No Child Left Behind, the Common Core Standards, and Race to the Top, which emphasize higher-order thinking. Jablon argues that democratic, inquiry-based classrooms are well-suited for such goals, as they "simultaneously and interrelatedly [help] students acquire and synthesize content, skills and habits of mind."[9]

Democratic classrooms, with their emphasis on individual and community reflection and discussion, also provide an ideal forum for students and teachers to undertake the challenging but necessary work of identifying and addressing issues of inequity and injustice within the classroom itself. Such issues are not only more relevant than injustice "out there," affecting the "marginalized Other," but also more within the students' immediate power to correct.

Here is a place where issues of intersectionality among the privileged become important to study. Are certain students always getting picked on, made fun of, or shortchanged? Are certain voices always getting heard at the expense of others?

If a key element of being an Activist Ally, by Swalwell's definition, is "soliciting and listening to the stories of marginalized peoples over one's own opinions," then students and teachers alike, she says, should practice "respectful listening among classmates and attending to injustices at the most local level of the classroom and the school."[10] One of the main differences that Swalwell finds between what she calls "conventional social justice pedagogy," versus a classroom that *embodies* as well as just teaches about the values of Activist Allyship, is this more inclusive and equitable sharing of power and agency between students, and between students and the teacher.[11]

If students can learn to listen to, cooperate with, and cede privilege to the marginalized people sitting several seats away—that is a real and tangible social justice action. If students and teachers alike develop an understanding that ultimately, the classroom is as much the students' space as the teacher's, this transformation of privilege and power dynamics can teach them far more about inclusivity and social justice than any abstract study of critical race theory.

Of course, when it comes to power dynamics, teachers are hardly the chief decision-makers. Significant power rests with a teacher's colleagues, with the school administration and, particularly in affluent suburban and independent school environments, with the community of parents.

NAVIGATING TREACHEROUS LANDSCAPES

It is easy to lampoon or demonize hyperconcerned parents, but the fact remains that these students are not your own children. Think of the most odious political or social belief you can imagine, and then imagine your own child being forced to spout it back to their teacher in order to get a good grade. If you become a teacher who requires that sort of thing, then a parent has every right to be upset. The fact is that you and your students' parents are really on the same side, in that you both, ideally, want for their children—theirs, not yours—to be broad-minded critical thinkers, equipped to be active participants in civic and corporate life.

In our highly polarized national climate where every idea gets quickly shoved into one or the other partisan "box," teachers attempting to engage privileged white students in the study and practice of social justice work can easily run into trouble with colleagues, supervisors, and parents suspicious of a "liberal, progressive agenda."

That kind of pigeonholing does a terrible disservice to the history of Republican efforts to combat racism; Republicans were among the strongest proponents of the Civil Rights Act of 1964. Republican governor George Romney was one of the foremost opponents of and crusaders against redlining. Every African American who served in the U.S. Senate belonged to the Republican Party until Carol Moseley Brown was elected in 1992. The infamous pivot to the so-called Southern Strategy in the late 1960s may have shifted much of the Republican Party's approach toward racial equity, but that does not, or at least, should not, somehow brand the pursuit of social justice as an inherently "blue" position.

Neither is the Democratic Party free, by any means, of racist or classist elements. Recall the opposition of the "Dixiecrats" to Civil Rights, the staunchly Democratic Boston government's opposition to school integration (sharing no small part of responsibility for the ensuing busing riots), the blackface photos of Virginia's Democratic governor Ralph Northam, or the regressive welfare and criminal justice reforms under President Bill Clinton that, in the analysis of Dartmouth history professor Matthew Delmont, proved "ruinous for many Black Americans."[12]

Teaching social justice does not, and should not, have anything to do with promoting any particular political party. Yet the reality remains that teachers have to tread carefully in an environment where accusations of "being too political" can ruin careers. By that same token, as detailed in chapter 1, teachers have every ethical and pedagogical reason alike to steer well clear of indoctrination.

If you want to plunge down the rabbit hole of when and how teachers can express political opinions on controversial matters, I recommend the American Civil Liberties Union's *Free Speech Rights of Public School Teachers* (2015), and Diana Hess and Paula McAvoy's *The Political Classroom: Evidence and Ethics in Democratic Education* (2014). But ultimately, the best insurance against accusations of political indoctrination—or, worse, *legitimate* accusations of political indoctrination—is to facilitate, encourage, and demand an atmosphere of critical exploration and inquiry.

As Matthew Kay advises, "deal in probing questions, not declarative statements."[13] Be even-handed in that you let no one, especially not students who readily leap to espouse social justice–oriented views, off the hook from having to justify and defend their beliefs. Kay writes:

We must spar. Not because every half-formed idea is worth twelve rounds, but because students need to learn how to articulate their opinions amid direct scrutiny. They must not wilt at the slightest pressure from perceived authority. Also, we hope to inspire a generation of students who realize that most ideas improve through pruning.

At the same time, a teacher must

remember that good sparring partners know when to ease up. They are getting paid to test the fighter's skills, to help them prepare for a contest—not to knock them out of the practice ring. I must not, in my challenging of students' ideas, seek to actually beat them. Only to jolt them into deeper reflection. [14]

Some good practices here include:

- Cultivate an earned reputation as an even-handed devotee of intellectual rigor, someone who lets no one off the hook, but who also shows equal compassion to all.
- When using examples drawn from current events or political figures, employ a balance across the political spectrum (e.g., if you are inviting the students to critically evaluate the actions of a Republican president, make sure you select similar or analogous actions of a Democratic president to critique as well).
- Include readings and perspectives from writers and thinkers from many social and political positions, especially those whom you personally disagree with.
- Have a crystal-clear grading policy—transparent and accessible to students, parents, and administrators—that demonstrates achievement based on specific skill-based goals, not political positions.

Students of all political persuasions, as well as those who consider themselves to be apolitical, need to feel safe and able to learn and succeed in your classroom. You may wish to (with permission) record your class sessions, or to enlist a colleague to observe your class discussions, in order to double-check if you are giving equal respect to all students, and whether you are even-handedly checking students who attempt to silence others' voices.

This is easier said than done as, especially in our current political climate, the mere act of voicing some positions may register as abusive in the minds of those who hold contrary beliefs. Lean heavily at all times on the four discussion norms outlined in the introduction to this book: speaking only for one's own experience, validating the experiences of others, asking questions rather than making accusations, and understanding that the same words may be received differently by different people.

There are also some communities, some administrators, who plain will not stand for anything other than a mirror reflection of their own hardened political position, and who may penalize you for anything that appears to deviate. Remember YKYS-YMVY. Ultimately, you need to decide what particular balance you will strike between doing your job well, and keeping yourself from getting fired, where you won't be able to do your job (and perhaps, feed your family) at all.

THE CONSERVATISM (SMALL C) OF "SUCCESSFUL" SCHOOLS

Regardless of the dominant partisan affiliation of the community, there is an inherent conservatism in affluent schools that has nothing to do with the political sense of that word. Students at such schools often boast impressive scores on state tests, SATs, and APs, and have near 100 percent graduation rates and college acceptance; in the eyes of state evaluators, magazines that rank schools, real estate agents, and parents seeking to move to the district, this is evidence of success.

Proposals for radical, or even small, changes to programming or school culture face an uphill battle in an environment where, unlike the case with "failing" urban or rural schools, suburban and independent school administrators, teachers, and parents can have every reason to feel, "if it ain't broke, don't fix it." This means that there is very little pressure on teachers in affluent schools to adopt particularly innovative pedagogical strategies, and the defaults, the paths of least resistance—highly teacher-centered, lecture-based approaches favoring memorization and recall—can predominate as a result. It is tempting for those teachers to conclude that these traditional methods are in fact responsible for their students' excellent test performance.

Yet median family income has long been shown to be one of the strongest predictors of SAT scores,[15] and some studies have been able to use U.S. Census data to successfully predict the percentages of students who score well on standardized tests based on just three demographic variables: percentage of families in a community above a certain income threshold, percentage of people in a community in poverty, and percentage of people in a community with bachelor's degrees.[16]

While rigid, teach-to-the-test methods can result in higher scores specifically on Advance Placement exams, the research is less clear as to whether those AP scores themselves are actually predictors of college success and completion, or merely a correlated variable, since students with high AP scores are disproportionally already academically successful individuals from affluent families.[17]

Independent and suburban schools, unlike many of their urban or rural counterparts in our present era of "school accountability," have little outside pressure to institutionalize the practice of collecting and analyzing student data to inform instruction. If they did employ such practices, they could test whether changing pedagogy or classroom structures have any impact upon the metrics of test scores. If income and wealth (and their corollaries, like good nutrition, high levels of both parental education and parental involvement) really are the key variables in student achievement as it is currently measured, then more inquiry-based, student-centered approaches to teaching would likely not threaten the status quo of a school's performance.

But without such experimentation and analysis, a combination of the fear of ruining a good thing, adherence to tradition for tradition's sake, and the sway of particularly influential faculty or administrators' idiosyncratic predilections can all create barriers to innovation within the very districts that should feel the most freedom to innovate and experiment. (Alternatively, with no one looking over their shoulders, suburban teachers can fall into the trap of *thinking* they are employing innovative and transformational practices when in fact their methods remain traditional. [18])

As a result, teachers of privileged students may not only feel less impetus to employ the kind of practices this book has been advocating as ideal, if not prerequisite, for meaningful social justice work, but can in fact develop an aversion to them. Administration and parents can intensify this hesitancy by ratcheting up the pressure to produce the kind of standardized assessment results that, to them, signal "success"—at the very same time that they pressure teachers to scale back on nightly readings and homework load in the name of reducing student stress levels.

As discussed previously, the realities of socioeconomics mean that such assessment scores are unlikely to be jeopardized by innovative pedagogies. So many white, privileged students arrive at high school already more than prepared to meet the low bar of many of these tests. However, the flip side of this reality is that those test scores are just as unlikely to be *boosted* by the use of those pedagogies.

In underprivileged, low-performing schools, increased student achievement on these tests is the proof in the pudding that a teacher can use to justify innovative and atypical practices, but teachers at affluent, high-performing schools won't have that tool in their arsenal. Instead, the weight of tradition, and/or internal politics, will often dictate which teachers and what approaches receive the blessing of their administrators and colleagues. Therefore, would-be innovators need to quickly become conversant in the internal politics of their school as well as the external politics of their community.

Instead of test scores, here's the kind of data you'll need to defend your pedagogy in affluent schools:

- Samples of student work (through the kinds of assessments that reveal higher-order thinking).

- Clear connections to state and Common Core standards, both as evidence of learning and as defense of your practices.
- Public activities, such as holding project fairs and inviting local media. Public recognition is not only rewarding and empowering for students, but also brings good PR to the school and thus makes administrative support more likely.

Building coalitions with fellow faculty is vital; the lone wolf, tradition-breaking teacher so iconic in Hollywood films doesn't last long at real-life high-powered schools. Find like-minded colleagues, especially those who, for whatever reason, have the institutional gravitas to legitimate any teaching approach simply because of who they are.

To the extent that your work/life balance permits, attend meetings and stay until the end. Take minutes. Volunteer for the jobs no one else wants. Help support colleagues in achieving their own goals. Be sure to frequent student athletic events, school plays, PTA fund-raisers; become a known face in the community.

This isn't just a matter of gaining political capital within the institution. These are also the best ways to get to know your colleagues, your students, and their families. It will help you learn the kind of local cultural references vital for constructing analogies and connections for your students, and will help you get to know and develop empathy for your fellow adults in and outside the building. In the end, all of this helps you become a more effective teacher.

That sort of empathy is also necessary for understanding the angst and anguish that undergirds some of the more outrageous behavior from the parents of privileged students.

UNDERSTANDING "LOCO PARENTIS"

Parental involvement in a child's education is one of the largest, if not the largest, determining factors in their academic success.[19] The vast resources of suburban schools do not derive solely from the school budget, but also from the substantial supplementation provided by parents.

* * *

Parental Paradox

Parental involvement was simultaneously one of the greatest aids, and one of the greatest challenges, in my job at Oak Hills. Whenever I needed any resources—new sets of books, bringing a Shakespeare troupe to campus, organizing a TEDx conference—parent and community groups readily came through with funding. On a day when we kept school open despite a bomb threat, a volunteer guard of parents joined the faculty in round-the-clock patrolling the halls. Some of these parents had even kept their children home that day, but had come themselves to help provide security.

Parents volunteer routinely as chaperones for field trips, organizers for student club fund-raisers, and for years provided the entire faculty with a buffet dinner on conference nights. That self-interest plays a role in this generosity does not detract from it; what parent wouldn't take every opportunity, if they could, to make sure their children had the best possible educational experience?

On the other hand, the same flexible professional schedules and proliferation of stay-at-home-parenthood that give affluent families enough free time to be supportive also give them the free time, if they are so inclined, to take independent initiative to "hold teachers accountable."

The following is just a sampling of the large repertoire of stories that teachers at suburban and independent schools shared with me during the course of my research:

- *A parent who brought in a stack of every quiz their child had taken all year and went through them in front of the teacher one by one, calculator out, double-checking their grading.*
- *A parent who, after a teacher confiscated the rubber ball their son was tossing around during class, filed a complaint against that teacher with the principal for "stealing their son's property."*
- *A parent who confronted a health education teacher, demanding that the school's sex-ed class be split in two sections, to be taught differentially: one for the "good" kids and one for the "bad" ones.*
- *A parent who interrupted a class and angrily demanded the teacher step out into the hallway and justify their choice of course readings right then and there.*

Egregious cases like these are thankfully the exception, but they are a near-universal experience for teachers of affluent students.

Nationwide trends[20] demonstrate that parents are invested in their children's education across the socioeconomic and geographic spectrum, but it manifests differently in different socioeconomic settings. Suburban and urban parents, for example, are more likely to directly interact with their children's teachers (including visiting classrooms) than rural parents. This does not mean rural parents are not invested in their children's education—in fact, they attend organized school events (athletic games, school plays, etc.) at a greater rate than either their urban or suburban counterparts.

This picture matches my experience of parent-teacher relations in my rural, at the time working-class, hometown, where schools seemed to me to

operate largely as a black box. One of my elementary school teachers regu-
larly showed up to work with alcohol on his breath and once dangled a
misbehaving student by his ankles out the second-story window. When I told
a friend's mother, her response was something on the order of, "the kid
probably deserved it."

Interestingly enough, when I wound up attending an elite independent
secondary school, teachers seemed to have similar carte blanche; at least for
those of us attending on scholarships, teachers were deities to be appeased,
gatekeepers of our advancement, to whom we had to prove our meritocratic
mettle. Our presence there was precarious, and rocking the boat was seen as
a tremendous risk of biting the charitable hand that fed us. Schools like Oak
Hills are something of a different story, for reasons discussed below.

* * *

Most suburban families are not nearly as wealthy as the self-assured gentry
of private school boarding students, but are still economically and politically
empowered enough to not feel at the mercy of school policy, and educated
enough to be suspicious and critical of those who would claim knowledge of
how to best educate their children. They constitute what Nicholas Lemann, a
Columbia University journalism professor, calls the "Mandarin Class," the
"products of the new formal education system [who] went to outstanding
colleges and then on to professional schools."[21]

Because "practically speaking, what the Mandarins have done is take over
a chunk of territory that was previously controlled by an inbred group of self-
styled gentlemen," they are disliked and viewed as upstarts by that Old
Guard, yet are viewed with equal distaste by the working classes, who "think
of them as privileged, conceited teacher's pets who are prone to concocting
corrupt arrangements behind closed doors."[22] This situation, combined with
the newness (and thus, perceived precariousness) of their high socioeconomic status, produces a certain level of anxiety. Unlike the Old Guard, there is
no sense of inevitability of their children continuing in the lifestyle their
parents had worked so hard to earn, and this anxiety has only intensified
since the Great Recession in 2008.

Parents in affluent districts may therefore harbor mixed feelings about
their children's teachers. They still see teachers as gatekeepers, perhaps of a
better life for their children, but at minimum a continuance of the current
one. Parental respect for teachers, therefore, wars constantly with their suspicion of teachers as nincompoops who someone has inexplicably placed in
charge of their children's future. Perhaps because of the characteristically
low pay and prestige of the teaching field, some parents cannot help but be
plagued on some level by the question that English teacher and slam poet

Taylor Mali summed up as: "What's a kid going to learn from someone who decided his best option in life was to become a teacher?"[23]

Such parents may expect teachers to challenge and prepare their children for the future . . . but perhaps not if doing so conflicts with ensuring their children's smooth movement along the conveyor belt from high school to college. So long as we keep that conveyor moving, parents will spare no effort to support us. But if we "create" bumps or jams along that belt, even if that bump was of the student's own making, at least some parents are going to declare war.

CONSEQUENCES FORBIDDEN

Recall the first chapter's story of Susannah, the "Airplane Girl," whose many unexcused absences were mysteriously "resolved" all of a sudden at the year's end. Oak Hills is no outlier in this practice; across the country, there are comparable schools where as many as 40 percent of students miss 10 to 50 classes a semester and still graduate.[24] Students at affluent schools are less likely to have an enforced dress code (hats and hoodies included) than students in urban schools, and less likely to have their school enforce a no cell-phone policy.[25]

Suburban schools are far less likely to deal with (white) misbehaving students through the use of detentions or suspensions.[26] Suburban teachers shared stories with me of students who routinely parked in teachers' parking spaces without consequence, who committed vandalism on small and large scales, who threatened or even committed acts of physical violence, all of which resulted in little more than a "stern talking to" from a counselor or administrator. An African American or Latinx student in a typical urban school committing some of these same acts would likely have been expelled and/or criminally prosecuted.

It is fortunate that most privileged, white students at affluent schools, most of the time, comply with the basic operational rules of the building, because often when they test the limits, those limits tend to dissolve. Teachers in such schools can find their disciplinary and motivational repertoire restricted to a series of "carrots," as there are few "sticks" that parents will tolerate.

* * *

When the Stakes Are Too High for Learning

"How can you do this to my son's future?" an anguished mother once demanded to know when her son's plagiarized paper earned a zero (which was at the time school policy and not just my own). I had no luck with the argument that her son had been the one to make the poor decision to copy his

essay wholesale off the internet, that he was 15 years old and wasn't it better that he made it now, in a low-stakes environment like school, where he could learn from it?

But this is not a low-stakes environment in the eyes of some parents. As college admissions become increasingly selective, the stakes become "just too high"—this was the explanation I was given once when a parent yanked her daughter out of my course entirely the first time (in January!) she failed an assignment.

The tragedy is just how much this culture hurts or even precludes learning. Without the ability to make mistakes, face consequences, and learn from them, young people cannot mature and grow, emotionally or intellectually.

This aversion is especially intense in classes designated as honors or Advanced Placement. It is not that privileged white students fear hard work; many shuffle six such classes at once, plus a varsity sport and extracurriculars. They routinely forego sleep and use sports drinks and caffeine pills to get through their classes. If assigned a five-page paper, they will sometimes write an eight- or ten-page one.

No, the place where these students are most likely to give pushback is when their teachers ask them questions without clear answers, engage them in discussion of texts with ambiguous meanings. They, and sometimes their parents, will push back on assignments that don't have a clear map of "write these specific things and you will earn an A" to follow. They are masters at crossing t's and dotting i's, and see it as something wrong with our teaching if we ask them to consider and experiment with how a Q, or a Z, or even π could alter the picture. Even though my "infinite revision" policy is designed to make intellectual experimentation a risk-free proposition in my classes, I find that so many students just can't get past their anxieties about their GPA.

This phenomenon, too, is hardly idiosyncratic to Oak Hills. Research has demonstrated that students, especially boys, assigned to honors classes become less likely to push the envelope intellectually, perhaps because they fear any move that would cast doubt upon their worthiness to be in an advanced group.[27] As essayist and former Yale professor William Deresiewicz puts it, "if you're afraid to fail, you're afraid to take risks, which begins to explain the . . . most damning disadvantage of an elite education: that it is profoundly anti-intellectual."[28]

I can't count how many students have told me, in one form or another, how they would love to read more from an author who fascinated them, or to research an area of personal interest as a supplement to the curriculum, or to stay after school for an extended discussion. However, they felt they could do none of this without jeopardizing their ability to complete the assignments that counted for grades.

Or to not complete them, as the case may be.

"Come on, Dr. Nurenberg," a dejected student once told me when I had caught him cheating, and told him that I would rather he have earned a B on his own best efforts than an A based on dishonesty. "If I earn a B, Harvard admissions isn't going to care if I worked hard and earned it. They want to see the A. Period."

That single moment was one of my absolute nadirs, made so by the fact that, in so many ways, this young man had assessed the situation correctly. Standing up for the value of learning, in the middle of this climate, must have cast me in the role of the portly Captain Renault from Casablanca—hands full of his winnings, he shuts down Rick's Café because he is "shocked, shocked to find out there is gambling going on in here."

* * *

As any psychologist will attest, predictable and fair consequences are a vital part of an adolescent's development. Schools and parents should work in concert to provide loving but firm limits and boundaries—despite teenagers' protests (which, to be fair, is their job, too), they suffer mental and emotional distress in an environment without them. Yet schools serving the "Mandarin elite" are moving farther and farther from such accountability, ironically, in the name of students' mental well-being. Meanwhile, schools primarily serving underprivileged students of color spent the last decade enforcing zero-tolerance, high-consequence, school-to-prison pipeline tactics.[29]

Neither extreme is healthy for students; parents at all ends of the socioeconomic and racial spectrum have a shared interest in finding a healthy middle ground for all schools. In this middle ground, children of all races and backgrounds would attend well-resourced schools that promoted learning, including learning from the consequences of their mistakes. But affluent parents can become suspicious of policies that encourage school equality, which they can see as "a serious threat to the birthright of the children of the Mandarin class."[30]

What they might be failing to see is that this "birthright" of privilege is also keeping their children from experiencing important developmental lessons in accountability and resiliency, stunting their growth into confident and capable young adults.

LIBERATING THE PRIVILEGED

Why do people want to become educators?

Anyone who thinks teaching is a cushy job with 2:30 p.m. dismissals and "summers off" is quickly disabused of that notion if they ever try their hand at the profession.

> Despite the conventional wisdom that K–12 teachers work shorter days (the
> average U.S. school day is 6.7 hours, according to the National Center for
> Education Statistics) . . . in addition to a full day in front of the classroom,
> teachers are expected to arrive at school at least an hour before school begins,
> and many stay an average of three to five hours beyond the traditional school
> day for meetings, grading, and other administrative or volunteer activities.
> That doesn't even include the amount of time they spend counseling students,
> serving as role models and doing work that goes above and beyond the tradi-
> tional job description . . . [and] most teachers devote a good portion of their
> summer "break" to preparing for the upcoming school year. That includes two
> to four weeks for continuing education, three weeks for curriculum planning,
> and another four weeks for training, classroom setup and preparation. [31]

This doesn't even take into account the challenge of essentially making five
presentations a day, 180 days a year, with insufficient resources, to an audience whose default preference is to be anywhere and do anything else. This is
all before factoring in the relentless "teacher-bashing" rhetoric daily dis-
played by politicians and other media figures; Donald Trump, Jr.'s public
characterization of teachers as "losers" in February 2019 was a prominent,
but far from atypical, example.

But concurrent with teacher bashing is the equally powerful and pervasive narrative that lionizes amazing teachers who help their students to
transcend lives of deprivation and violence, to love learning, and to acquire
the skills needed for a better future. Usually this translates to images of white
teachers helping urban students of color. Regardless of the insidiously racist,
paternalistic, and often inaccurate strokes in which that picture is painted, it's
one of the few beliefs about teachers—about anything, really—that unites
Americans of all political persuasions.

So who are the amazing teachers of white, privileged students? Those
who enable the Mandarin class to maintain its socioeconomic fortunes? This
is the dominant message suburban teachers receive, and it is a seductive one.
The rewards for doing so are numerous: the respect of peers and community,
fond remembrance by well-resourced families.

It is tempting to follow the path of Professor Slughorn, J. K. Rowling's
teacher from the *Harry Potter* series, who mercenarily makes relationships
with "go-getter" students so he can get favors from them when they later
ascend to positions of influence. There are worse vices to be guilty of. Teaching remains a difficult job, no matter the socioeconomics of the setting, and
the good teaching and mentorship Slughorn gives his promising young
charges is genuine.

But there is a reason why Professors Dumbledore and McGonagall are the
heroic teachers of the *Harry Potter* series, while Slughorn is comic relief.
They are the teachers who, despite every incentive to do otherwise, take risks
and push their students toward challenging acts of personal evolution. They

insist that their students not only excel in their classes but also work toward battling sinister forces both within and beyond the school walls, and provide the inspiration, preparation, and support to help them do that.

As Dumbledore tells Harry, "there will be a time when we must choose between what is easy and what is right,"[32] and he is determined, even when it earns the ire of his superiors and costs him his job, to prepare Harry to make those right choices.

Truly amazing teachers of privileged white students are those who not only help those students acquire skills to be economically competitive, but who also help their students transcend lives of cynicism and strategic compliance to love learning, and to acquire the skills they need to make a better world. Those students' current world is too often one that drives them to eating disorders, nervous breakdowns, and self-harm. Even at its least toxic, it manifests as *weltschmerz*, a world-weariness that no teenager should be burdened by, as Madeline Levine observes in her ever-increasing caseload of affluent teenaged patients:

> [w]hile at first they may not appear to meet strict criteria for a clinical diagnosis, they are certainly unhappy. Most of these adolescents have great difficulty articulating the cause of their distress. They describe "being at loose ends" or "missing something inside." . . . While they are aware that they lead lives of privilege, they take little pleasure from their fortunate circumstances. They lack the enthusiasm typically seen in young people.[33]

This mission, to help students find that "missing something inside," is incredibly difficult. The idea that students' malaise may be the product of the very system that also advantages them is counterintuitive. Teaching students how to identify, critique and, if they so choose, work to change that system requires preparation that few teacher education programs provide.

Teachers of privileged white students must undergo significant, time-consuming, and challenging work to understand their own identity and the history and privilege they inherit, and to develop genuine knowledge about and respect for those they have been raised to see as the "Other," so that they can then guide their students on that same journey. They need to help their students not only learn about the injustices and inequities in society, but also learn what personal relevance and stake those students themselves hold in understanding and combatting those injustices. They need to help their students develop strategies and skills to work for equity without attempting to be "saviors." They have to cocreate democratic, student-centered, and highly discussion-focused spaces, governed by effective norms that permit students to have difficult, emotionally charged conversations in a productive way.

Teachers of privileged white students have to do all of this without unintentionally replicating the very patterns of oppression they are seeking to undermine. They also have to do all of this without getting fired.

Why bother? For the same reason teachers take on any of our many impossible tasks. Because our students need it, and because the reason we are there is to help them.

James Baldwin writes about how privilege traps the privileged in a "history they do not understand; and until they understand it, they cannot be released from it."[34] Social justice education is not just about training the privileged to become benefactors to an oppressed Other. At its best, it is about helping them to recognize the historical and present conditions that perpetuate a system that, in different ways, harms all of us. Our students may go on to teach others, who will then teach still others. This is the faith that all of us—educators, parents and mentors—live by.

The aims and strategies in this book are in some sense aspirational; I certainly don't pull it all off in my own classroom, at least not every day, although on my best days I've done pieces of all of it. Regularly, in my teaching practice and undoubtedly in the course of writing this book, I fail to check my own privilege, I fall victim to my own implicit bias, and I unintentionally reinforce rather than erode inequity.

But fortunately, it's not up to me alone. The debate about whether or not the "master's house can be broken down by the master's tools" is a false one—the world needs both approaches. Remember Freire's and Swalwell's determination that what ultimately serves the cause of social justice most is cooperation across the spectrum of privilege, socioeconomic status, and race. Swalwell writes,

> Because activist allies have made a connection between the oppression of marginalized groups and their own humanization, fighting injustice is not just about helping Others, but improving their own lives. Their privilege . . . is thus seen as a set of resources to be mobilized for the purposes of mutual transformation in societal improvement.[35]

Working with, and if necessary being guided by, marginalized people, privileged white Americans can leverage their advantages to aid those common goals.

I will close by sharing an anecdote about Elena, one of my white eleventh graders who pursued the justice project (described in chapter 6). She picked for her issue of injustice the frequent police shootings of unarmed black men in the United States. For the part of this project that involved identifying and learning from a "local organization or group of people directly affected by the issue who are working to change it," Elena approached an organization affiliated with Black Lives Matter.

At the time, the height of the Ferguson unrest had barely subsided, and sympathy protests were happening around the country. A group of African American students at Oak Hills had even staged a vocal disruption of classes earlier in the year. For her act of activism, Elena joined that local Black Lives Matter group in a protest in downtown Boston with the intention, she later wrote, to just hang back and take notes.

However, according to the narrative in her project journal, a moment came during the protest when the phalanx of police officers present began to advance threateningly upon the crowd. Elena heard an organizer at the megaphone shout, "White allies to the front!" and soon found herself stepping forward, holding hands with other white people, forming a barrier between the police and the demonstrators of color. After a moment, the police ceased their forward march. After a few more moments, the protest chants resumed, and the police encroached no further.

In her reflections, Elena realized that she had used her privilege, along with her fellow white protesters, to aid the cause of justice by maintaining a safe space for her more marginalized partners to continue making their own voices heard. She hadn't grabbed the microphone, hadn't tried to take over the protest and start speaking "for" the marchers of color. In short, Elena had demonstrated she understood what it meant to be an Activist Ally, in a more genuine, authentic, and powerful way than any classroom exercise or written exam could reveal.

What stands out most in my mind, though, was her demeanor while reporting the event to the class the next day. Elena had always presented as a shy, taciturn girl. For months she had been struggling with depression in the wake of a sports-related concussion that had kept her from participating in the after-school athletics that she described as the best part of school. She had missed a number of classes that semester for "mental health days." But the day after the protest, Elena presented as ebullient, radiant, speaking with a confidence I had never before seen her express.

She looked, and felt, empowered. I don't think it an exaggeration to say that, in the course of learning and pursuing social justice, she hadn't just aided a group of marginalized people—she had liberated herself. It was a beautiful sight to see.

Schools have an opportunity, and a duty, to help all students—the privileged included—engage with this pedagogy of freedom.

NOTES

1. In "Social Aims," 1875, republished in Emerson, 1917.
2. Swalwell, 2013, 124.
3. Ibid., 112–13
4. Freire, 2000, 74.
5. Ibid., 31.
6. Rock, Gregg, Ellis, and Gable, 2008, 32.
7. See Stiggins, 2005.
8. Emdin, 2017, 288.

9. Jablon, 2014, 41.

10. Swalwell, 2013, 112–13.

11. Swalwell, 112. Although this book lacks the space to treat the topic of restorative justice (RJ) mechanisms in detail, there is a rich literature on how RJ can help create a more equitable and inclusive classroom and school disciplinary culture.

12. Delmont, 2016.

13. Kay, 2018, 228–9.

14. Ibid.

15. The College Board, 2013.

16. Tienken, Colella, Angelillo, Fox, McCahill, and Wolfe, 2017.

17. Pope and Levine, 2013, review a number of studies on this issue. Their article offers an in-depth critique of the AP exams from a number of other angles as well. And yes, I realize there is some irony in the authors of this work being from Challenge Success, a program I referred to somewhat disparagingly earlier in this book. The world is a complicated place. See also Wainer, 2011; Ferenstein and Hershbein, 2016.

18. de Waal-Lucas, 2007.

19. Hill and Tyson, 2009.

20. Prater, Bermúdez, and Owens, 1997; Witte and Sheridan, 2011.

21. Lemann, 2000, 188.

22. Ibid.

23. Mali, 2002.

24. St. George and Moyer, 2019.

25. DePina, 2003.

26. Fenning and Rose, 2007; Skiba et al., 2012; Wallace, Goodkind, Wallace, and Bachman, 2008.

27. Catsambis, Mulkey, and Crain, 2001.

28. Deresiewicz, 2008.

29. Thankfully, urban schools are now finally moving away from such policies. See Falk, 2016.

30. LaPiana, 2000.

31. Murray, 2013.

32. Rowling, 2002, 724.

33. Levine, 2006.

34. Baldwin, 1963/1985, 8.

35. Swalwell, 2013, 100.

Afterword

When I first began working at Oak Hills, we didn't hold classes on the Jewish High Holidays, but eventually a faculty meeting was convened to debate the merits of changing that policy, ostensibly so the school year could end earlier in June. I was silent during this debate. I didn't have it in me to be the "Jewish Avenger" that day. I did, however, eventually propose that the motion on the floor, "Elimination of Religious Holidays," be renamed to reflect what it was really about: "Elimination of *Jewish* Religious Holidays." After all, no one was putting Christmas on the chopping block.

The response, predictably, was similar to the sentiments expressed in those student letters about the Colors Forum (see chapter 6); calling attention to the inequity was itself considered an attack.

A white, gentile colleague rose to his feet, face red with the same kind of anger I recognized all too well from my white students, and said, "Oh, come on. Christmas is an *American* holiday!"

I didn't feel like taking the bait, so I kept quiet.

But then a Christian colleague rose up right after and said, "Excuse me, but I find that statement offensive. Who are you to say what holidays are or aren't American?"

The tenor of the discussion changed immediately. Now that another Christian had voiced the same concern I had, the issue on the floor had been magically transformed from David Nurenberg's "Jewish problem," easily dismissible, into a problem affecting the entire community, one that the entire community now needed to solve.

Right or wrong, voices of privileged allies are sometimes prerequisite legitimating "keys" for unlocking the gates of justice. That is why it is so vital to have teachers willing and able to help privileged white students develop the skills to become such allies. It is not a matter of arguing that this mission is, or is not, as vital as training teachers for educating disadvantaged children for academic and career success. Rather, I am arguing we may never be able to accomplish the latter without also pursuing the former.

Venture capitalist Nick Hanauer, founder of the public-policy incubator Civic Ventures and the nonprofit League of Education Voters, shared in an *Atlantic* article the realization he had come to after he had

> devoted countless hours and millions of dollars to the simple idea that if we improved our schools . . . American children, especially those in low-income and working-class communities, would start learning again . . . poverty and inequality would decrease, and public commitment to democracy would be restored. [1]

Hanauer eventually came to regard this idea as "tragically misguided," and that "we have confused a symptom—educational inequality—with the underlying disease: economic inequality." He worries that the popular crusade to "save" America's most underprivileged students "appeals to the wealthy and powerful because it tells us what we want to hear: that we can help restore shared prosperity without sharing our wealth or power." Ultimately, he writes, a truly just America "will require wealthy people to not merely give more, but take less."[2]

Throughout this book I have tried to make the case that the only way the privileged will agree to take less, to share more power, is if they see this to be in their best interests, and if they actually learn the specific mechanisms of how to do so.

I will freely acknowledge that this effort, written by a single white author, does not—despite my best attempts to acknowledge, integrate, and amplify many voices of people of color throughout—represent the kind of cross-racial, cross-privilege partnership necessary to fully address injustice and inequity.

I therefore invite my reader to consider this book as one of those "keys," like the one my Christian colleague provided at the faculty meeting, a privileged white "foot in the door" that can open it wider to admit further discourse and ideas. If anyone else finds it even slightly easier to fit through that doorway because of what I've done, I will consider my efforts worthwhile.

NOTES

1. Hanauer, 2019.
2. Ibid.

Bibliography

"5 Keys to Rigorous Project-Based Learning." *Edutopia*, June 25, 2014. https://www.edutopia. org/video/5-keys-rigorous-project-based-learning.

"AAA Statement on Race." American Anthropological Association, May 17, 1998. https:// www.americananthro.org/ConnectWithAAA/Content.aspx?ItemNumber=2583.

Abong, Fred. "The Fallacy of the Empathic Fallacy: Unpacking 'Nope.'" *The Savage Philosopher* blog), May 7, 2017. http://www.fredabong.com/blog/2017/5/7/the-fallacy-of-the-empathic-fallacy-unpacking-nope.

Abourjilie, Charlie. *Developing Character for Classroom Success: Strategies to Increase Responsibility, Achievement and Motivation in Secondary Students.* Boone, NC: Character Development Group, 2000.

Abudi, Gina. "The Five Stages of Project Team Development." Project-Management.com, October 9, 2018. https://project-management.com/the-five-stages-of-project-team-development/.

Achebe, Chinua. *Things Fall Apart.* New York: Penguin, 1994 (first published 1958).

Adichie, Chimamanda Ngozi. "The Danger of a Single Story." TEDGlobal, 2009. https://www. ted.com/talks/chimamanda_adichie_the_danger_of_a_single_story/transcript?language=en.

———. "The Headstrong Historian." *New Yorker*, June 23, 2008. https://www.newyorker. com/magazine/2008/06/23/the-headstrong-historian.

Ahmed, Sara. "A Phenomenology of Whiteness." *Feminist Theory* 8, no. 2 (2007): 149–68.

Aisch, Gregor, Larry Buchanan, Amanda Cox, and Kevin Quealy. "Some Colleges Have More Students from the Top 1 Percent Than the Bottom 60. Find Yours." *New York Times*, January 18, 2017. https://www.nytimes.com/interactive/2017/01/18/upshot/some-colleges-have-more-students-from-the-top-1-percent-than-the-bottom-60.html.

American Civil Liberties Union. *Free Speech Rights for Public School Teachers.* ACLU Washington, October 9, 2015. https://www.aclu-wa.org/news/free-speech-rights-public-school-teachers.

American Mosaic Project. "The Role of Prejudice and Discrimination in Americans' Explanations of Black Disadvantage and White Privilege." University of Minnesota, 2003. https:// www.racialequitytools.org/resourcefiles/uminnesota.pdf.

Anderson, Elijah. "The White Space." *Sociology of Race and Ethnicity* 1, no. 1 (2015): 10–21. https://sociology.yale.edu/sites/default/files/pages_from_sre-11_rev5_printer_files.pdf.

Applebee, A. N. *Book-Length Works Taught in High School English Courses.* ERIC Clearinghouse on Reading and Communication Skills, 1990.

Baldwin, J. *The Fire Next Time.* New York: The Modern Library, 1985 (first published 1963).

———. "On Being 'White'. . . and Other Lies." In *Black on White: Black Writers on What It Means to Be White*, ed. David R. Roediger. New York: Schocken Books, 1998. https:// collectiveliberation.org/wp-content/uploads/2013/01/Baldwin_On_Being_White.pdf.

Baloche. Linda, *The Cooperative Classroom: Empowering Learning*. Upper Saddle River, NJ: Pearson, 1997.

Barlow, Rich. "BU Research: A Riddle Reveals Depth of Gender Bias." *BU Today*, January 16, 2014. https://www.bu.edu/today/2014/bu-research-riddle-reveals-the-depth-of-gender-bias/.

Bartolomé, Lilia. "Beyond the Methods Fetish: Toward a Humanizing Pedagogy." *Harvard Educational Review*, Summer 1994. https://www.hepg.org/her-home/issues/harvard-educational-review-volume-64,-issue-2/herarticle/toward-a-humanizing-pedagogy_349.

Bass, B., I. Fette, P. Mans, M. Seth, J. Sullivan, and P. Washburn. "News bias explored: The art of reading the news." University of Michigan, 2003. http://umich.edu/~newsbias/manifestations.html

Battle, E. S., and J. B. Rotter. "Children's Feelings of Personal Control as Related to Social Class and Ethnic Group." *Journal of Personality* 3, no. 4 (1963): 482–90.

Benz, Robert J. "Teaching White Supremacy: How Textbooks Have Shaped Our Attitudes on Race." *Huffpost.* November 19, 2017. https://www.huffingtonpost.com/entry/teaching-white-supremacy-how-textbooks-have-shaped_us_5a0e4f65e4b023121e0e9142.

"Best Practices to Reduce Stereotype Threat in the Classroom." Wayne State Office for Teaching and Learning, March 2014. https://otl.wayne.edu/teaching/best_practices_to_reduce_stereotype_threat_in_the_classroom.pdf.

Bethea, Lamar. "What It's Like Being the Only Black Student in Class." *The Tab*, May 31, 2016. https://thetab.com/us/2016/05/31/like-black-student-class-11145.

Bishop, Rudine Sims. "Mirrors, Windows, & Sliding Glass Doors." *Perspectives* 6, no. 3 (1990): ix–xi. Reprinted by *Prism*. http://prism.scholarslab.org/prisms/35977eaa-6c50-11e7-9dec-005056b3784e/visualize?locale=es.

Black Student Union, Cambridge Rindge and Latin School. "Cambridge's Minority Reports: Volume 1." YouTube, accessed May 5, 2019. https://www.youtube.com/watch?v=zV43Bw58jSQ.

Bleiberg, Efrain. "Normal and Pathological Narcissism in Adolescence." *American Journal of Psychotherapy* 48, no. 1 (1994): 30–51.

Blumenfeld, Warren. "Dominant Group Privilege: Contextual, Conditional, Intersectional." The Good Men Project, September 21, 2013. https://goodmenproject.com/social-justice-2/cc-dominant-group-privilege-contextual-conditional-intersectional/.

Bonilla-Silva, E. *Racism without Racists: Color-Blind Racism and the Persistence of Racial Inequality in America*. Lanham, MD: Rowman & Littlefield, 2017.

Boulding, Elise. *Building a Global Civic Culture: Education for an Interdependent World*. Syracuse, NY: Syracuse University Press, 1990.

Brasher, Joan. "Teacher's Race Affects Gifted Program Selections." *Research News @Vanderbilt*, January 18, 2016. https://news.vanderbilt.edu/2016/01/18/teachers-race-affects-gifted-program-selections/.

Bringle, R., and J. Hatcher. "A Service Learning Curriculum for Faculty." *Michigan Journal of Community Service-Learning* 2 (1995): 112–22.

Brown, Jennifer. "He Seemed to Have It All: Arapahoe High School Senior's Suicide Rattles Emotionally Fatigued, Frightened Community. Colorado's Teen Suicide Rates Have Reached a Crisis Level." *Colorado Sun*, October 25, 2018.

Browne, Anthony. *Voices in the Park*. New York: DK Publishing, 2001.

Bui, Quoctrung, and Conor Dougherty. "Good Schools, Affordable Homes: Finding Suburban Sweet Spots." *New York Times.* March 30, 2017. https://www.nytimes.com/interactive/2017/03/30/upshot/good-schools-affordable-homes-suburban-sweet-spots.html?_r=0.

Bump, Philip. "The Source of Black Poverty Isn't Black Culture, It's American Culture." *The Atlantic*, April 1, 2014. https://www.theatlantic.com/politics/archive/2014/04/the-source-of-black-poverty-isnt-black-culture-its-american-culture/359937/.

Burden, P. *Classroom Management: Creating a Successful K–12 Learning Community*. New York: John Wiley & Sons, 2016.

Butin, D. W. "Of What Use Is It? Multiple Conceptualizations of Service Learning within Education." *Teachers College Record* 105, no. 9 (2003): 1674–92.

Butler, Valerie. "Kicking It Up a Notch: Becoming a Culturally Relevant Science Educator." *The Node* (blog), January 19, 2017. http://thenode.biologists.com/kicking-notch-becoming-culturally-relevant-science-educator/education/.

California Newsreel. "Race: The Power of an Illusion: Online Companion" PBS, 2003. http://www.pbs.org/race/000_General/000_00-Home.htm.

Carpenter, Louise. "Revealed: The Science Behind Teenage Laziness," *Telegraph*, February 14, 2015. http://www.telegraph.co.uk/news/science/sciencenews/11410483/Revealed-the-sci
ence-behind-teenage-laziness.htm.

Catsambis, S., L. Mulkey, and R. Crain. "For Better or For Worse? A Nationwide Study of the Social Psychological Effects of Gender and Ability Grouping in Mathematics." *Social Psychology of Education* 5, no. 1 (2001): 83-115.

Chall, J. S. *The Academic Achievement Challenge: What Really Works in the Classroom?* New York: Guilford, 2000.

"Challenge Day." Challenge Day, n.d. Accessed April 26, 2019. https://www.challengeday.org/our-programs/schools/#challengeday.

"Challenge Success." Challenge Success, n.d. Accessed April 26, 2019. http://www.challengesuccess.org/.

Chang, A. The data proves that school segregation is getting worse. Vox, 2018, March 15. Retrieved January 3, 2020 from https://www.vox.com/2018/3/5/17080218/ school-segrega-tion-getting-worse-data

Chicago: Glass, Ira. "548: Cops see it differently, Part two." *This American Life*. Chicago Public Media, Feb. 13, 2015.

Chodos, Alan. "The Lessons of March 4." *Inside Higher Ed*, March 4, 2019. https://www.insidehighered.com/views/2019/03/04/50th-anniversary-protest-scientists-points-similarities-and-differences-position.

Chowkwanyun, Merlin, and Jordan Segall. "The Rise of the Majority-Asian Suburb." *The Atlantic*, August 24, 2012. https://www.theatlantic.com/politics/archive/2012/08/the-rise-of-the-majority-asian-suburb/428610/.

Cole, Nicki Lisa. "Does Hollywood Have a Diversity Problem?" ThoughtCo, March 18, 2017. https://www.thoughtco.com/diversity-in-hollywood-3026690.

Cole, Teju. "The White-Savior Industrial Complex." *The Atlantic*, March 21, 2012. https://www.theatlantic.com/international/archive/2012/03/the-white-savior-industrial-complex/254843/.

"Collaborative Culture: Norms." EL Education, n.d. Accessed May 10, 2019. https://eleducation.org/resources/collaborative-culture-norms.

The College Board. "Total Group Profile Report." CollegeBoard.org, 2013. http://secure-media.collegeboard.org/digitalServices/pdf/research/2013/TotalGroup-2013.pdf.

Conway, Michael. "The Problem with History Classes." *The Atlantic*, March 16, 2015. https://www.theatlantic.com/education/archive/2015/03/the-problem-with-history-classes/387823/.

Cooper, Alexia, and Erica L. Smith. "Homicide Trends in the United States, 1980–2008." Bureau of Justice Statistics, November 2011. https://www.bjs.gov/content/pub/pdf/htus8008.pdf.

Costa, Arthur L., and Bena Kallick, eds. *Learning and Leading with Habits of Mind: 16 Essential Characteristics for Success*. ASCD, 2008. http://www.ascd.org/publications/books/108008/chapters/Learning-Through-Reflection.aspx.

Council for American Private Education. "Facts and Studies." CAPENET, 2016. http://www.capenet.org/facts.html.

Crenshaw, Kimberlé Williams, Priscilla Ocen, and Jyoti Nanda. "Black Girls Matter: Pushed Out, Overpoliced, and Underprotected." African American Policy Forum, 2015. http://static1.squarespace.com/static/53f20d90e4b0b80451158d8c/t/54d23be0e4b0bb6a8002fb97/1423064032396/BlackGirlsMatter_Report.pdf.

Crosley-Corcoran, Gina. "Explaining White Privilege to a Broke White Person." *Huffpost*, May 8, 2014. https://www.huffingtonpost.com/gina-crosleycorcoran/explaining-white-privilege-to-a-broke-white-person_b_5269255.html.

Cross, Amanda. "My Personal Experience with Being the Only Black Student in Class." *The Happy Arkansan* (blog), August 4, 2017. https://thehappyarkansan.com/blog/only-black-student-in-class/.

Cruz, N. I., and D. E. Giles, Jr. "Where's the Community in Service-Learning Research?" *Michigan Journal of Community Service Learning* 7 (2000): 28–34.

Dahl, Natalie. "How to Talk about White Privilege with White People." FreshU, 2017. https://www.freshu.io/natalie-dahl/how-to-talk-about-white-privilege-with-white-people.

D'Ambrosio, U. "Ethnomathematics and Its Place in the History and Pedagogy of Mathematics," in *Ethnomathematics: Challenging Eurocentrism in Mathematics Education*, ed. A. B. Powell and M. Frankenstein, 13–24. Albany: State University of New York Press, 1997.

de Bono, E. *De Bono's Thinking Course*. London: MICA Management, 1994.

Delgado, Richard, and Jean Stefancic. "Images of the Outsider in American Law and Culture: Can Free Expression Remedy Systemic Social Ills?" *Cornell Law Review* 77 (1992): 1258.

Delialioğlu, Ömer. "Student Engagement in Blended Learning Environments with Lecture-Based and Problem-Based Instructional Approaches." *Journal of Educational Technology & Society* 15, no. 3 (2012): 310–22.

Delmont, Matthew. "When Black Voters Exited Left." *The Atlantic*, March 31, 2016. https://www.theatlantic.com/politics/archive/2016/03/exit-left/476190/.

DePina, A. "Comparing Suburban School Culture in Metropolitan Hartford: How Does the Formal and Hidden Curriculum Vary across Two High Schools?" Educational Studies Senior Research Project. Hartford, CT: Trinity College, 2003.

Deresiewicz, W. "The Disadvantages of an Elite Education." *American Scholar*, June 1, 2008. https://theamericanscholar.org/the-disadvantages-of-an-elite-education/#.XfpnEGRKg2w.

Devine, Patricia G., Patrick S. Forscher, Anthony J. Austin, and William T. L. Cox. "Long-Term Reduction in Implicit Race Bias: A Prejudice Habit-Breaking Intervention." *Journal of Experimental and Social Psychology* 48, no. 6 (2012). https://www.ncbi.nlm.nih.gov/pmc/articles/PMC3603687/.

de Waal-Lucas, A. "Teaching in Isolation: An examination of the Treatment of Multicultural Content in a Predominantly White and Affluent Suburban School." *Social Studies Research and Practice* 2, no. 1 (2007): 1–21.

DiAngelo, R. *White Fragility: Why It's so Hard for White People to Talk about Racism*. Boston: Beacon Press, 2018.

"District Progress Report." Wellesley Public Schools, 2018. https://wellesleyps.org/district-information/district-progress-report/.

Du Bois, W. E. B. *Black Reconstruction in America, 1860–1880*. New York: Free Press, 1995 (first published 1935).

Edmondson, Ella L. J., and Nkomo, Stella M. *Our Separate Ways: Black and White Women and the Struggle for Professional Identity*. Cambridge, MA: Harvard Business Review Press, 2003.

Edutopia. "Applying Math Skills to a Real-World Problem." YouTube, September 23, 2010. https://www.youtube.com/watch?v=hxufdpcfpJY.

Eligon, John. "The 'Some of My Best Friends Are Black' Defense." *New York Times*, February 16, 2019. https://www.nytimes.com/2019/02/16/sunday-review/ralph-northam-blackface-friends.html.

Emdin, Christopher. *For White Folks Who Teach in the Hood . . . and the Rest of Y'all Too*. Boston: Beacon Press, 2017.

Emerson, R. W. *Letters and Social Aims* (Vol. 8). New York: Houghton, Mifflin, 1917.

Falk, Terry. "Why Schools Are Abandoning Zero Tolerance." *Urban Milwaukee*, September 8, 2016. https://urbanmilwaukee.com/2016/09/08/op-ed-why-schools-are-abandoning-zero-tolerance/.

Farber, Katy. "Reflecting on Your PBL." Tarrant Institute for Innovative Education, May 9, 2018. https://tiie.w3.uvm.edu/blog/reflecting-on-your-pbl-how-did-it-go/#.XKd-Y-tKjdc.

Fellner, James. "Decades of Disparity: Drug Arrests and Race in the United States." Human Rights Watch, March 2, 2009. https://www.hrw.org/report/2009/03/02/decades-disparity/drug-arrests-and-race-united-states#_ftn21.

Fenning, P., and J. Rose. Overrepresentation of African American students in exclusionary discipline the role of school policy. *Urban Education* 42, no. 6 (2007): 536–559.

Ferenstein, Gregory, and Hershbein, Brad. "How Important Are High School Courses to College Performance? Less Than You Might Think." Brookings Institution, July 20, 2016. https://www.brookings.edu/blog/brown-center-chalkboard/2016/07/20/how-important-are-high-school-courses-to-college-performance-less-than-you-might-think/.

Fernandez, Manny, and Christine Hauser. "Texas Mom Teaches Textbook Company a Lesson on Accuracy." *New York Times*, October 5, 2015. https://www.nytimes.com/2015/10/06/us/publisher-promises-revisions-after-textbook-refers-to-african-slaves-as-workers.html.

Fernando, Spencer. "It's Time to Stop with the Microaggressions BS." SpencerFernando.com, February 3, 2017. https://www.spencerfernando.com/2017/02/03/microaggressions-bs-political-correctness/.

Foster, Deborah. "A Guide to White Privilege for White People Who Think They've Never Had Any." Politicus USA, January 26, 2014. http://www.politicususa.com/2014/01/26/guide-white-privilege-white-people-theyve.html.

Francis, David R. "Employers' Replies to Racial Names." National Bureau of Economic Research, September 2003. https://www.nber.org/digest/sep03/w9873.html.

Freire, Paolo. *Pedagogy of Freedom: Ethics, Democracy, and Civic Courage.* Lanham, MD: Rowman & Littlefield, 1998 (first published 1974).

———. *Pedagogy of the Oppressed.* New York: Continuum, 2000 (first published 1970).

Fugard, Athol. *Master Harold . . . and the Boys.* New York: Viking Penguin, 1984.

Fusion Comedy. "How Microaggressions Are Like Mosquito Bites—Same Difference." YouTube, October 5, 2016. https://www.youtube.com/watch?time_continue=3&v=hDd3bzA7450.

Gamoran, Adam. "The Variable Effects of High School Tracking." *American Sociological Review* 57, no. 6 (1992): 812–28.

Geary, Daniel. *Beyond Civil Rights: The Moynihan Report and Its Legacy.* Philadelphia: University of Pennsylvania Press, 2015.

Gilboy, M. B., S. Heinerichs, and G. Pazzaglia. Enhancing Student Engagement Using the Flipped Classroom. *Journal of Nutrition Education and Behavior* 47, no. 1 (2015): 109–14.

Glass, Ira. "683: Beer Summit." *This American Life.* Chicago Public Media, September 20, 2019. https://www.thisamericanlife.org/683/beer-summit.

Goodman, Diane. "Cultural Competence for Social Justice." DianeGoodman.com, 2013. http://www.dianegoodman.com/documents/Cultural_Competence_for_Social_Justice-handout.pdf.

———. *Promoting Diversity and Social Justice: Educating People from Privileged Groups.* New York: Routledge, 2011.

"Gordon Allport's Contact Hypothesis." Facing History and Ourselves, n.d. Accessed May 12, 2019. https://www.facinghistory.org/sounds-change/gordon-allports-contact-hypothesis.

Gordon, Amelia, and Derek Burtch. "Give Students the Power to Be Change Agents." Erase the Space, n.d. Accessed May 12, 2019. https://www.erasethespace.org/about-us.

Gordon, B. "Knowledge Construction, Competing Critical Theories, and Education." In *Handbook of Research on Multicultural Education*, ed. J. Banks and C. Banks, 184–99. New York: Macmillan, 1985.

Gould, Elise, and Jessica Schieder. "Poverty Persists 50 years after the Poor People's Campaign." Economic Policy Institute, May 17, 2018. https://www.epi.org/publication/poverty-persists-50-years-after-the-poor-peoples-campaign-black-poverty-rates-are-more-than-twice-as-high-as-white-poverty-rates/.

Grant, Laurens, dir. "Stay Woke: The Black Lives Matter Movement." Documentary, 2016. https://www.youtube.com/watch?v=-QukU6_VWk8.

Graves, Joe. "Science and Social Justice." *Beacon* (blog), August 25, 2016. https://www3.beacon-center.org/blog/2016/08/25/science-and-social-justice/.

Great Schools Partnership. "21st Century Skills." Glossary of Education Reform, 2016. https://www.edglossary.org/21st-century-skills/.

Gutiérrez, Rochelle. "Is the Multiculturalization of Mathematics Doing Us More Harm Than Good?" In *Multicultural Curriculum: New Directions for Social Theory, Practice, and Policy*, ed. Ram Mahalingam and Cameron McCarthy, 199–221. New York: Routledge, 2013.

Gutstein, Eric. "Home Buying While Brown or Black: Teaching Mathematics for Racial Justice." In *Rethinking Mathematics: Teaching Social Justice by the Numbers*, ed. Eric Gutstein and Bob Peterson, 62–63. Milwaukee, WI: Rethinking Schools, 2013. https://eclass.edc.uoc.gr/modules/document/file.php/PTDE110/MATH%20AND%20SOCIAL%20JUSTICE.pdf.

Gyasi, Yaa. *Homegoing*. New York: Vintage, 2016.

Hammond, Claudia. "Despising the Poor." *The Psychologist*, May 11, 2016. https://thepsychologist.bps.org.uk/despising-poor.

Hammond, Zaretta. "Four Tools for Interrupting Implicit Bias." Culturally Responsive Teaching and the Brain, April 9, 2015. https://crtandthebrain.com/four-tools-for-interrupting-implicit-bias/.

Hampton, Henry, dir. *Eyes on the Prize II: America at the Racial Crossroads, 1965–1985*. Alexandria, VA: PBS Home Video, 2010 (originally released 1990).

Hanauer, Eric. "Better Schools Won't Fix America." *The Atlantic*, July 2019. https://www.theatlantic.com/magazine/archive/2019/07/education-isnt-enough/590611/.

Harris, Fred, and Alan Curtis. "The Unmet Promise of Equality." *New York Times*, February 28, 2018. https://www.nytimes.com/interactive/2018/02/28/opinion/the-unmet-promise-of-equality.html.

Heer, Nick. "Diversity of Tech Companies by the Numbers: 2016 Edition." Pixelenvy. August 9, 2016. https://pxlnv.com/blog/diversity-of-tech-companies-by-the-numbers-2016/.

Hess, Diana, and Paula McAvoy. *The Political Classroom: Evidence and Ethics in Democratic Education*. New York: Routledge, 2014.

Hill, Nancy E., and Diana F. Tyson. "Parental Involvement in Middle School: A Meta-Analytic Assessment of the Strategies That Promote Achievement." *Developmental Psychology* 45, no. 3 (2009): 740–63. https://www.ncbi.nlm.nih.gov/pmc/articles/PMC2782391/.

Hobson, Mellody. "Color Blind or Color Brave?" TED2014, March 2014. https://www.ted.com/talks/mellody_hobson_color_blind_or_color_brave/up-next?language=en.

Hoenig, Chris. "Major League White: How Pro Sports Aren't What They Seem." DiversityInc, April 30, 2014. https://www.diversityinc.com/news/major-league-white-pro-sports-arent-seem.

Hong, Lu, and Scott E. Page. "Groups of Diverse Problem Solvers Can Outperform Groups of High-Ability Problem Solvers." *Proceedings of the National Academy of Sciences*, November 16, 2004. https://www.pnas.org/content/101/46/16385.full.

"How Racist Is Boston?" *The Daily Show with Trevor Noah*, September 12, 2018. http://www.cc.com/video-clips/xjpyqi/the-daily-show-with-trevor-noah-how-racist-is-boston-.

Hyde, Jesse. "The Lone Peak Story: What You Didn't Know about Affluence and Teen Suicide." *Deseret News*, December 14, 2016.

Hyland, Nora E. "Detracking in the Social Studies: A Path to a More Democratic Education?" *Theory into Practice* 45, no. 1 (2006): 64–71.

"The Illusion of Race." AAAS Science Net Links, n.d. Accessed May 10, 2019. http://sciencenetlinks.com/lessons/the-illusion-of-race/.

Ingolfsland, Jason. "25 Richest Celebrities with the Highest Net Worth." List25, 2019. https://list25.com/25-richest-celebrities-with-the-highest-net-worth/.

Ingraham, Christopher. "Black Men Sentenced to More Time for Committing the Exact Same Crime as a White Person, Study Finds." *Washington Post*, November 16, 2017. https://www.washingtonpost.com/news/wonk/wp/2017/11/16/black-men-sentenced-to-more-time-for-committing-the-exact-same-crime-as-a-white-person-study-finds/?utm_term=.261d6eb70d87.

Jablon, Paul C. "Analogous Interrelationships and Role-Playing: Engaging the Previously Disengaged in Science." Unpublished paper presented at the Association for Science Teacher Education international conference, Sacramento, California, January 2010.

———. *The Synergy of Inquiry*. Huntington Beach, CA: Shell Education, 2014.

Joelson, Richard. "Locus of Control." *Psychology Today*, August 2, 2017. https://www.psychologytoday.com/us/blog/moments-matter/201708/locus-control.

Johnson, David W., and Roger T. Johnson. *Teaching Students to Be Peacemakers*. Minneapolis: Interaction Book Company, 1997.

Kang, Sonia, Katy DeCelles, András Tilcsik, and Sora Jun. "Whitened Résumés: Race and Self-Presentation in the Labor Market." University of Toronto, 2016. http://www-2.rotman.utoronto.ca/facbios/file/Whitening%20MS%20R2%20Accepted.pdf.

Kay, Matthew R. *Not Light, but Fire: How to Lead Meaningful Race Conversations in the Classroom*. Portsmouth, NH: Stenhouse Publishers, 2018.

Kelsky, Karen. "How to Support Students of Color." *Chronicle Vitae*, January 31, 2017. https://chroniclevitae.com/news/1683-how-to-support-students-of-color.

Khan, Shamus Rahman. *Privilege: The Making of an Adolescent Elite at St. Paul's School*. Princeton, NJ: Princeton University Press, 2012.

Kohl, Herbert. *I Won't Learn from You: And Other Thoughts on Creative Maladjustment*. New York: The New Press, 1995.

Krehbiel, Randy. "Oklahoma Legislative Committee Questions Legality of Advanced Placement Courses in Public Schools." *Tulsa World*, February 17, 2015. https://www.tulsaworld.com/news/government/oklahoma-legislative-committee-questions-legality-of-advanced-placement-courses-in/article_2b257556-b62c-5a92-862e-8e9821a29bbc.html.

Kriedler, W. *Conflict Resolution in the Middle School: A Curriculum and Teaching Guide*. Cambridge, MA: Educators for Social Responsibility, 1994.

Ladson-Billings, Gloria. "Just What Is Critical Race Theory and What's It Doing in a Nice Field Like Education?" *International Journal of Qualitative Studies in Education* 11, no. 1 (1998): 7–24.

Lander, Christian. *Stuff White People Like: A Definitive Guide to the Unique Taste of Millions*. New York: Random House, 2008.

LaPiana, William P. "Testing, Class, and Material Success, or How We Got to Be Professors." Humanities and Social Sciences Net, August 2000. https://www.h-net.org/reviews/showrev.php?id=4403.

Larmer, John, and John R. Mergendoller. "The Main Course, Not Dessert." Buck Institute for Education, 2011. https://www.bie.org/object/document/main_course_not_dessert.

Larmer, J., J. Mergendoller, J., and S. Boss. *Setting the Standard for Project-Based Learning*. Alexandria, VA: Association for Supervision and Curriculum Development, 2015.

"Lateral Thinking in Maths: Why You Cannot Cram for a Maths Exam." BestTuition. January 4, 2018. https://besttuition.com.au/2018/01/04/lateral-thinking-in-maths-why-you-cannot-cram-for-a-maths-exam/.

Lee, H. D. P. *The Republic*. New York: Penguin, 2003.

Lemann, Nicholas. "America's New Class System." *TIME*, June 24, 2001. http://content.time.com/time/magazine/article/0,9171,135534,00.html.

———. *The Big Test*. New York: Farrar, Straus and Giroux, 2000.

Levine, Madeline. "The Price of Privilege Exerpt [sic]." *San Francisco Chronicle*, June 5, 2006. http://madelinelevine.wpengine.com/the-price-of-privilege-exerpt/.

Lewis, Amanda E., and John B. Diamond. *Despite the Best Intentions: How Racial Inequality Thrives in Good Schools*. Oxford: Oxford University Press, 2015.

Lieber, Carol Miller. *Conflict Resolution in the High School: 36 Lessons*. Cambridge, MA: Educators for Social Responsibility, 1998.

———. *Getting Classroom Management RIGHT: Guided Discipline and Personalized Support in Secondary Schools*. Cambridge, MA: Educators for Social Responsibility, 2009.

Loewen, James W. *Lies My Teacher Told Me: Everything Your American History Textbook Got Wrong*. New York: The New Press, 1995.

Loewen, James, and Edward Sebesta, eds. *The Confederate and Neo-Confederate Reader: The "Great Truth" about the "Lost Cause."* Oxford: University Press of Mississippi, 2010.

Loewus, Liana. "The Nation's Teaching Force Is Still Mostly White and Female." *Edweek*, August 15, 2017. https://www.edweek.org/ew/articles/2017/08/15/the-nations-teaching-force-is-still-mostly.html.

Logan, John R., and Julia Burdick-Will. "School Segregation and Disparities in Urban, Suburban, and Rural Areas." *Annals of the American Academy of Political and Social Science* 674, no. 1 (2017): 199–216. https://www.ncbi.nlm.nih.gov/pmc/articles/PMC5804745/.

Lopez, German. "Black Kids Are Way More Likely to Be Punished in School Than White Kids, Study Finds." *Vox,* April 5, 2018. https://www.vox.com/identities/2018/4/5/17199810/school-discipline-race-racism-gao.

Luthar, Suniya S., Phillip J. Small, and Lucia Ciciolla. "Adolescents from Upper Middle Class Communities: Substance Misuse and Addiction Across Early Adulthood." *Development and Psychopathology* 30, no. 1 (2018): 315–35.

Mali, Taylor. "What Teachers Make." In *What Learning Leaves.* Newtown, CT: Hanover Press, 2002. Reproduced at Taylor Mali Poems. https://taylormali.com/poems/what-teachers-make/.

Marcus, Jon. "Facts about Race and College Admission." The Hechinger Report, July 6, 2018. https://hechingerreport.org/facts-about-race-and-college-admission/.

Markham, T. *Project-Based Learning Handbook: A Guide to Standards-Focused Project-Based Learning for Middle and High School Teachers.* Novato, CA: Buck Institute for Education, 2003.

Martin, Courtney. "Why Are White People So Bad at Talking about Race?" *Bright,* September 7, 2018. https://brightthemag.com/white-fragility-why-are-white-people-so-bad-at-talking-about-race-robin-diangelo-white-privilege-dbd5b92ba210.

Martin, Michelle. "Microaggressions: Be Careful What You Say." National Public Radio, April 3, 2014. https://www.npr.org/2014/04/03/298736678/microaggressions-be-careful-what-you-say.

Massachusetts Department of Elementary and Secondary Education. "2017 Massachusetts School Report Card Overview CAMBRIDGE RINDGE AND LATIN." 2017. http://profiles.doe.mass.edu/reportcard/SchoolReportCardOverview.aspx?fycode=2017&orgcode=00490506&.

Maynard, James. "Suicide Rates Differ Greatly Between Rural and Urban Youths." *Tech Times,* March 9, 2015. https://www.techtimes.com/articles/38487/20150309/suicide-rates-differ-greatly-between-rural-urban-youths.htm.

McIntosh, Peggy. "White Privilege: Unpacking the Invisible Knapsack." *Peace and Freedom,* August 1989. Reprinted at https://www.racialequitytools.org/resourcefiles/mcintosh.pdf.

———. "White Privilege and Male Privilege: A Personal Account of Coming to See Correspondences through Work in Women's Studies." Working Paper 189, 1988. Retrieved December 12, 2019 from nationalseedproject.org.

McNeir, Gwennis. "Outcome-Based Education." ERIC Digest, No. 85, 1993. https://files.eric.ed.gov/fulltext/ED379765.pdf.

Miner, H. M. "Body Ritual among the Nacirema." *American Anthropologist* 58, no. 1 (June 1956): 503–7. https://www.sfu.ca/~palys/Miner-1956-BodyRitualAmongTheNacirema.pdf.

Miranda, Lin-Manuel and J. McCarter. *Hamilton: The Revolution.* New York: Grand Central Publishing, 2016.

Miringoff, Lee M., Barbara L. Carvalho, and Mary E. Griffith. "Being a Better Person and Weight Loss Top 2018 New Year's Resolutions." *Marist College Institute for Public Opinion,* December 20, 2017. http://maristpoll.marist.edu/wp-content/misc/usapolls/us171106_HBO/Complete%20Survey%20Findings_Marist%20Poll_December%202017.pdf#page=1.

MIT Registrar. "MIT Student Diversity by School." Institutional Research Office of the Provost at MIT, 2018. http://ir.mit.edu/diversity-dashboard.

Mitchell, Gail. "Why Hasn't the Hip-Hop Boom Pushed More Black Executives to the Top?" *Billboard,* April 13, 2018. https://www.billboard.com/articles/business/8313035/hip-hop-boom-black-executives-music-business-labels

Mitchell, Heidi. "Who Gets More Mosquito Bites." *Wall Street Journal,* July 15, 2013. https://www.wsj.com/articles/SB10001424127887324425204578601621658128936.

Morgan, Rachel E. "Race and Hispanic Origin of Victims and Offenders, 2012–15." Bureau of Justice Statistics, October 2017. https://www.bjs.gov/content/pub/pdf/rhovo1215.pdf.

Morrison, Toni. *Song of Solomon.* New York: Vintage, 2004 (first published 1977).

Moynihan, Daniel Patrick. *The Negro Family. The Case for National Action.* Washington, D.C.: US Department of Labor, Office of Policy Planning and Research, 1965.

Muoio, Deb. "Locus of Control and the Wealth Mindset." *Arch Profile* (blog), October 29, 2015. http://blog.archprofile.com/archinsights/locus-of-control-wealth-mindset.

Murray, Corey. "How Many Hours Do Educators Actually Work?" *Ed Tech Magazine,* August 2013. https://edtechmagazine.com/k12/article/2013/08/how-many-hours-do-educators-actually-work.

Neiwert, David. "White Supremacists' Favorite Myths about Black Crime Rates Take Another Hit from BJS Study." Southern Poverty Law Center, October 23, 2017. https://www.splcenter.org/hatewatch/2017/10/23/white-supremacists-favorite-myths-about-black-crime-rates-take-another-hit-bjs-study.

Ngoma, Heather. "How Teachers Can Reduce Stereotype Threat in the Classroom." *Rutgers Center for Effective School Practices.* Rutgers Graduate School of Education, n.d. https://cesp.rutgers.edu/blog/how-teachers-can-reduce-stereotype-threat-classroom.

Nguyen, Josh. "Why Is White the Default?" *Medium,* May 25, 2017. https://medium.com/gender-theory/why-is-white-the-default-23a5d0df5564.

Nishi, Akihiro, Hirokazu Shirado, David G. Rand, and Nicholas A. Christakis. "Inequality and Visibility of Wealth in Experimental Social Networks." *Nature* 526 (October 15, 2015): 426–29. https://www.nature.com/articles/nature15392.

Nutt, Amy Ellis. "Why Kids and Teens May Face Far More Anxiety These Days." *Washington Post,* May 10, 2018. https://www.washingtonpost.com/news/to-your-health/wp/2018/05/10/why-kids-and-teens-may-face-far-more-anxiety-these-days/?utm_term=.3c82e9a5e04e.

Oakes, Jeannie. *Keeping Track: How Schools Structure Inequality.* New Haven, CT: Yale University Press, 1985.

Olsen, Hanna Brooks. "Please Admit You Don't Like Poor People So We Can Move On." *Medium,* July 5, 2018. https://medium.com/@mshannabrooks/please-admit-you-dont-like-poor-people-so-we-can-move-on-f4e964087b16.

Ong, Aihwa. *Buddha Is Hiding: Refugees, Citizenship, the New America.* Berkeley: University of California Press, 2003.

Open Source Shakespeare. *King Lear.* Accessed May 12, 2019. https://opensourceshakespeare.org/views/plays/play_view.php?WorkID=kinglear&Scope=entire&pleasewait=1&msg=pl.

Ortner, Tuulia M., and Fons J. R. Van De Vijver. *Behavior-Based Assessment in Psychology: Going Beyond Self-Report in the Personality, Affective, Motivation, and Social Domains.* Boston: Hogrefe Publishing, 2015.

Orwell, George. "Shooting an Elephant." *New Writing* 2 (1936): 501–6. http://orwell.ru/library/articles/elephant/english/e_eleph.

Osler, Johnathan. *Social Justice Math Manual—Radical Math.* Last updated November 18, 2019. http://www.radicalmath.org/docs/SJMathGuide.doc.

"Our Approach." Challenge Success, n.d. Accessed May 9, 2019. http://www.challengesuccess.org/about/our-approach/.

Parker, Kim, Juliana Menasce Horowitz, Anna Brown, Richard Fry, D'Vera Cohn, and Ruth Igielnik. "Demographic and Economic Trends In Urban, Suburban and Rural Communities." Pew Research Center, May 22, 2018. http://www.pewsocialtrends.org/2018/05/22/demographic-and-economic-trends-in-urban-suburban-and-rural-communities/.

Parra, Flavia C., Roberto C. Amado, José R. Lambertucci, Jorge Rocha, Carlos M. Antunes, and Sérgio D. J. Pena. "Color and Genomic Ancestry in Brazilians." *Proceedings of the National Academy of Sciences* 100, no. 1 (2003): 177–82.

Partnership for 21st Century Learning (P21). "Frameworks for 21st Century Learning." Battelle for Kids, 2016. http://www.battelleforkids.org/networks/p21/frameworks-resources.

Pawlak, Justyna, and Lidia Kelly. "Polish Lawmakers Back Holocaust Bill, Drawing Israeli Outrage, U.S. Concern." *Reuters,* January 31, 2018. https://af.reuters.com/article/worldNews/idAFKBN1FK3ER.

Perkins, Annie. "The Mathematicians Project: Mathematicians Are Not Just White Dudes." Arbitrarily Close, August 21, 2016. https://arbitrarilyclose.com/2016/08/21/the-mathematicians-project-mathematicians-are-not-just-white-dudes/.

Perry, Jeffrey B. "The Developing Conjuncture and Some Insights from Hubert Harrison and Theodore W. Allen on the Centrality of the Fight Against White Supremacy." *Cultural Logic: A Journal of Marxist Theory & Practice* 17 (2010).

Perry, Theresa. *Young Gifted and Black: Promoting High Achievement Among African-American Students*. Boston: Beacon Press, 2004.

Phillips, Katherine W., Gregory B. Northcraft, and Margaret A. Neale. "Surface-Level Diversity and Decision-Making in Groups: When Does Deep-Level Similarity Help?" *SAGE Journals*, October 1, 2006. https://journals.sagepub.com/doi/abs/10.1177/1368430206067557.

Piff, Paul K., Daniel M. Stancato, Stéphane Côté, Rodolfo Mendoza-Denton, and Dacher Keltner. "Higher Social Class Predicts Increased Unethical Behavior." *Proceedings of the National Academy of Sciences*, March 13, 2012. https://www.pnas.org/content/109/11/4086.

Plessy v. Ferguson (1896), Digital History, 2019. http://www.digitalhistory.uh.edu/disp_textbook.cfm?smtID=3&psid=1103.

Pope, D., and M. Levine. "The Advanced Placement Program: Living Up to Its Promise." Stanford Graduate School of Education, August 23, 2013. http://www.challengesuccess.org/Portals/0/Docs/ChallengeSuccess-AdvancedPlacement-WP.pdf.

"Poverty in Black America," Black Demographics, 2014. https://blackdemographics.com/households/poverty/.

Prater, Doris L., Andrea B. Bermúdez, and Emiel Owens. "Examining Parental Involvement in Rural, Urban, and Suburban Schools." *Journal of Research in Rural Education* 13, no. 1 (1997): 72–75. http://jrre.vmhost.psu.edu/wp-content/uploads/2014/02/13-1_8.pdf.

"Private School Enrollment." National Center for Education Statistics. Last updated January 2018. https://nces.ed.gov/programs/coe/indicator_cgc.asp.

Putnam, J. W., ed. *Cooperative Learning and Strategies for Inclusion: Celebrating Diversity in the Classroom*. Baltimore, MD: Paul H. Brookes Publishing, 1993.

"Race: The Power of an Illusion Viewing Guide." Facing History and Ourselves, 2003. https://www.facinghistory.org/chunk/race-power-illusion-viewing-guide.

"Racial and Ethnic Achievement Gaps." Stanford Center for Education Policy Analysis, February 2015. https://cepa.stanford.edu/educational-opportunity-monitoring-project/achievement-gaps/race/.

Randhawa, Kuldip S. *Absolute Privilege to Deprive: "Discovery of White Privilege."* Bloomington, IN: AuthorHouse, 2015.

Rebora, Anthony, Donna Ogle, and Laura Lang. "Common Core: Reading and Writing Across the Curriculum." *Education Week*, November 14, 2012. https://www.edweek.org/media/2012-11-14commoncorereadingandwriting.pdf.

Richard, Orlando, Amy McMillan, Ken Chadwick, and Sean Dwyer. "Employing an Innovation Strategy in Racially Diverse Workforces: Effects on Firm Performance." *SAGE Journals*, March 1, 2003. https://journals.sagepub.com/doi/abs/10.1177/1059601102250022.

Riley, Jason L. "50 Years of Blaming Everything on Racism." *Wall Street Journal*, March 7, 2018. https://www.manhattan-institute.org/html/50-years-blaming-everything-racism-10991.html.

Rock, M. L., M. Gregg, E. Ellis, and R. A. Gable. "REACH: A Framework for Differentiating Classroom Instruction." *Preventing School Failure: Alternative Education for Children and Youth* 52, no. 2 (2008): 31–47.

"The Role of Science in Advancing Racial Equity." Union of Concerned Scientists, September 2, 2016. https://www.ucsusa.org/center-science-and-democracy/role-of-science-in-advancing-racial-equity.

Rosin, Hanna. "The Silicon Valley Suicides: Why Are So Many Kids with Bright Prospects Killing Themselves in Palo Alto?" *The Atlantic*, December 2015. https://www.theatlantic.com/magazine/archive/2015/12/the-silicon-valley-suicides/413140/.

Rowling, J. K. *Harry Potter and the Goblet of Fire*. New York: Scholastic Paperbacks, 2002.

Schmitt, Glenn R. "Demographic Differences in Sentencing: An Update to the 2012 *Booker* Report." U.S. Sentencing Commission, November 2017. https://www.ussc.gov/sites/default/

files/pdf/research-and-publications/research-publications/2017/20171114_Demographics. pdf.

Schneider, Jack. "The Urban-School Stigma." *The Atlantic*, August 25, 2017. https://www. theatlantic.com/education/archive/2017/08/the-urban-school-stigma/537966/.

Schulson, Michael. "Should 'Race' Be Taught in High School Biology?" *UnDark*. September 12, 2018. https://undark.org/article/biology-textbooks-race-high-school/.

Seider, Scott. "Social Justice in the Suburbs: Engaging Privileged Youth in Social Action." *Educational Leadership* 66, no. 8 (2009): 54–58.

Shafer, Leah. "Talking About Race in Mostly White Schools." *Harvard Graduate School of Education*, April 20, 2017. https://www.gse.harvard.edu/news/uk/17/04/talking-about-race-mostly-white-schools.

Shapiro, T. M. *The Hidden Cost of Being African American: How Wealth Perpetuates Inequality*. New York: Oxford University Press, 2004.

Sherman, Erik. "Hiring Bias Blacks and Latinos Face Hasn't Improved in 25 Years." *Forbes*, September 16, 2017. https://www.forbes.com/sites/eriksherman/2017/09/16/job-discrim ination-against-blacks-and-latinos-has-changed-little-or-none-in-25-years/#6328340351e3.

Sleeter, Christine E. "The Academic and Social Value of Ethnic Studies: A Research Review." National Education Association Research Department, 2011. http://www.nea.org/assets/ docs/NBI-2010-3-value-of-ethnic-studies.pdf.

Skiba, R. J., L. A. Shure, L. V. Middelberg, and T. L. Baker. "Reforming School Discipline and Reducing Disproportionality in Suspension and Expulsion." In *Handbook of School Violence and School Safety*, 516–529. London: Routledge, 2012.

Smith, K. "Positive Reinforcement . . . A Proactive Intervention for the Classroom." College of Education, University of Minnesota, 2010. http://ceed.umn.edu/wp-content/uploads/2017/ 05/Positive-Reinforcement.pdf.

Soergel, Andrew. "Most of America's Businesses Run by White Men." *US News & World Report*, September 1, 2016. https://www.usnews.com/news/articles/2016-09-01/most-of-americas-businesses-run-by-white-men-says-census-bureau.

Spatig-Amerikaner, Ary. "Unequal Education: Federal Loophole Enables Lower Spending on Students of Color." Center for American Progress, August 2012. https://www. americanprogress.org/wp-content/uploads/2012/08/UnequalEduation.pdf.

Srogi, L. A., and L. Baloche. "Using Cooperative Learning to Teach Mineralogy (and Other Courses, Too!)." In *Teaching Mineralogy*, eds. John B. Brady, David W. Mogk, and Dexter Perkins III. Mineralogical Society of America Monograph, 1997. http://www.minsocam. org/msa/openaccess_publications/#Teaching_Mineralogy.

St. George, Donna, and Justin Moyer. "Can You Skip 47 Days of English Class and Still Graduate from High School?" *Washington Post*, May 25, 2019. https://www. washingtonpost.com/local/education/can-you-skip-47-days-of-english-class-and-still-graduate-from-high-school/2019/05/25/be3318ca-1b84-11e9-88fe-f9f77a3bcb6c_story. html?utm_term=.93c0cace1558&wpisrc=nl_most&wpmm=1.

"The Status of Rural Education." National Center for Education Statistics, Last updated May 2013. https://nces.ed.gov/programs/coe/indicator_tla.asp.

Steele, Claude. *Whistling Vivaldi: How Stereotypes Affect Us and What We Can Do*. New York: W. W. Norton & Company, 2011.

Stiggins, Richard J. *Student-Involved Assessment for Learning*. New York: Abe Books, 2005.

Stinson, D. W. "Negotiating the 'White Male Math Myth': African American Male Students and Success in School Mathematics." *Journal for Research in Mathematics Education* 44, no. 1 (2013): 69–99.

Stotsky, Sandra. "Academic Guidelines for Selecting Multiethnic and Multicultural Literature." *The English Journal* 83, no. 2 (1994): 29–30. http://www.csun.edu/~krowlands/Content/ Academic_Resources/Literature/Canon/Stotsky-choosing%20multicultural%20literature. pdf.

———. "Changes in America's Secondary School Literature Programs." *Phi Delta Kappan* 76, no. 7 (1995): 605–13.

Stroessner, Steve, and Catherine Good. "Stereotype Threat: An Overview: Adaptations from ReducingStereotypeThreat.Org." 2011. https://diversity.arizona.edu/sites/default/files/stereo

type_threat_overview.pdf.

Sue, Derald Wing. "Microaggressions: More Than Just Race." *Psychology Today*, November 17, 2010. https://www.psychologytoday.com/us/blog/microaggressions-in-everyday-life/201011/microaggressions-more-just-race.

Sutton, Rosemary. "Teachers' Anger, Frustration, and Self-Regulation." In *Emotion in Education*, ed. Paul Schutz and Reinhard Pekrun, 259–74. Amsterdam: Academic Press, 2007.

Swalwell, Katy M. *Educating Activist Allies: Social Justice Pedagogy with the Suburban and Urban Elite*. New York: Routledge, 2013.

Swartz, E. "Emancipatory Narratives: Rewriting the Master Script in the School Curriculum." *Journal of Negro Education* 61, no. 3 (1992): 341–55.

Tate, W. F. "Race, Retrenchment, and the Reform of School Mathematics." *Phi Delta Kappan* 75, no. 6 (1994): 477–85.

Tatum, Beverly Daniel. *Can We Talk About Race? And Other Conversations in an Era of School Resegregation*. Boston: Beacon Press, 2008.

Thomas, Angie. *The Hate U Give*. New York: HarperCollins, 2017.

Tienken, Christopher H., Anthony Colella, Christian Angelillo, Meredith Fox, Kevin R. McCahill, and Adam Wolfe. "Predicting Middle Level State Standardized Test Results Using Family and Community Demographic Data." *Research in Middle Level Education* 40, no. 1 (2017). https://www.tandfonline.com/doi/full/10.1080/19404476.2016.1252304.

Toshalis, E. *Make Me!: Understanding and Engaging Student Resistance in School*. Cambridge, MA: Harvard Education Press, 2015.

Tuckman, Bruce W. "Developmental Sequence in Small Groups." *Psychological Bulletin* 63, no. 6 (1965): 384–99. doi:10.1037/h0022100.

Twenge, Jean M., A. Bell Cooper, Thomas E. Joiner, Mary E. Duffy, and Sarah G. Binau. "Age, Period, and Cohort Trends in Mood Disorder Indicators and Suicide-Related Outcomes in a Nationally Representative Dataset, 2005–2017." *Journal of Abnormal Psychology* 128, no. 3 (2019): 185–99.

Tyson, H., and A. Woodward. "Why Students Aren't Learning Very Much from Textbooks." *Educational Leadership* 47, no. 3 (1989): 14–17.

Ukpokodu, O. "How Do I Teach Mathematics in a Culturally Responsive Way? Identifying Empowering Teaching Practices." *Multicultural Education*, March 22, 2011. Reprinted in The Free Library. https://www.thefreelibrary.com/How+do+I+teach+mathematics+in+a+culturally+responsive+way%3F...-a0274955684.

"Understanding Implicit Bias." The Ohio State University Kirwan Institute for the Study of Race and Ethnicity, 2015. http://kirwaninstitute.osu.edu/research/understanding-implicit-bias/.

"Uniform Crime Reporting (UCR) Program." FBI, n.d. https://www.fbi.gov/services/cjis/ucr.

Urist, Jacoba. "Who Should Decide How Students Learn about America's Past? *The Atlantic*, February 24, 2015. https://www.theatlantic.com/education/archive/2015/02/who-should-decide-how-students-learn-about-americas-past/385928/.

Van der Veer, R., and J. Valsiner. *Understanding Vygotsky: A Quest for Synthesis*. Hoboken, NJ: Blackwell Publishing, 1991.

Van Houtte, Mieke, and Peter A. J. Stevens. "Sense of Futility: The Missing Link between Track Position and Self-Reported School Misconduct." *Youth & Society* 40, no. 2 (2008): 245–64.

Van Susteren, Greta. "In Defense of Arizona's Ethnic Studies Law." *Fox News,* May 13, 2010. https://www.foxnews.com/story/in-defense-of-arizonas-ethnic-studies-law.

Vollman, Alexandra. "Changing the Face of Climate Science." Insight into Diversity, 2017. https://www.insightintodiversity.com/changing-the-face-of-climate-change-science/.

Wainer, Howard. *Uneducated Guesses: Using Evidence to Uncover Misguided Education Policies*. Princeton, NJ: Princeton University Press, 2011.

Walker, John. "These 7 Microaggressions Could Ruin Someone's Day." MTV, July 17, 2014. http://www.mtv.com/news/1871828/look-different-microaggression-videos/.

Wallace, David Foster. "Authority and American Usage." In *Consider the Lobster and Other Essays*, 66–127. New York: Little, Brown, 2006.

Wallace, J. M., Jr, S. Goodkind, C. M. Wallace, and J. G. Bachman. "Racial, Ethnic, and Gender Differences in School Discipline among US High School Students: 1991–2005." *The Negro Educational Review* 59, no. 1–2 (2008): 47.

Wells, Spencer. *The Journey of Man: A Genetic Odyssey.* Princeton, NJ: Princeton University Press, 2002.

"What Are the Essential Parts of a WebQuest?" Concept to Classroom, 2004. https://www.thirteen.org/edonline/concept2class/webquests/index_sub3.html.

"What Is Critical Race Theory?" UCLA School of Public Affairs, November 4, 2009. https://spacrs.wordpress.com/what-is-critical-race-theory/.

"What Kids Are Reading," Renaissance, 2019. https://www.renaissance.com/learning-analytics/wkar/.

"What Is PBL?" PBL Works, Buck Institute for Education, n.d. Accessed May 12, 2019. https://www.pblworks.org/what-is-pbl.

"Which One of These Things Is Not Like the Other?" Facing History and Ourselves, n.d. Accessed May 20, 2019. https://www.facinghistory.org/chunk/which-one-these-things-not-others.

Whitbourne, Susan Krauss. "Yes, the Rich and Famous Really Are That Narcissistic." *Psychology Today*, January 22, 2019. https://www.psychologytoday.com/us/blog/fulfillment-any-age/201901/yes-the-rich-and-famous-really-are-narcissistic.

Williams, Trisha. "White Advocates for All." *BGD: Amplifying the Voices of Queer & Trans People of Color* (blog), October 18, 2016. https://www.bgdblog.org/2016/10/white-advocates-for-all/.

Wise, Tim. *White Like Me: Reflections on Race from a Privileged Son.* New York: Soft Skull Press, 2011.

Witte, Amanda L., and Susan M. Sheridan. "Family Engagement in Rural Schools." National Center for Research on Rural Education, June 2011. https://r2ed.unl.edu/resources/downloads/2011-wp/2011_2_Witte_Sheridan.pdf.

Wood, L. Todd. "I'm Mad as Hell and I'm Not Taking It Anymore." *Washington Times*, September 26, 2017. https://www.washingtontimes.com/news/2017/sep/26/black-america-blames-white-america/.

Yates, Tuppett M., Allison J. Tracy, and Suniya S. Luthar. "Nonsuicidal Self-Injury among 'Privileged' Youths: Longitudinal and Cross-Sectional Approaches to Developmental Process." *Journal of Consulting and Clinical Psychology* 76, no. 1 (2008): 52.

Zinn, Howard. *A People's History of the United States.* New York: HarperCollins, 2015 (first published 1980).

About the Author

David Nurenberg, PhD, is an associate professor and core faculty member at Lesley University's Graduate School of Education, as well as a high school English teacher, writer, and educational consultant. Over his 20 years as an educator, David has developed and taught a wide variety of interdisciplinary courses with strong project-based learning and social justice education components.

David's published work has appeared in several prominent peer-reviewed journals including *The Harvard Educational Review*, *NCTE's English Education*, *American Secondary Education*, and *High School Journal*, as well as in general-audience publications such as *Education Week* and *The Jewish Advocate*. He is also the host of the education-themed podcast, *Ed Infinitum* (www.ed-infinitum.com).

Both through Lesley University and independently, David consults with middle and secondary schools seeking to develop, improve, and expand their work with student-centered pedagogy, inquiry, and project-based learning, cooperative learning, and more. For more information, visit www.doctornurenberg.com.